Berber Culture on the World Stage

JANE E. GOODMAN

Berber Culture on the World Stage

From Village to Video

INDIANA UNIVERSITY PRESS
Bloomington and Indianapolis

This book is a publication of

Indiana University Press
601 North Morton Street
Bloomington, IN 47404-3797 USA

http://iupress.indiana.edu

Telephone orders   800-842-6796
Fax orders   812-855-7931
Orders by e-mail   iuporder@indiana.edu

© 2005 by Jane E. Goodman

The paper used in this publication meets the minimum requirements of American National Standard for Information Sciences—Permanence of Paper for Printed Library Materials, ANSI Z39.48-1984.

Manufactured in the United States of America

Library of Congress Cataloging-in-Publication Data

Goodman, Jane E., date
  Berber culture on the world stage : from village to video / Jane E. Goodman.
    p. cm.
Includes bibliographical references and index.
  ISBN 0-253-34629-0 (cloth : alk. paper) — ISBN 0-253-21784-9 (pbk. : alk. paper)
  1. Berbers—Algeria. 2. Algeria—Ethnic relations. 3. Algerians—France—History. 4. Music—Performance—Algeria. I. Title.
  DT283.2.G66 2005
  305.89′33065—dc22

                                                                                    2005006229

1 2 3 4 5   10 09 08 07 06 05

For my father, Richard, and my late mother, Arlene

Contents

Acknowledgments

This work would not have been possible without the generous assistance, hospitality, and interest of a great many people. I take this opportunity to thank them. In some cases, I omit their last names to protect their privacy.

Fanny Colonna introduced me to Algeria and welcomed me into her home on numerous occasions. Without her support, I may never have chosen Algeria as a field site. I am deeply grateful.

The ethnomusicologist Mehenna Mahfoufi, whose own work centers on Kabyle women's songs, made contacts for me in his former field site and home village, and introduced me to most of the singers and poets with whom I worked. Fully aware that our work would overlap to some degree, he nevertheless encouraged my project from start to finish. I thank him for his ongoing support and friendship.

The Djouadou family, Abderrahmane, Zoubida, Taos (setsi), Larbi, Hacina, and Zakkia, opened their homes and themselves to me, both in Algeria (for ten months in 1993) and the suburbs of Paris (for nine months in 1994 and 1996). They patiently bore with me as I learned to speak Kabyle, met my many questions with generous and thoughtful discussion, and supported my work on every level—showing me how to dance Kabyle-style, assisting me with translations, and making contacts for me with other community members. I owe Abderrahmane, Zoubida, and their family a profound debt that only lifelong friendship can begin to repay.

I thank the family of Yamina Tameqwrant ("old"), Bachir, Yamina Tamezyant ("young"), Mohamed, and Abdullah Djouadou, who invited me for many couscous dinners and evenings of conversation. Yamina Tameqwrant graciously recorded and explained her songs, and Bachir spent hours passionately discussing with me the intricacies of local and national politics. Bachir also helped me to develop a census of the village, arranged for me to visit other sites in Kabylia, and bequeathed to me his substantial collection of newspaper clippings on Berber politics. I thank the family of Amar, Zhor, Jejjiga, Na Zahara, Nouara, Hakim, Sabrina, and Karina Djouadou, who invited me sight unseen into their home in Algeria in the summers of 1990 and 1992 and helped me to establish a base in their community. I thank Noura Haddab, who offered her friendship as both of us moved between Algeria and France, and who helped me understand the complexities of diasporic life for young women. Hamid Kacet and Belqacem Beloucif provided invaluable assistance with my work on the village community in Paris. Finally, I extend my thanks to the many other men and women from both the Algerian and Parisian sides of my host village who offered their friendship and support, including: Zhor and her family, Na Jejjiga and her family,

Unisa and her family, Rosa, Dehbia, Dalila, Amara, Karim, and Saada. I was fortunate to be able to spend time in several other Kabyle villages as well, and thank in particular Aldjia, Fatima, Farid, Kamal, and their families. Ahmed Semah allowed me to video the children's chorus he directed. Ammar Lakehal and Ramdane Achab shared with me their memories of the early years of Berber activism in Algeria during periods of follow-up research in Montreal and Paris. Eduardo, Adriana, Pablo, and Anahí facilitated my research in Paris in 1988 and 1990. Halima Belhandouz was an invaluable friend, sounding board, and colleague throughout the research and writing process.

My work on new Kabyle song would not have been possible without the support of its creators. Ben Mohamed spent hours patiently explaining his song texts to me; chapters 2 and 5, in particular, bear the fruit of these conversations. Thanks also to Ben's family—Dominique and Ania—for their generous hospitality and for many enjoyable evenings. Idir took time out of his busy performance schedule to meet with me; his music, which I first fell in love with in 1980, not only provided much of the material for this study but also has added a great deal of pleasure to my life. Lounes Aït Menguellet shared with me both his songs and his stage, allowing me to sing in his 1994 concerts at the Olympia Theater in Paris, and we spent many hours talking about his creative process. I am also grateful to Ferhat Imazighen Imula, the late Matoub Lounes, and members of the group Djurdjura for their time, interest, and assistance.

Perhaps the most understated presence in this work is that of Boualem Rabia, a poet, musician, and teacher who is deeply committed to the revitalization of the Kabyle language and culture. Boualem painstakingly helped me to translate dozens of songs and graciously shared with me his extensive knowledge of village repertoires. Boualem also gave generously of his time, meeting with me almost weekly from April to November of 1993. I hope that his faith in me will be at least partially borne out by this work.

Transcribing Berber songs would have been exceedingly difficult without the help of Boualem Rabia, Ben Mohamed, Ramdane Achab, Hacina Djouadou, Noura Haddab, Lakhdar, Jaffar, Mennad, and, in particular, Soraya. I extend to them my heartfelt thanks. I am also grateful to the late Mustapha Aouchiche, founder of the bookstore Editions Berbères in Paris, for lending to me from his personal collection documents that are out of print and unavailable in French libraries, and to the Berber Cultural Association (Association de Culture Berbère, ACB) in Paris for allowing me to use their space for interviews and for generally facilitating my work.

In Algeria, the Department of Amazigh Studies at the University of Tizi Ouzou Hasnaoua facilitated my stay by hosting me as a visiting scholar and providing library facilities. In France, I had the benefit of working with two ongoing research groups: the Groupe de Sociologie Politique et Morale at the Ecole des Hautes Etudes en Sciences Sociales, under the direction of Fanny Colonna, and the Groupe de Recherches Berbères at the Institut National des Langues et Civilisations Orientales, under the direction of Salem Chaker. I thank the members of both groups for their intellectual and logistical support.

Earlier versions of chapters 4, 5, and 6 of this work were drafted at the University of Michigan–Ann Arbor, where I was a fellow at the Advanced Study Center in the spring of 1997. I thank the members of the seminar "Nation, Community, and Culture in the Aftermath of Empire" for their valuable input and support. I also thank Ann Stoler for allowing me to sit in on her course on the anthropology of colonialism, which helped to enrich chapter 4. My aunt Lillian Goodman's financial support enabled me to extend my stay.

Dick Bauman and Ilana Gershon read the nearly completed manuscript on extremely short notice and reassured me that I did indeed have a book in this material. John Bowen generously read two drafts; his comments helped me to reshape the manuscript. Carol Greenhouse provided invaluable assistance at a difficult turning point. For their comments on specific chapters, I thank in particular Paula Amad, Katherine Hoffman, Sam Kaplan, Philip Parnell, and Teri Silvio. Finally, I am indebted to Rebecca Tolen, my editor at Indiana University Press, who helped me to transform the manuscript into what I believe is a far more readable book. Any remaining lapses or lacunae are entirely my responsibility.

This book would not have been possible without the support of Judith Irvine, Richard Parmentier, and Brinkley Messick. Special thanks to Judy for her faith in me over the years; to Rick for provocative discussions of intertextuality; and to Brink for introducing me to North Africa and for providing a sounding board for my readings in the colonial literature. Susan Slyomovics offered many beneficial suggestions. Janina Fenigsen, Benjamin Soares, Kate Zirbel, and, later, Ilana Gershon provided electronic and telephone lifelines during the often isolating writing process. I was also fortunate to have the support of Kabyle friends in Boston, especially Nadia Ouahes and Makhlouf Redjdal, who commented on parts of several chapters, as well as virtual communication with a community of Imazighen via the discussion forum Amazigh-net, whose members generously answered my questions about topics ranging from quarter-tone guitar tuning to word usage.

My father, Richard Goodman, and my late mother, Arlene Goodman, offered more support, financial and otherwise, than I can ever adequately repay. I thank them for always encouraging me to pursue my interests, and for helping me to keep my cars and computers running!

Funding support for the research on which this project is based was generously provided by the Fulbright Institute for International Education; the Wenner-Gren Foundation for Anthropological Research; the Social Science Research Council; the American Institute for Maghribi Studies; the Sachar Fellowship Program and the Department of Anthropology at Brandeis University; the Advanced Study Center at the University of Michigan; and the Department of Communication and Culture and the Dean of Faculties Office at Indiana University. Writing was completed with a generous fellowship from the Indiana University President's Arts and Humanities Initiative.

Chapter 1 of this volume elaborates on "Reinterpreting the Berber Spring: From Rite of Reversal to Site of Convergence," *Journal of North African Studies*

9 (3): 60–82. Chapter 2 is an expanded version of "From Village to Vinyl: Genealogies of New Kabyle Song," *Emergences: Journal for the Study of Media and Composite Cultures* 13 (1/2): 75–93. Chapter 4 is a development of "Writing Empire, Underwriting Nation: Discursive Histories of Kabyle Berber 'Oral Texts,'" *American Ethnologist* 29 (1): 86–122. Parts of chapter 5 were first published in "Singers, Saints, and the Construction of Postcolonial Subjectivities in Algeria," *Ethos* 26 (2): 204–228, and in "Writing Empire, Underwriting Nation: Discursive Histories of Kabyle Berber 'Oral Texts,'" *American Ethnologist* 29 (1): 86–122. Chapter 6 is a significant expansion of material that appeared in "'Stealing Our Heritage?': Women's Folk Songs, Copyright Law, and the Public Domain in Algeria," *Africa Today* 49 (1): 84–97.

Note on Orthography and Translation

Kabyle Berber orthography uses a modified version of the Roman alphabet and follows a phonemic system, with one letter representing one phoneme. I adopt the orthographic conventions set forth in J. M. Dallet's *Dictionnaire kabyle-français* (Kabyle-French Dictionary) (Dallet 1982, xxvi–xxxii), with the following exceptions. For proper names, I retain the spellings used by the individuals in question. When reproducing texts found in earlier works, I retain the orthography of the original text. To aid the English-speaking reader, for the words *Amaziɣ* and *Tamaziɣt,* used respectively to refer to a pan-Berber people and language, I employ "gh" rather than γ when these words are embedded in English sentences, as is common in French-language publications (including those by Berbers). Following Dallet, I generally indicate phonological assimilation with an underscore between words. For example, in the phrase *ad teççeḍ* ("you will eat"), the *d* assimilates as follows into the *t: at_ teççeḍ.* I use a superscripted "w" to indicate labiovelarization of the preceding consonant.

When the use of Kabyle orthography would unduly obscure a term that is otherwise well known in the literature, I supply the conventional orthography. For example, for the Kabyle term *ccix* (religious leader), I also provide the Arabic transliteration *shaykh.* For the word *tajmaɛt* (a men's village assembly), which occurs frequently in the book, I change the ɛ to an ʿ (*tajmaʿat*) except when it appears in Kabyle texts.

All English translations are my own unless otherwise indicated.

Berber Culture on the World Stage

Introduction

September 17, 1993. I grab my camcorder and set off with two young male college students, who have arranged for me to videotape the performance of a children's chorus called Tilelli, a neologism meaning "Freedom." The chorus was the creation of a newly formed Amazigh (Berber) cultural association, one of over 1,000 that had sprung up in Algeria's Kabyle Berber region since 1989, when sweeping changes in the nation's constitution opened the way for the formation of civic organizations without government authorization. After an hour's drive over winding mountain roads, we reach the small village of 1,600 and are greeted by the chorus director and his cohort of young male cultural militants. I am taken first to the seat of the association—a room in the village's former mosque—where I am encouraged to begin filming. I train my camcorder on the walls of the room, pausing first at a large banner with the phrase, "Oh our sons, Algeria is our land" (*ay arrac-nneɣ, Lẓẓayer tamurt-nneɣ*) handlettered in blue in the Tamazight (modern Berber) language. I then lower the lens to the floor, where I find an orderly display of cultural objects, each indexed by number: an assortment of clay jugs, several woven baskets, a goatskin bag, iron tools, a leather saddle. Affixed to some of the objects are small white cards bearing their Berber names. Finishing my exploration of this small exhibit, I turn toward the group of men and I am startled to find myself part of the picture. Their camcorder has me fixed in its frame. The young men are also filming the event: An American woman has come to view their culture. We are all part of the day's documentation. All of us are on stage.

As they continue to film me, I focus again on the wall, where I find another banner: "He who wants Tamazight must learn to write it" (*W' ibɣan tamaziɣt ad yissin tira-s*). I recognize the words, slightly modified, as the lyrics of one of the songs of Idir, a popular singer and founder of the politicized Berber world music genre known as "new Kabyle song." Later on, the Tilelli chorus would perform a rendition of Idir's song, which is inspired by a local women's wedding tune. Moving across white walls outlined in tile, my camera next pauses at a large sheet of paper taped to the wall. It bears a passage, handwritten in French, titled "Of the talents of the Berber race and its noble qualities." Advancing slowly through the passage, I locate its author at the end: Ibn Khaldun, a fourteenth-century chronicler of North African societies who produced the first-known written account of Berber groups (Khaldun 1925). Doubtless unknown to the copyist, who had drawn the quote from a 1972 book titled *Algeria in Antiquity,* the passage in question had been translated into French in the 1840s under the orders of the French minister of war, becoming one of the first of thousands of colonial documents on North Africa's Berber populations.

Moving on, I find, through my camcorder's lens, several newspaper articles affixed to the wall, all written in French: "Jordan and the Bulls Are Favored"; "Magic Johnson—the Reasons I Retired"; "Elsa—plus pastel que destroy." Grouped with this amalgam of world youth culture is a fourth article titled "Matoub Lounes: I Am Here for the Berber Spring"—a reference to April 1980 demonstrations in which thousands of Kabyles, galvanized by government cancellation of a talk on traditional Berber poetry, turned out en masse in the first significant public outcry against state repression of Berber language and culture in independent Algeria. This cultural association, I later learn, had formed in April 1989, its anniversary designed to coincide with the Berber Spring, which they and hundreds of other Berber associations throughout North Africa and the diaspora commemorate each year. I see, through my camera's lens, pictures of these and other commemorative events carefully laid out and labeled in a large photo album: a four-year record of cultural exhibits, village-wide soccer and volleyball tournaments, chorus performances. I am told that the association lends both its small exhibit and its chorus—pending, for the girls, notarized paternal permission—to regional and national Amazigh cultural festivals.

As the time for the scheduled concert approaches, we move outside and walk down to the school where the event is to be held, filming as we go: figs drying in the warm fall sun, new houses under construction, soaring mountain peaks, parked cars. Once again I find myself inscribed into the event, coming face-to-face with a sign taped up along our path:

> NOTICE: The Freedom Chorus of the Association will present its repertoire in the school cafeteria on Friday September 17 at 10:30, in honor of the presence of an American woman doing research on new Kabyle song. Come one and all.

As we set up in the cafeteria, the Freedom Chorus of twelve young girls (ages eleven–twelve) and seven older boys (ages sixteen–seventeen) take their places on a stage made from several long tables pushed together. Accompanied by guitar, frame drum (bendir), and flute players, they begin to sing their own arrangements of the politicized repertoire of popular new Kabyle singers, many of whose songs are sourced in familiar village repertoires. While my camcorder is trained primarily on the chorus—capturing their innovative, if slightly off-key, harmonies of these familiar songs as well as their original Kabyle rendition of Beethoven's "Ode to Joy"—it also takes in the audience. Young boys and men make up about four-fifths of the crowd, with young girls and a few older women seated together in the front. An association member continues to video the events. Occasionally, the eyes of our two camcorders cross, each revealing itself through the other's lens.

What stands out about this event is its readiness for travel. The show was set to go, the script in place, from the visit to the cultural exhibit to the concert to a follow-up interview with the chorus director. It all seemed to unfold effortlessly, as if this kind of scenario had been enacted countless times. The events were camera-ready: The textualized, museum-like nature of the exhibit itself as well as the organization and staging of the concert had been prepackaged as if to be captured on film. That the event was conceived for distant audiences was apparent even in its advertising: The show billed itself in terms of its American guest. By 1993, Kabyles knew precisely what it took to achieve visibility on a world stage. If they had carved out a spot on a burgeoning global map of indigenous identities, it was because it had become second nature for Berbers to represent themselves in terms that would be instantly recognizable beyond Algerian borders. "Culture" was the currency through which such recognition could be attained.

This scenario opens up the terrain of inquiry on which this book is situated. I am interested in how Berber cultural identity is being constituted through and for a world stage. For under a unifying rubric of Berber culture, this event was inescapably global, littered with references from colonial history to contemporary youth culture. Local artifacts were displayed through practices borrowed from museums. The concert took shape around an organization of performance familiar to folk-rock audiences across the world. The songs the chorus performed had already traveled far and wide. Most were associated with new Kabyle song, which emerged in the 1970s in connection with phenomena as diverse as ethnographic film, postcolonial theory, pan-African ideology, and western folk-rock. The cultural association was enabled through Algerian law, in turn modeled on the charters of other states. The newspapers, cassette recordings, photographs, microphones, even the poster advertising the show were among the media that made this day possible. The video recordings themselves were destined for at least two locations. Only one would be traveling with me to America. The other was being produced for local consumption. It would presumably enter the village's own archive, joining the hundreds of documents that the cultural association had been producing about itself over the last four years.

The videotapes reveal more than just a record of the culture on display that September day. Each tape also contains a sidelong glance at the other and a trace of itself refracted through the other's lens. Who was watching whom? What were we each looking at? Were we seeing the same thing? Why was I making yet another ethnographic document on Kabylia, a region already subjected to over a century of colonial and anthropological scrutiny? Why were the young men taping an exhibit and concert that they had presumably seen numerous times? How were these two endeavors connected—how, in other words, were both anthropological analysis and indigenous activism served by the tapes of this day's proceedings? And why were we each so intent on capturing the other in the process of recording? Was it the show itself that most interested us, or the fact that the show was seen by the other as an event worthy of being documented on film?

Why Culture?

Starting this discussion with an account of a performance of Berber cultural identity suggests a prior question: Why culture? Culture is, after all, only one possible rubric through which a social group can achieve visibility. The Algerian case makes this particularly apparent. During the 1980s and 1990s, struggles for Berber cultural identity developed alongside a growing Islamist movement. Berberists and Islamists both constituted themselves in opposition to the army-backed National Liberation Front (Front de Libération Nationale, FLN), which had governed Algeria single-handedly since independence in 1962. Both groups sought to transform the very foundations of the Algerian polity. Berbers, a linguistic minority, called for constitutional changes that would acknowledge the nation's cultural and linguistic pluralism. They envisioned a secular and democratic Algeria in which Berber (Tamazight) would be elevated alongside Arabic to the status of a national and official language, to be used in the nation's courts, schools, and places of business. Islamists also targeted the state, calling for a republic to be governed by Islamic shariʿa law. At various points both Berberists and Islamists were involved in significant clashes with state forces. Their activities were circumscribed, their activists were jailed, and their members were subjected to harassment and surveillance. These two movements were also demographically similar, drawing from the same constituency of young men disillusioned by Algeria's high unemployment rate, severe housing shortages, and failed educational system. They disseminated their messages via mediated products such as cassettes, pamphlets, and, later, videos. And both groups organized performances—from gala events with charismatic leaders held in soccer stadiums to small gatherings in local venues—to mobilize members and attract new recruits.

Despite their many commonalities, the two movements formulate their claims to authority and legitimacy in substantially different ways. The Islamist movement defines itself through religion, while the Berberist movement understands itself through culture—even though most Berbers also consider themselves Muslims. Indeed, culture has become the rallying cry used by Berbers to contest the rise of political Islam in Algeria. Why should that be the case? How did "Berber culture"—a concept that barely could have been articulated before the mid-nineteenth century—come to be so readily subjected to representation that a performance of culture could be mounted for a visiting American scholar on a few days' notice? How have Berbers learned to see themselves in terms of culture?

Interest in Berber culture dates to the period of French colonialism in Algeria (1830–1962). The French looked at Algeria with a kind of dual vision. Whereas they viewed Arabs through a lens of religion, they saw Berbers through a lens of culture. Even so, on the eve of Algerian independence, most Berbers did not single out their culture for special attention. Nor did they do so during the initial formation of the new Algerian state in the early 1960s. Colonial history alone does not explain why Berbers today are increasingly constituting their identities in cultural terms. Moreover, most Berbers never bought into French claims that they were less attached to the Muslim religion than their Arab counterparts. Although the Berber-Arab relationship is usually characterized in terms of polarization, Algeria's Berber and Arab populations may have more similarities than differences. In addition to their common adherence to the Muslim faith (albeit with divergences in practice), Arabs and Berbers have related ways of organizing family structures and gender relations. Why, then, has culture become so important to the development of contemporary Berber identity?

Berber cultural identity has developed through a long history of precise linkages and connections to other peoples, products, and places. Yet as cultural identity is singled out by Berbers as a way to achieve recognition in a global arena, such interconnections tend to be erased from view. Working against this erasure, I foreground the processes, products, and performances that have enabled Berber identity to become globally recognizable. To do so, I move from the 1990s, when Berber cultural activists had become a force to be reckoned with across North Africa and the diaspora, to the 1860s, when discrete domains of Berber social life were just beginning to be carved out and marked as "culture" by French colonial agents. While I look closely at the specificities of the Arab-Berber relationship in Algeria, my focus also extends to the wider networks of circulation and exchange through which Berbers have formulated their identities in cultural terms. Central among these is the phenomenon of world music, through which the musics and cultures of various parts of the ex-colonized world have been brought into relation with the West. World music brings together indigenous and Western harmonies, rhythms, instruments, and styles; it is associated with particular ethnic groups, usually from nonwestern countries; and it is marketed and distributed in the West as well as in the region of origin (Guilbault 1993: 36). The music sung by the Tilelli chorus—new Kabyle song— played a key role in enabling Kabyles to develop a sense of cultural identity when it emerged in the 1970s. Other networks were also in play. National systems such as public schools and universities, which were significantly expanded in virtually all ex-colonized nations in the years following independence, provided crucial pathways through which ideas about Berber culture were formulated and disseminated. The well-traveled routes between Algeria and the Kabyle diaspora in France provided another way for Berberist ideas and products to circulate. In attending to these networks, which are not particular to Algeria or to Arabs and Berbers per se, I move beyond an approach to Algerian history that narrates the relationship between Arabs and Berbers solely in terms of a dichotomy that has been widening since precolonial times.

Berbers through History

Berber populations today generally define themselves through indigeneity and language.[1] These criteria emerged gradually, taking on different meanings in relation to a series of political upheavals that would bring into being what is now North Africa. As far as the historical record is concerned, Berbers constitute the region's autochthonous inhabitants. They once occupied a widespread territory extending from the Siwa Oasis in what is now Egypt on the east to the Canary Islands on the west, and from the Mediterranean coast on the north to just below the Sahara Desert on the south. Today, this region includes parts of Egypt, Libya, Niger, Mali, Burkina Faso, and Mauritania and virtually all of Algeria, Morocco, and Tunisia. From early on, various parts of this region were also settled by a series of newly arriving populations. The most important of these were the Romans, who ruled for seven centuries (146 B.C.–439 A.D.); the Byzantines (533–647); the Arabs (arriving in several waves, primarily during the seventh and eleventh centuries); the Turks, who reached as far as present-day Tunisia and Algeria (1515–1830) during the expansion of the Ottoman Empire; and most recently, the French (1830–1962 in Algeria; 1881–1956 in Tunisia; 1912–1955 in Morocco). Prior to the French colonial conquest, the Arabs arguably had the most enduring impact on Berber populations. Whereas the Romans remained largely in urban centers and ruled outlying tribal groups through native leaders, the Arabs sought to unite the entire region under the banner of Islam. Aside from a small number of Latin-speaking inhabitants presumed to be Christian and allowed to retain their beliefs if they paid a poll tax (Brett and Fentress 1996: 83), the rest of the population was forced to submit simultaneously to both the Arab conquerors and the God of Islam. It was at that point that "Berbers"—identified as those indigenous groups who did not speak Latin— began to be conceived of as a separate people (Brett and Fentress 1996: 83).

The term "Berber" itself is almost certainly of external origin. Although not all experts agree on its precise etymology and history, it likely derives from the Latin *barbarus* (Greek *barbaroi*), which the Romans bestowed on various indigenous groups to describe the "strangeness" of their tongue (Brett and Fentress 1996: 4, 83). "Berber" does not refer to a single, unified language but serves as an umbrella term to describe a number of related linguistic varieties. These varieties or "dialects" (as they are popularly called) are linked to the Hamito-Semitic language family, which comprises Semitic languages (including Arabic) as well as old Egyptian (Brett and Fentress 1996; Chaker 1996).[2]

Because Arabic came to serve as the primary language of trade and commerce, it gradually became a lingua franca (Brett and Fentress 1996: 125–126), supplanting Berber in many parts of the region. Only in more remote areas did Berber remain the primary tongue. Today, Berber-speaking populations are found primarily in the high mountains of north-central Algeria and Morocco and in southernmost regions of the Sahara Desert. This comprises, in Algeria, the Kabyles of the Djurdjura mountains, the Shawiya of the Aures mountains, and the Ibadites of the oases of the Mzab, as well as several smaller groups such as the Shenwa on Algeria's western Mediterranean coast and the Gourara of the desert city Timimoun. In Morocco, Berber-speaking populations inhabit the mountainous regions of the Rif and the Middle Atlas in the north and center, and the High Atlas and Anti-Atlas mountains as well as the Sus Valley in the south. Another large group of Berber speakers is comprised of the Tuareg populations in the Saharan regions of Niger, Mali, southern Algeria, and Burkina Faso.[3] In Algeria, Berber speakers make up at least 20 to 25 percent of the population; Kabyles represent about two-thirds of those (Chaker 1989: 10). In Morocco, approximately 40 percent of the population is Berberophone (Brett and

Fentress 1996; Chaker 1989). Aside from older women who never attended school, most Berber speakers today have at least some facility with Arabic; many also speak some French, particularly in Kabylia.

Historically, these groups did not call themselves "Berbers" but had their own terms of self-referral. Kabyles, for instance, refer to themselves as "Leqbayel," Shawiyas as "Ishawiyen," and so on. Each group speaks a different variety of Berber. Although these language varieties share many syntactic and morphological correspondences, lexical and phonological variations are significant enough that intergroup communication is far from automatic. These localized Berber varieties have discrete names, usually formed by adding "t" (feminine diminutive) to the beginning and end of the singular form of the group name: for example, *aqbayli* (Kabyle individual) becomes *taqbaylit* (Kabyle language). Usage of the term "Berber" by the populations themselves began to become more generalized under French rule. When the French arrived in Algiers in 1830, they ousted the Turks from power and rapidly gained control over most of northern Algeria. Kabylia was the exception: It would take almost thirty more years and several intensive military campaigns before, in 1857, the mountainous Kabyle Berber region on the Mediterranean coast—its westernmost border a mere sixty miles from Algiers—fell to the French.

The Kabyle Myth

From early on, the French viewed North Africa through a Manichean lens. Arab and Berber became the primary ethnic categories through which the French classified the population (Lorcin 1995: 2). This occurred despite the fact that a diverse and fragmented populace comprised not only various Arab and Berber tribal groups but also Turks, Andalusians (descended from Moors exiled from Spain during the Crusades), Kouloughlis (offspring of Turkish men and North African women), blacks (mostly slaves or former slaves), and Jews.[4] Of the various Berber groups, Kabyles were singled out for special attention—probably because of their geographic proximity to Algiers and France. In what came to be called the Kabyle Myth, a number of the French military men charged with governing the new colony contended that Kabyles were closer to the French than were Algerian Arabs and demonstrated greater promise of being able to assimilate into the French polity (Ageron 1960; Lorcin 1995, 1996; Silverstein 2002, 2004b).

The Kabyle Myth was driven by perceived sociological and religious differences between Arabs and Kabyle Berbers that the French molded into an ideological hierarchy. First, the French attributed to Kabyles romanticized qualities of industriousness and frugality. Because the Kabyles were a sedentary, mountain-dwelling population living in small villages, they reminded the French of the peasants living in France's own picturesque countryside. In contrast, Arabs were caricatured as nomadic, tent-dwelling peoples lacking stability and purpose. This claim would have been unsustainable had nomadic Berber popu-

The French were attracted to the picturesque mountaintop villages they found when they conquered the Kabyle region in the mid-nineteenth century. This shot of the village At Lahcène was taken in 1993.

lations of the Sahara and sedentary Arab city and plains dwellers been taken into account. Yet it appeared to hold true for the Kabyle region and thus took on valence in the French colonial imagination.

Second, although the French were well aware that Kabyles were Muslims, they viewed Kabyles as less "fanatical" in their religious practice than their Arab counterparts. Some French administrators looked to the region's Roman history for signs that the Berbers may once have been Christianized. A few even contended that Berbers had Roman or Gallic origins. French missionaries established outposts and schools throughout Kabylia in an intensive (and ultimately failed) attempt to convert Kabyles to Christianity. The French army men who administered the region also made much of a particular social institution found in every Kabyle village—the *tajmaʿat*, or weekly assembly, where all the village's men would come together to deliberate matters of concern to the village as a whole and to establish and enforce laws governing social behavior. Although in practice these assemblies were controlled by powerful groups of patrilineages, the French interpreted them as a kind of primitive democracy that appeared to augur well for the assimilation of Kabyles into the French state. Some went so far as to see the tajmaʿat institution as inspired by Roman law (Ageron 1960: 317–318). In contrast, Arabs were perceived as Muslim zealots whose reliance on Quranic law made them unlikely candidates for democratic training.

Law was one way the French sought to promote the secular tendencies they perceived in the tajmaꜥat. The army officers assigned to Kabylia during the 1860s—many of them ardent Berberophiles—maintained the tajmaꜥat structure under French oversight. One erudite officer, Colonel Adolphe Hanoteau, set out to collect and codify the various tajmaꜥat laws with the full support of the Ministry of War (Hanoteau and Letourneux 1872–73; see Goodman 2002b). The years 1870–1871 marked a major shift. In France, the Third Republic replaced Louis Napoleon's Second Empire, which fell during the war with Prussia. In Algeria, military rule was replaced by a civilian regime more interested in extending the privileges of French settlers than in preserving indigenous customs. Legal administration of the Kabyle region was placed directly in the hands of French judges, who were initially charged with applying Colonel Hanoteau's compendium of Kabyle laws. While the attempt to administer Kabylia through a codified version of indigenous law was short-lived, it nonetheless worked to further differentiate Kabyles from Algerian Arabs, as it was in part via the category of "customary law" that notions of Berber custom began to be articulated.

Schooling was the other primary venue in which the French differentiated Kabyles from Arabs. Several Berberophiles in the government targeted education as the primary vehicle through which Kabyles could best assimilate into the French polity. French schools were built in the Kabyle region a generation earlier than elsewhere in Algeria, with the first schools opening in the early 1880s (Ageron 1960; Lorcin 1995; Mahé 2001; cf. Colonna 1975). It may appear contradictory that the French on the one hand promoted Kabyle political and legal institutions while on the other hand they sought to inculcate Kabyles with a republican education. In fact, however, both initiatives shared the goal of developing what the French perceived as a latent secularism in Kabyle society.

The Kabyle Myth may have been most pernicious in its separation of Kabyles and Arabs with regards to Islam (Lorcin 1995). To perceive Kabyles as somehow only superficially Muslim was to disregard important dynamics of Kabyle social life. Alongside a more orthodox or scriptural Islam centered on the five pillars of faith (the profession of faith, prayer, alms-giving, fasting, and the pilgrimage to Mecca), North African populations—both Berbers and Arabs—have long practiced a form of popular Islam related to the Sufi mysticism known in some parts of the Arab East. In brief, North African popular Islam centers around a series of holy figures known in French as *marabouts* (*imrabden* in Kabyle Berber), sometimes translated as "saints" (Cornell 1998). These individuals—some of whom claim descent from the Prophet Muhammad—traveled across North Africa from the fourteenth to the sixteenth centuries, arriving in Kabylia during the 1500s. The typical mark of a marabout was his ability to perform miracles such as curing the sick or causing water to spring up from dry ground. In that they were believed to have a privileged relationship to the supernatural, marabouts were understood as intermediaries between God and the populace. Marabouts also played key political roles, serving as mediators between competing tribal factions and providing a safe haven for travelers (Berque 1955; Eickelman 1976, 2002; Gellner 1969). Following a marabout's death, a shrine was generally erected around his tomb; these shrines were thought to contain *baraka,* a magical substance believed to have transformative powers because it was infused with the holy man's blessing. The descendants of a marabout generally maintain these ancestral shrines, some of which grew into large lodges or *zawiyas* that became important regional sites of religious instruction and pilgrimage (see Eickelman 1976). Whereas the mosque serves as a location for the collective practice of Islam's five daily prayers and for coming together for Friday sermons or on other Muslim holy days, the shrine is more typically visited for guidance in personal matters or simply as a way to escape from the pressures of daily life.

In practice, the distinction between mosques and shrines articulates with gender divisions animating Kabyle society, with women more likely to frequent the shrines while men gather in mosques (although men also pay visits to the shrines on special occasions). This gendered organization of religious practice is also found throughout many Arab regions of North Africa. At the risk of over-simplifying what was certainly a much more complex social reality, before the arrival of the French the greatest divide in Algerian society with regard to religion may not have been between Berbers and Arabs but between men and women and, by extension, between a more orthodox or scriptural and a more popular form of Islamic practice (see Brett and Fentress 1996: 264–269).

From a sociological point of view, the *imrabden* (a marabout's descendants) have until recently occupied a unique position in Kabyle society. Forbidden to own agricultural lands and exempt from collective village labors, they were provided for by ordinary Kabyle villagers (*leqbayel*) in exchange for offering religious education as well as consultations on matters ranging from infertility to intravillage disputes. Marabout families did not generally refer to themselves as "Kabyles" (*leqbayel*), for to do so would have been to deny their sacred ancestry. The Kabyle Myth's attempt to characterize Kabyle social practice as secular, then, also utterly disregarded the interdependencies between "ordinary" Kabyles (*leqbayel*) and marabouts (*imrabden*) that constituted a key sociological dynamic of every Kabyle village.

Language and Nationalism

Berber-Arab differences were newly articulated during the rise of Algerian nationalism in the 1930s and 1940s, this time by Algerians themselves. Three articles of faith—"Islam is our religion, Algeria is our country, Arabic is our language" (Ageron 1991: 94, citing the *Kitāb al-Jazaʿir* or Book of Algiers)— served as the foundation of the anticolonial nationalist movement. Arab Algerian nationalists increasingly gravitated toward the type of Reform Islam being developed in Egypt and elsewhere in the Middle East, which sought to "purify" the religion by returning to its original texts and tenets. Kabyle nationalists objected to the ways Reform Islam linked together the Arabic language and the Muslim faith to the exclusion of the Maghreb's Berber dimensions. Efforts of Kabyle nationalists to articulate the anticolonial struggle around the notion of an "Algerian Algeria" (*Algérie algérienne*) rather than an "Arab and Muslim Algeria" (*Algérie arabe et musulmane*) failed, leading to the marginalization of most Kabyle leaders (Ouerdane 1990). Yet for the first time, Kabyles—albeit primarily elites—began to formulate their identity in cultural, linguistic, and historical terms. This set the stage for the development of a specifically Berber nationalist consciousness. Whereas Arab nationalists sought to locate the beginnings of the Algerian nation with the Arab conquests of the seventh and eleventh centuries, Kabyles countered that the present-day Maghrebi countries had formed out of what was once a vast Berber land, giving Berbers greater historical legitimacy. To counter the image that Berbers were a mere collection of disparate tribes speaking mutually incomprehensible dialects (hardly a foundation for a nationalist polity), they introduced an indigenous term of self-referral—Imazighen, translated as "free men"—and claimed that the various Berber varieties had once constituted a single, pan-Maghrebi language called Tamazight. These terms do have Berber origins; they are still used as the primary terms of self-referral in Morocco's Middle Atlas region and have more restricted uses among other populations (Chaker 1987b). There is no evidence, however, that they were used in Kabylia before the 1940s.[5]

Within the Berber-Amazigh pair, Berber is clearly the unmarked or "default" term, employed more commonly in both general usage and scholarship. The *Berber Encyclopedia* (*Encyclopédie berbère*), founded in 1984 by contemporary scholars who share a commitment to the survival and standardization of the Berber language, employs "Berber" in its title and contains no alphabetic entry for it, while the entry for "Amazigh" is extensive (Chaker 1987b). Most Kabyles today refer to themselves unproblematically as either "Leqbayel" or "Berbères." "Amazigh," in contrast, calls attention to itself as an ideological choice, signaling that the speaker deliberately rejects perceived pejorative associations that "Berber" can carry and advocates a particular political vision of the Maghreb's future. For this reason, I retain the terms "Kabyle Berber" or simply "Berber" throughout most of this study. Unless otherwise noted, by "Berber" I refer only to Kabyles and not to other Berber groups. By "Berberist" I mean Kabyles advocating for linguistic and cultural rights in Algeria. Following current usage, I employ the terms "Amazigh," "Imazighen," and "Tamazight" to refer to contemporary efforts to create a transnational community with a standardized language and common political-cultural platform. While "Amazigh" may now be more common than "Berberist," that was not the case in the Kabyle region during the years of most concern in this work. I rarely heard Kabyles in Algeria refer to themselves as Imazighen, although the term had a bit more currency in the diaspora.

Berbers found themselves once again marginalized on linguistic grounds following the departure of the French in 1962 after a bloody eight-year war. Kabyles led the effort to standardize Tamazight so that it could hold its own alongside Modern Standard Arabic. Activists also tried to promote the notion of Amazigh identity among the populace at large. New Kabyle song was a key medium through which notions about Amazigh identity were disseminated. The new Kabyle singers I worked with all make reference to an Amazigh people and have written songs in support of Tamazight, and some included these terms in their song titles or stage names (for example, one singer named himself Ferhat Imazighen Imula). Whether the new, transnational Tamazight language (based heavily in Kabyle Berber, which itself has yet to be standardized) is understood by more distant Berber populations remains unclear. Indeed, orthographic choices themselves are still contested. In Algeria, Tamazight has been developed using a modified version of the Roman alphabet, while many Moroccans have lobbied for an orthography based in the Arabic alphabet and, more recently, the Tifinagh alphabet—the latter developed by Tuareg populations but never used by other Berber groups.

From the 1960s to the 1980s, Berber activists clashed on numerous occasions with state forces. Hundreds of Kabyles, ranging from key political figures to young teens rounded up at Berberist demonstrations, were periodically imprisoned and sometimes tortured. In 1976, following months of public debate, the Berber language and culture received almost no recognition in Algeria's new constitution, and prominent Berberist leaders were jailed. In March 1980, the government cancelled a lecture on Berber poetry by the Kabyle scholar Mouloud Mammeri. In response, students staged weeks of demonstrations and strikes in the regional capital of Tizi Ouzou (and, later, in Algiers). The events turned violent, culminating in a police attack on university dormitories that led to further insurgency. Following these events, now known as the Berber Spring, the Berber Cultural Movement (Mouvement Culturel Berbère, MCB) was born.

Berbers and Islamism

Even as the Berber Cultural Movement intensified the struggle for Berber language and culture during the 1980s and 1990s, Berber activists also found themselves contending with a growing Islamist movement. Islamist supporters in Algeria, inspired by related movements throughout the Arab world, look to shariʿa law and to the life and writings of the Prophet Muhammad as models for both state government and social behavior. For Islamists, the Arabic language is fundamental to Algeria's Muslim identity; the Berber language and heritage have no place in their vision. Berberists thus had to carve out a new position that would enable them to continue to argue for Berber as a component of Algerian identity without rejecting Algeria's Islamic dimension—which would be tantamount to losing all legitimacy in the eyes of the Algerian public. "Secular democracy" became the rallying cry around which they articulated this new vision. By secular democracy, Berbers refer not only to a separation of religion and state or to democratically elected public bodies, but also to a "project of society" (*projet de société*) designed to replace "retrograde" ways of thinking and acting with "forward-looking" mentalities and behaviors. Formulated as a modernizing initiative, secular democracy was a project to be achieved at both state and local levels.

Meanwhile, throughout the 1980s, social tensions were rising, fueled by skyrocketing unemployment and rapid inflation. In widespread rioting in early

Young men gather to demonstrate for Berber rights in Tizi Ouzou on April 20, 1993. Their banner reads, "No Democracy without Tamazight."

October 1988, thousands of demonstrators, primarily young men, attacked symbols of the state and particularly the ruling FLN. Six days of rioting were ultimately halted by the military, but at a high cost: Tanks fired on crowds of civilians, killing up to 500 and injuring many more. The government regained control only by promising democratic reforms. The state constitution was amended to permit new citizen associations and political parties. Almost overnight, some sixty parties formed, including the Islamic Salvation Front (Front Islamique de Salut, FIS), legalized in September 1989. The first multiparty elections in the state's twenty-eight-year history were scheduled for June 1990.

The Islamic Salvation Front soon became the most prominent of the new national parties. Able to galvanize the thousands of disenchanted youth who had taken to the streets in October, it became the primary opposition in most parts of the country. Kabylia was the exception. Here, loyalties were largely split between two secularist parties, the radical RCD (Rassemblement pour la Culture et la Démocratie, or Assembly for Culture and Democracy), headed by the leftist psychiatrist Said Sadi, and the more moderate FFS (Front de Forces Socialistes, or Socialist Forces Front), led by the revolutionary war hero Ait Ahmed. The Islamist FIS swept the June 1990 municipal elections everywhere but in Kabylia.[6] Eighteen months later, on December 26, 1991, the FIS handily won the first round of national parliamentary elections. The second round, which would have given the FIS control over the National Assembly, was abruptly cancelled with a coup d'état. On January 11, 1992, President Chadli Ben Djedid, in power since 1979, was forced to resign. Control of the government was assumed by a new entity called the High Council of State (Haut Conseil d'Etat, HCE). The HCE invited Mohammed Boudiaf, an exiled war hero who had come out on the losing end of a post-independence power struggle some three decades earlier, to serve as its first chair. Called back from Morocco, Boudiaf enjoyed a measure of popular support, but not from FIS members: Boudiaf outlawed the FIS in March 1992 and disbanded the municipal assemblies it controlled. Those FIS members who were not arrested and sent to holding camps in the Sahara Desert went underground, formed a militia known as the Islamic Salvation Army (Armée Islamique de Salut, AIS), and began low-level guerrilla warfare, targeting police officers and other representatives and institutions of the state.

On June 29, 1992, Boudiaf was assassinated. On August 26, the first large-scale "terrorist" incident took place, the bombing of the Algiers International Airport, which left 11 dead and 128 injured. What ensued was a civil war that, while never recognized as such by the Algerian state, would leave well over 100,000 dead by the end of the 1990s. Secularist intellectuals, reporters and newspaper editors from the liberal (French-language) press, artists and singers, and, eventually, foreigners were among those singled out by Islamist armed groups as especially desirable targets.[7] I began research in Algeria in early August 1992, between Boudiaf's assassination and the airport bombing, and left in December 1993, four days after the *fatwa* (authoritative religious decree) declaring that foreigners were legitimate candidates for assassination went into effect.[8]

As the FIS increasingly galvanized populist support, cultural associations became important vehicles for Kabyles, where they sought to lay the groundwork for the secular-democratic "project of society" that they envisioned. Similar to the role neighborhood mosques were playing in Islamist areas, these associations worked to bring national ideology to bear on local practice. One of the most contentious sites where ideological differences were being played out was gender. That the choral performance I witnessed included both boys and girls was no accident. It was at once a provocative refusal of Islamist calls for a gender-segregated public sphere and a way to begin to change the social organization of the village, which was itself largely ordered around gender divisions. The chorus's repertoire also worked to articulate the cultural association's vision of the nation's future. The children sang songs drawn from the recordings of new Kabyle singers who had played a pivotal role in Berber consciousness-raising for the two previous decades. The name of the chorus—Tilelli, or Freedom—spoke as well to the kinds of linkages through which Berbers were articulating their demands for recognition. The term is resonant with associations to democracy, liberty, and equality—all characteristics of secular democracy and cornerstones of modernity. It also evokes a transnational community and provides it with historical legitimacy: *tilelli* is a neologism created by Berber scholars engaged in developing Tamazight as an official or standard form of Berber that could reunite pan-Berber populations across North Africa.

Beyond Berbers and Arabs

As the Tilelli performance and cultural exhibit make apparent, a good deal more has been entailed in the development of contemporary Berber identity than a simple opposition between Berbers and Arabs. While Arab and Berber identities have clearly formed in close relation to each other, both have also emerged through interconnections that extend much farther afield. France has obviously served as an important point of reference through which both groups assess and critique themselves and each other. Berberists have even been pejoratively labeled the "Party of France" (*hizb Fransa*) by some Arab-Algerian nationalists, who interpret Kabyles' relative facility with the French language (developed through decades of immigration as well as through the Algerian school system) and their lack of support for the particular form of Arabo-Islamist ideology propounded by the state as signs that they align with the former colonial power. Berbers counter with accusations that the state has modeled itself after the nations of the Arab East rather than looking to Algeria's indigenous traditions. Any number of examples of this kind of triangulation, in which the relationship between Arabs and Berbers is defined via a third term, can be found in Algerian history (one of the earliest being perhaps the Kabyle Myth).

Yet Berber identity in Algeria has developed through interconnections that branch further still. I turn to a series of products and performances taken as especially representative of Berber identity in order to tease out the ways a contemporary Kabyle Berber cultural modernity has been forming through encounters that extend well beyond Algerian borders. These range from colonial-era poetry collections to new Kabyle songs and from wedding performances based in Kabyle villages to multimedia events in Paris. By examining the specific ways these products and performances are configured, I show how Berber identity has been made to appear singular and unique precisely through cultural motion—that is, through various relationships and connections formed between Kabyles in Algeria and the Algerian and French states, the Kabyle diaspora, and more globalizing circuits. In saying that Berber identity formed through encounters with extralocal formations, my argument is entirely distinct from the position of the Algerian state, which long viewed the Berber identity project as a neocolonialist plot motivated exclusively from without (in particular, from France). The state's position is rooted in the untenable Jacobin belief that nations come prepackaged with a single language, religion, and culture that formed in isolation from the rest of the world. Arabo-Islamic Algerian identity could be similarly understood as emerging through encounters with extralocal forces, although the particulars would of course differ.

In order to move beyond the apparent singularity of Berber identity discourse, I consider the complexity of its constitutive networks (cf. Latour 1993). I seek to identify what Jean-Loup Amselle has called the "branching interconnections" (*branchements*) (Amselle 2001) through which a notion of Berber culture has taken on meaning and substance. Based on the premise that interconnection is one of the conditions of possibility for the construction of cultural identity, *branchement* describes both the state of being connected and the acts of connecting, linking up, or plugging in. In its most basic sense, *branchement* is what enables the transmission of electrical current. More recently, the term's semantic reach has extended to digital media, evoking the decentered, thread-like branching through which the World Wide Web is organized. From a perspective of *branchement*, it is the very process of setting themselves in relation to an Other that enables social groups both to define themselves in terms of a singular cultural identity and to gain a newly reflexive awareness of their own apparent uniqueness. At the same time, seeing themselves through the Other produces not a mirror image but a refractive effect that also generates a sense of difference (cf. Bhabha 1994).

As a way of conceptualizing cultural motion, the metaphor of *branchement* has much to recommend it. It describes not a unidirectional flow but a network of exchange. Imagine the branching that occurs along a power grid. Some lines are regularly traveled while others may be used intermittently. Some remain permanently connected while others may cross without meeting. Currents may reverse direction, temporarily switch over to other lines, or be disconnected altogether. Adding new lines may either reinforce or draw power away from existing connections. In that it can describe a force field that extends simultaneously in multiple directions, the term is a good deal more potent than a concept like Ulf Hannerz's "ecumene" (Hannerz 1989, 1992), which posits a unidirectional flow from center to periphery. In contrast, *branchement* allows for precise tracking of the connective processes through which some locations may become more central than others. It also can accommodate the disjunctiveness of the model of cultural flows proposed by Arjun Appadurai (1990) without defining in advance, as Appadurai does, the contours of the various landscapes of motion in terms of ethnicities, ideologies, finances, media, and technologies (see Tsing 2000). Finally, the term captures the energetic nature of exchange: To extend the metaphor, "plugging in" can spark new synergies. Flows, in other words, are not passive but productive.

If *branchement* conveys a sense of the dynamic network of pathways through which culture moves, it does so through a spatial metaphor that does not consider differences among the ways particular channels form and operate. For instance, the linguistic politics of the Algerian public school system in the 1970s constitutes an entirely different kind of channel or "branch" than a set of Berber poetry collections that spans the nineteenth and twentieth centuries. Each enabled Berber culture to emerge in new ways as a tangible presence that could be reflexively grasped and experienced, but they did so through distinct institutions and media. The nature, shape, and history of a particular channel demands as much attention as what might flow through it (Tsing 2000). Equally seriously, *branchement* has no way to account for the relationship between cultural motion and the way that motion is described in discourse. One of the conditions of possibility for the development of a sense of unique cultural identity is the erasure of the very interconnections that enabled its emergence. By itself, *branchement* cannot speak to this erasure. In other words, it cannot account for the gap between how things circulate and the ways they are (or are not) represented.

To address these concerns, I move from a vocabulary of electrical science to one of physics, from current to force, drawing on Greg Urban's provocative suggestion that culture travels in relation to the ways it is discursively characterized. Such discourse can take either "accelerative" or "inertial" form (Urban 2001). "Metaculture"—the way a cultural item is talked about in relation to its past and its future—is what provokes one or the other kind of motion. Consider the artifacts on display in the cultural exhibit described above. When these were in daily use, they were passed from generation to generation through the "inertial force" of habit: The pots and jugs moved along social and discursive pathways that had been carved out by their prior movement (storage, food preparation). Their past usage, in other words, determined their future travels. It would take a new kind of "accelerative force" to propel these artifacts into novel circuits, where they could be self-consciously laid out and labeled as signs of a shared identity. Part of what enabled this resignification was the evaluation to which the objects were subjected. Whereas the objects-in-use were characterized in terms of their past ("this kind of jug is used to store olive oil because it has always been used that way"), the displayed objects were cast in terms of a future that foregrounded their novelty: They were now signs of a modern Berber culture that sharply demarcated itself from the past ("come and see these objects, which provide evidence of our heritage"). As this metacultural interpretation finds its way into an object, the interpretation itself becomes "a force in the world" (Urban 2001: 37).

This study is loosely situated around several accelerative moments, or points where Berber identity has seemed to branch rapidly in new directions. I begin with the Berber Spring of 1980, which for the first time focused international attention on the Berber predicament and resulted in a widespread "coming to awareness" (*prise de conscience*) of Amazigh identity among Kabyles themselves. I then turn to an earlier point of acceleration that helped to set the stage for the Berber Spring: the smash success of the first new Kabyle song to receive airplay outside Algeria, the singer Idir's 1973 hit *A vava inouva* (Oh, my father). Based around a traditional women's story, the song drew attention to Berber poetic and musical traditions even as it recast them as world music. Both of these moments are popularly narrated as springing almost out of nowhere—as sudden eruptions that reversed or at least unsettled the order of things. In contrast, I identify the multistranded but often occluded pathways that enabled these moments to be constituted as pivotal. The third accelerative moment I take up is the aftermath of the events of October 1988 in Kabylia and the Kabyle diaspora, which coincided with the period of my fieldwork. I focus in particular on how Kabyle activists were seeking to counter Islamist calls for gender segregation by developing performance opportunities for young women that challenged not only Islamists but also the gender organization of Kabyle society itself. To include girls and women in political performances was to bring family- and village-based norms and practices into relation with national interests and transnational ideologies.

Indigenous Texts, World Music, and the Foundations of Modernity

To ask how Berber culture was configured for a world stage is also to ask why Western consumers have been so interested. How did I come to be filming a performance by a children's chorus in a Kabyle mountain village? My own interest in Berber culture has been mediated from the outset by historically grounded assumptions and understandings similar to those that have informed the Amazigh cultural revival itself. In the 1980s, I performed with the Boston-based women's ensemble Libana, which is dedicated to researching and performing women's songs from around the world. As a Libana member I had already trooped, tape recorder in hand, to the homes of members of ethnic communities in the Boston area willing to share their songs with us. Before I ever dreamed of visiting Algeria, I had already painstakingly transcribed the words to Kabyle songs, wondering how we would learn to pronounce them correctly. I had stood on stages in Boston and New York, Michigan and Montreal, announcing that Libana's next number was from the Kabyle Berber region. I had witnessed the tears of male Kabyle audience members after the show, thanking us for bringing them "home."

The story that interests me here is that the contemporary fascination with world cultures, ethnicities, traditions, and identities—an interest shared both by members of the ethnic groups in question and by American and European performers and audiences—seems so very natural. Why are we all so persuaded of the compelling importance of, for instance, a woman's lullaby? Why did I go, camcorder in hand, to trace these small, sometimes whispered, wisps of culture? Why are so many others doing the same thing? Why are American audiences spellbound by the melancholic strains of an Armenian song performed by Libana? Why do tapes of traditional music from around the world fill entire catalogs and merit their own section in Tower Records or HMV? And why do we find libraries and archives full of the traces of those who quested after these songs and poems before us, in some cases more than a century ago? What was I doing in 1992 by tape-recording the very same women's satirical song that a French army colonel had written down in the 1860s?

To ask these questions is to inquire into the ways indigenous texts became central to the development of modernity itself (Bauman and Briggs 2003). The world music phenomenon in which both Idir and Libana have participated is but one in a series of projects dedicated to the recovery of indigenous voices. This enterprise has its foundations in the work of the eighteenth-century philosopher Johann Gottfried Herder, who maintained that to encounter such voices was to be in contact with a pure or authentic human essence not yet tainted by the perceived corruptions of modernity (Bauman and Briggs 1999). Collecting poems and songs was one way colonial agents attempted to grasp and monitor what they understood as a native "spirit" (Goodman 2002c; Raheja 1996). Assembling such texts into performances of folk heritage has been a key way nationalist regimes demonstrate their own rootedness in a timeless past (Anderson 1991). Recording and preserving "oral texts" (as scholars now call them) as specimens of other cultural realities has long been central to the disciplines of folklore, anthropology, and ethnomusicology (Bendix 1997). Indeed, what Steven Feld has called the "benign and hopeful" ethnomusicological project to collect and record the musics of the world's peoples, which came into vogue in the 1960s, gave birth to the term "world music" itself (Feld 2000: 146).

These projects share more than a benevolent interest in the voices of the Other. They participate in a regime of textuality predicated on a radical separation between modernity and its antecedents. One form this separation has taken is to differentiate sharply between texts that have been authored by individuals and those thought to be the collective heritage of groups. This distinction almost always coincides with other axes of hierarchical difference, such as male–female or urban–rural. Whereas individually authored texts are treated as private property that can be used by others only with legal dispensation and usually payment, texts construed as heritage are thought to belong to humanity itself. Even though in local practice such texts may be associated with particular individuals or be used only in specific kinds of settings, Western copyright law allows anyone to publish or record them with virtual impunity. To look into the reasons for the success of contemporary world music, then, is to come up against assumptions about authorship, ownership, and property rights that have been sedimented into the very foundations of modernity (see Coombe 1998).

World music's success is also dependent, of course, on media and dissemination technologies. Sound recordings of indigenous songs and poems remained largely in the hands of specialists until the advent of the cassette recorder in the 1960s. Not only did cassettes give singers like Idir an easy and affordable way to record their grandmothers' songs as source material for their own texts, but also it meant that the recordings of these singers could travel to far wider audiences than was previously the case. Consider that Idir's song *A vava inouva* reached me in Boston in 1980 on a cassette tape sent by an Argentine friend living in Paris, who wanted me to hear some of the most popular tunes on the Parisian airwaves. Libana's own repertoire of Kabyle songs was initially drawn from LP and cassette recordings by the Kabyle women's group Djurdjura, readily available to us from the local Tower Records store. Cassette recordings could also circulate with greater ease in Kabyle villages, many of which lacked not only record players but also the electricity to run them. Battery-operated cassette recorders presented a more affordable option.

If in the West Idir's songs were hailed as signs of modernity's Others, in Algeria they were understood as vehicles of modernity. The songs gave many Kabyles a sense that their culture counted—that is, that Berber customs and traditions were not backward or outmoded but could form a part of a modern Algerian nation. They prompted a widespread revalorization of Berber heritage that had become second nature by the time I arrived in Algeria. The songs were also taken up into new performance initiatives (like the Tilelli chorus) and used to articulate visions of a modern Kabyle society that would not be constrained by patrilineally based gender norms. Close examination of the way these songs have operated within local practice can help to illuminate the emergence of a specifically Kabyle cultural modernity.

Also at stake for Kabyles in the music of Idir and other new Kabyle singers was the way it created a sense of rootedness for those living in the diaspora. Kabyles had been moving back and forth between France and Algeria since the first decades of the twentieth century, but in the 1970s immigration assumed a permanent character as women began joining their husbands and raising families. Some 500,000 Algerians of Kabyle origin reside in France today, constituting approximately one-third of all Algerian immigrants.[9] Several of my immigrant friends who grew up in Paris told me that it was by listening to Idir's music that they were able to connect with Kabyle culture as teenagers as well as to gain greater facility with the language itself. That the song *A vava inouva* had become a sign of their heritage for diaspora audiences was especially apparent to me during an Idir concert I attended at the Olympia Theater in Paris in June 1993. At the show's end, Idir was joined on stage by more than a dozen Kabyle singers. Passing the mike from one to the next, they each sang a single line of the song as the crowd roared. Clearly, it had become a piece of collective heritage to which all could lay claim.

Return to the Village

In taking up a range of sites, my hope is to provoke a critical rethinking of the practice of ethnography itself and, in particular, of what constitutes the "field" of anthropological research under contemporary circumstances. I take the field not as a place (or even a series of places) but as a problematic that emerges at the intersection of contemporary ideologies, historically shaped discursive formations, and situated discourse and performance practices. The notion of the village is one such problematic. Once construed as the locus classicus of ethnographic fieldwork, the village remains important to this study, but for new reasons: It is via the village that Berber culture has traveled to a world stage. Although only two of the book's eight chapters are specifically concerned with the goings-on in a particular village, a figure of the village inhabits this study from beginning to end. The village has served as a site of privileged source material for collectors of indigenous poetry, ethnographers, and world music singers alike. The song that put Kabylia on the international map, Idir's *A vava inouva*, centers around images of life in a traditional village, which is portrayed as separate from the surrounding world. Notions about the kinds of cultural productions apt to be found in villages help to found modern regimes of textuality, reinforcing the presumed divide between authored and collective works that underwrites intellectual property law. The village also constitutes a key, if contested, symbolic anchor for diasporic representations of Berber culture. Depictions of an originary village as a timeless entity untouched by the modern world serve as a way to measure the supposed degradations wrought by modernity.

In a world of nation-states in which political legitimacy requires a particular way of narrating the past (Bhabha 1990), the village and its attendant cultural mythology provide such an authorizing figure. Yet although the village is generally evoked as a locus of an originary cultural purity, this image of the village has formed through various branching interconnections that represent diverse ideological projects. The notion of an originary source serves to mask these interconnections, thereby naturalizing the social and political uses to which village cultural products are put. By tracking various poems, songs, and performances in the making, I show how they have been shaped to serve distinct political agendas even as their connections with those agendas are erased. In considering the ways cultural products can be severed from their constitutive networks, I call attention to the relationship between representation and circulation. For as Urban (2001) has made abundantly clear, some kinds of representations circulate better than others. That Berber culture has now achieved global visibility is testimony to the extraordinary attention Kabyles have devoted to how culture travels.

Without a representation of an originary village, the development of Berber cultural modernity would hardly have been imaginable. But the Kabyle village, of course, is also a geopolitical entity. Dozens of densely packed houses mark its place on the mountainous Mediterranean landscape. In that villages are patrilineally organized around nested groups of kin, to enter a village is to come into a tightly woven organization of social relationships. No outsider could pass unnoticed. Much of my fieldwork took place in a particular village in Kabylia, although that village, like many others, itself has a double existence: More than one-third of its population lives in Paris for most of the year. The populations on Algerian and Parisian "sides" of this village have ongoing material relationships, with commodities, cash, and corpses regularly traveling between them. With these populations, the project of cultural modernity is being mediated in new ways, as the collective representations of Berber identity that have journeyed to a world stage are resituated within local organizations of performance. At the same time, globalizing performance forms (such as children's choruses) are being taken up within the villages and used to constitute new kinds of relationships to self and family, village and nation. I return, then, from the world stage to village-based ethnography in order to develop an account of how Kabyles are performing modernity within lived social practice.

From the Berber Spring to the Parisian Stage

I approach the development of cultural modernity in Kabylia via three interconnected rubrics: circuits, texts, and performances. Part 1 concerns itself with three specific locations around which a sense of Berber identity has developed: the Berber Spring, the song *A vava inouva,* and the Kabyle village. Here, I focus specifically on the discrepancies between the plurality of networks through which culture circulates and the singular ways in which it is represented. Part 2 provides extended consideration of the ways indigenous texts have served the development of Kabyle cultural modernity, moving from colonial collections of poetry to world music song texts to local disputes about the ownership and authorship of new Kabyle songs with regards to copyright law. In part 3, I take up the ways Kabyles are constituting themselves in relation to modernity through performances in both Algeria and the diaspora in Paris.

Part 1 opens with the period of violence known as the Berber Spring, which surrounded the police attacks on student dormitories on April 20, 1980. This event is typically cast as a rite of reversal in which a repressed Kabyle population finally rose up against a dictatorial state. Suspending this interpretation, I ask what enabled April 20 to become constituted as a turning point for the Berber identity movement and a date around which Berbers worldwide now gather annually in commemoration and solidarity. Four phenomena converged around the university that spring: the Arabization program implemented in the Algerian public schools; a small network of cultural collectives established by elites in Paris during the preceding two decades; the modes of student governance being practiced at Algerian universities; and the international press and human rights organizations. But April 20 is not talked about as a site of convergence; rather, it is characterized as a rite of reversal. Why the split between the sets of intersecting phenomena, whose pathways had no preordained connection, and the ritual language with which April 20 is now talked about (cf. Latour 1993)? Here I move beyond the pathways themselves to consider how discourse travels. To be a good candidate for widespread circulation, an element of culture has to be packaged such that it can be readily detachable from its surrounds (Bauman and Briggs 1990). April 20 has been cast as such a detachable entity. The date serves as a tangible point of reference around which Berbers can articulate new concerns. It provides a recurring means of both educating new generations about the movement's history and mobilizing them for future activism. Now commemorated transnationally, April 20 enables Berber communities across North Africa, Western Europe, and North America to gather annually to envision a common Amazigh identity. In short, framed as a rite of reversal, April 20 travels far better than it would if described in terms of branching interconnections.

From the Berber Spring of 1980 I move to the 1970s, considering the development of Berber identity in relation to new Kabyle song. Chapter 2 centers around *A vava inouva*, the song that put Berber culture on an international stage. The song builds on a traditional Kabyle women's story to develop what its author called an "internal gaze" through which Berbers could see themselves in their own terms. This internal gaze turns out, however, to be densely mediated. The Kabyle legend was recast in relation to such diverse phenomena as a Tunisia-based ethnographic film, the 1969 Pan-African Festival in Algiers, the writings of such postcolonial luminaries as Frantz Fanon, Albert Memmi, and Amilcar Cabral, and the music of Cat Stevens and Simon and Garfunkel. The song enabled Kabyles to develop a self-reflexive vantage point on their culture by seeing it at a certain remove—much like the videographer who recorded me filming a concert that had been set up for me to video. Here again, interconnection constituted the condition of possibility for the development of a sense of unique Berber identity.

Chapter 3 turns from the world stage to the village life conjured as its opposite. Putting Berber culture into circulation for world audiences created local pressure to imagine home—the village—in particular ways. The image of the village as a fixed location of tradition masks the potentially destabilizing dynamics of village life that result in part from the long history of immigration between Algeria and France. I contrast the popular representation of the Kabyle village as a location of tradition with an ethnographic account of the continuous movement through which the village is actually constituted. My ethnographic discussion focuses on three locations within the village—the house, the men's assembly, and the wedding. These settings have been characterized through the lenses of nostalgia and loss by local inhabitants, colonial agents, and scholars alike. The nostalgia for these sites is significant in that it is precisely through the house, the men's assembly, and the wedding that people manage their own trans-Mediterranean mobility. Both villagers and ethnographers have traditionalized these sites so as to conceal the dynamic instability that in fact pervades village life at its core.

Part 2 is concerned with the centrality of indigenous texts to the construction of Berber identity. Chapter 4 moves from the 1980s to the 1860s, taking up the issue of how collections of Kabyle poetry have been made to mediate new forms of political consciousness. Since French colonel Adolphe Hanoteau published the first volume of Kabyle poetry in 1867, indigenous poems have been gathered by variously positioned individuals and oriented to divergent ideological horizons. A series of collectors who produced both print anthologies and (in one case) sound recordings of Kabyle poetry and song over more than a century propelled Kabyle poems into entirely new spheres of discourse, making them speak alternately to nineteenth-century pacification and civilizing missions, turn-of-the-century liberalist debates, nationalist agendas, and postcolonial identity projects. Their premise that texts serve as vehicles for an authentic indigenous voice obscures how the poems were made to participate in the construction of social difference.

Chapter 5 returns to the present, foregrounding the authorial processes entailed in transforming village women's poems and songs for a world stage. Whereas earlier collectors claimed to reproduce texts as they found them, contemporary singers and songwriters acted more like entrepreneurs or cultural brokers. They took what they considered original texts and pried them apart, reworking the texts to purge them of what they viewed as "backwardness" while making them speak to contemporary concerns. Their own evaluations of the texts they gathered are not presented "around" the text (for example, in framing essays or footnotes) but rather are folded into the new texts themselves. Reading backward from new songs to their village sources can reveal the particular processes through which this folding took place. In the discrepancies between a new text and its village antecedent, the local specificities of the modernizing project in which the new singers were engaged can be discerned.

Chapter 6 starts from a number of disputes I witnessed about whether those new songs that were drawn from village repertoires had been properly registered at the copyright agency. That is, were they listed by the singer as original authored creations or as coming from the public domain? What the term "public domain" appears to evoke for Kabyles is not a neutral zone in which songs belong to no one and from which songs can simply be plucked with impunity by anyone who chooses to do so. Rather, the term suggests a gendered space where the songs travel in strictly regimented ways. That is, songs are attached to specially designated events (such as weddings) and may be sung only by women of a certain age who bear a particular relationship to the event (close kin). If the singers can be called authors, the logic goes, then why not also the women? Here, then, the concept of public domain itself is what produces a sense of authorship, challenging one of the law's foundational conceits: that authorship and the public domain constitute inherently opposed domains of textuality that can be sharply demarcated. Overall, the chapter proposes a critical rethinking of the ways Western scholarship has conceptualized the public domain.

Part 3 highlights some of the dynamic tensions between the performance of Berber identity for a world stage and the social relations of its production in specific settings. Chapter 7 focuses directly on how the problematics of the village and trans-Mediterranean mobility materialize as aspects of concert performance. I compare performances produced by members of newly created Berber cultural associations in both Algerian and Parisian "sides" of the Kabyle village where I resided. On display were not only the particular shows at hand but also, more importantly, new forms of social relationship. Boys and girls would stand side-by-side onstage at an Algerian wedding as they sang some of the now-classic hits from the new Kabyle song repertoire. Young men and women from different village sections and patrilineal groups participated together in the opening events of the village's Paris-based association. Yet although men and women may have been sharing the same stage, they were facing in different directions. Young men were looking toward the nation. In positioning their sisters on a village stage, they placed themselves on a national stage, displaying their adherence to secular-democratic (rather than Islamist) principles. Young women, in contrast, faced primarily the village. In taking up new subject positions in front of their families, relatives, and future in-laws, they were evaluated not in terms of their allegiances to particular political ideologies but in relation to norms of morality that exerted the most pressure within the village itself.

Chapter 8 takes up the "village" as it was reconstituted on the Parisian stage in May 1994. The scene is the Olympia Theater; the star of the show, Lounis Aït Menguellet, one of the major figures of new Kabyle song. He performed before a painted backdrop of mountains, flanked by men's and women's backup choruses who stood before replicas of quintessential symbols of male and female social spaces (public benches, a fountain). The show was to be filmed for a commercial video, and this time I was in front of the camera's lens, joining four Kabyle women in the women's backup chorus. Looking from the stage to the video reveals a striking absence: The women's chorus was removed from the film, its only trace an occasional passing shot of five empty microphones. Starting from that trace image, the chapter explores some of the terrain that lies between the collective performance of Berber identity and the diasporic setting in which it was produced. Onstage, the women played traditional roles. Standing before a water fountain, they represented the ways Kabyle women would have sung together in a village setting. Behind the scenes, however, when the women articulated concerns arising from the conditions and constraints of their lives as Algerian women who were living, working, and raising families in Paris, they were silenced. Rather than pay the women what they asked for, the singer instead chose to delete them from the video. In his view, their demands threatened to destabilize the collective representation of Berber identity. It was only the idyllic village—understood as an originary source from which the Berber identity movement drew inspiration—that could transfer to video.

When I began long-term ethnographic fieldwork in 1992, I set out to do an ethnography of performance that would focus on new Kabyle song and the contemporary Berber movement. But the traces I kept finding of collectors who had gone before refused to remain silent. I could not separate today's performances from the histories through which Berber culture—and so-called folk cultures more generally—had been constituted. Ultimately, my focus expanded to include both the discrete discourse and performance genres through which Berber concerns with culture are being newly articulated, and the broader historical formations through which culture has come to carry such ubiquitous force. This study both participates in and seeks to elucidate the intertwined historical and contemporary interconnections that led to two camcorders filming each other filming a performance of culture in a Berber mountain village in 1993.

Part One.   *Circuits*

1   The Berber Spring

L'existence de plusieurs mouvements de jeunes risque d'aboutir à des orientations contraires et pas toujours conformes à la ligne du parti. La jeunesse algérienne brassée pendant la guerre de libération doit rompre aujourd'hui tout
cloisonnement et être organisée dans un rassemblement national sous une
direction unique et sous l'impulsion du parti.
> —La Charte d'Alger, 1964, Part III, Chapter 1, Article 22

[The existence of multiple youth movements risks producing opposing orientations that may not always conform to the party line. Algerian youth, stirred
up during the war, must today break with all forms of compartmentalization
and organize itself in a national union moving in a single direction and under
the impetus of the Party.
> —The 1964 Charter of Algiers, Part III, Chapter 1, Article 22]

April 20, 1980. One o'clock in the morning. Operation Mizrana has been launched,
the forces of repression invade all the sites that are being occupied [by striking
Kabyle students, hospital personnel, and factory employees]. Students, surprised in
their sleep, are assaulted in their beds; dogs are let loose on those who flee. Students
leave their dormitory rooms in their underwear. Professors are arrested in their
homes. All the personnel of the hospital, doctors and nurses, are arrested and replaced by military doctors. A spontaneous general strike is begun by the population of Tizi Ouzou. Kabylia is cut off from the world; access is forbidden to everyone and in particular to journalists.

The above account is drawn from a history of the Berber identity movement
produced on six hand-lettered posters by the Tafrara Cultural Association. Entitled "Chronology of the Contemporary Berber Struggle," the posters graced
the walls of the Mouloud Mammeri Cultural Center during the week of April
20, 1993, in what has become an annual commemoration of the 1980 Berber
Spring. I sat in front of the posters, copying by hand their account of what transpired.[1] The chronology begins on March 10, 1980, when Kabyle scholar and
activist Mouloud Mammeri (1917–1989) was to give a public lecture on the role
of poetry in traditional Kabyle society, the subject of his newly published book
Poèmes kabyles anciens (Old Kabyle Poems). The talk was to take place at Hasnaoua University in the city of Tizi Ouzou, the intellectual and commercial center of the Kabyle Berber region. A crowd of more than one thousand had gathered, but Mammeri never arrived. He was stopped at a police roadblock, brought

before the region's governor (*wali*), and informed that the event had been canceled. The reason: "risk of disturbing the public order." The cancellation sparked demonstrations and strikes at schools, universities, and businesses that would rock the Kabyle region for more than two months. Matters came to a head on April 20 when, at 4:15 in the morning, riot police stormed university dormitories, a factory, and the local hospital. Armed with tear gas and clubs, they arrested hundreds and wounded many more. Subsequent demonstrations, often violent, swept the region. Echoes were felt as far away as Paris, where some 600 demonstrated on April 25 at the Algerian embassy, against the orders of French authorities.[2] Widely commented on in the French press,[3] the events were reported to human rights organizations, including Amnesty International and the International League of Human Rights. Mammeri hoped his book would "serve as an instrument in the transmission of Berber culture" (Mammeri 1980: 47), but he could hardly have foreseen the catalytic impact of his canceled lecture. For while the period of violence resolved within several months, its memory mushroomed. The Berber Spring (Tafsut Imazighen, or simply Tafsut), as April 20 is now called, is commemorated unofficially each year in Algeria as well as in the Berber diaspora in Europe and North America. Tafsut is now one of the key sites through which a discourse on Amazigh identity circulates.

Before April 1980, such a discourse was not widely available. Consider Bachir's story. He had first heard the word "Amazigh" in 1976, at the age of 10, when Idir's new song *Muqleγ* ("I See") was played on the Kabyle radio station (Idir 1976b). The song's refrain goes like this:

Muqleγ tamurt umaziγ	I see the Amazigh land
Yugurten waleγ udem-ik.	Yugurtha,[4] I see your face.

"What was this Amazigh?" Bachir remembered wondering. For while the term "Amazigh"—used to signify a pan-Maghreb history, culture, and linguistic identity—circulated among intellectuals, it was not part of the vocabulary of most Kabyles in the 1970s, let alone their self-definition. As Bachir recounted it to me in November 1993, he thought that the term referred to a large tribal group located on the other side of the mountains from his village. He pictured lots of snow and wild, crazy men with long, unkempt hair and beards, who were barefoot, wearing loincloths and tunics, and holding sheaths and lances. Bachir's father told him that Amazigh referred to the Berbers, but Bachir was unconvinced: "I felt an incredible pity for those people," he told me. For Bachir, the Amazigh was a primitive savage, an Other who had little relevance for his own life.

Four years later, in April 1980, Bachir was in junior high school when he heard what he described as a frightening sound like a "swarm of bees." Turning to look out the window, he was initially terrified—a mob of young men was advancing, throwing stones, breaking windows, and chanting. As they drew closer, he made out their words: "I—ma—zi—ghen." For the first time, he made a visceral connection between the term and his own experiences: "It was at that moment," he said, "that I knew who I was." The next April, Bachir helped to

Wall paintings of the ancient Berber heroes Massinissa, Kahina, and Yugurtha, who are now revered for resisting invading forces. Azazga, April 1993.

organize Tafsut events at his school; in 1982, he was permanently suspended for his role in planning Tafsut activities. While Bachir's initial image of the Amazigh may be more graphic than most, his testimony is hardly unique. According to Hend, who in 1993 was a local representative of the ultra-secular RCD party: "We saw Amazigh as something else, as unconnected to our lives and traditions." Most of his parents' generation, said Hend, did not distinguish between Muslims and Arabs; for older Kabyles, to claim that "We are not Arab" was tantamount to renouncing their Muslim identity, an unthinkable prospect.

If the Berber Spring, or Tafsut Imazighen, is described as a turning point in individual testimonies, it is also cast as a point of origin in both popular and academic publications. In these accounts, April 20 is typically characterized in almost ritual terms as a liminal moment of reversal when a repressed population rose up against an absolutist, dictatorial state.[5] For example, a 1981 article in the grassroots journal *Tafsut* ("Spring"), which began publication after 1980, begins: "In the spring of 1980, following a series of provocations and aggressions on the part of the authorities, the demands [*revendications*] for Berber culture burst open in full daylight" (Tafsut 1981c: 13). Another starts, "The suffocation of popular cultures and the repeated attacks on democracy led during 1980 to the emergence of a mass movement" (Tafsut 1981b: 10). Even academic studies that otherwise provide nuanced and detailed analysis of the events draw on tropes of repression, rupture, and explosion. Amar Ouerdane, for instance, describes April 20 as a moment when "rupture with the central government [*le Pouvoir*] was consummated" (Ouerdane 1990: 193); Said Sadi describes the moment as one that "reversed the order of things" (Sadi 1983: 43). When accounts mention the institutional and conjunctural factors related to the Berber Spring, they do so almost parenthetically, within an overall frame of repression and explosion (e.g., Chaker 1989). Mammeri's canceled lecture is typically characterized as the spark that ignited the fire or the drop of water that made the vessel overflow.

The Berber Spring is also projected forward and backward, superimposed on other violent episodes in Kabyles' relation to the state. Thus, a deadly 1949 clash between Berberists and Arabo-Islamists over the question of Algeria's national language is construed by one scholar as "the first Berber Spring" (Ouerdane 1990: 47, 59). In this view, April 20, 1980, is already a repetition, a "reappearance of a demand [*revendication*] for Berber culture that had long been inhibited" (Harbi 1980: 31). Alternatively, the Berber Spring is seen as inflecting a later event. Thus, for example, a period of violence that began in April 2001, when state forces fired into a crowd, killing an eighteen-year-old Kabyle youth and sparking ongoing unrest that led to over one hundred deaths, is popularly termed the "Black Spring," despite the fact that the insurrection lasted for well over a year.

These accounts appear to be caught up in ways of conceptualizing history that may obscure more than they clarify. They recall the familiar Fanonian anticolonial liberation narrative that begins in repression and alienation, then moves through consciousness and awakening to resistance and struggle, ultimately culminating in realization (Scott 1999: 201–208; Fanon 1963). This narrative is articulated with a view of history that Hayden White has described in terms of fulfillment (White 2002). Here, particular events are made to stand out from their surrounds to become fraught with significance; through such events, both the individual and the community are said to emerge transformed. These charged and redemptive moments, extracted from the particular configuration of forces that produced them, can also be mapped onto each other such that a later event is interpreted as a fuller realization of an earlier one, which is then said to be annunciatory or prophetic.

To cast what happened in April 1980 solely in terms of opposition, resistance, or effervescence, however, is to obscure the important ways in which it was Kabyles' very mastery of state-based systems of governance and communication that enabled them to pull off a relatively organized and politically productive two-month insurgency (cf. Colonna 1996). Suspending the Fanonian lens through which the Berber Spring is typically understood makes it possible to elucidate the linked institutional and ideological processes through which April 20 became available for both political mobilization and individual self-constitution. This is not to contest the importance of 1980 in the history of the Kabyle relationship to the Algerian state, but it is to take issue with the way most narratives account for the Berber Spring. Such accounts obscure the ways that

Kabyles themselves had been gradually putting in place crucial networks, which they could draw on in 1980.

Why should April 1980 have become a turning point in the development of Berber consciousness? After all, a rhetoric of Amazigh identity was hardly new in 1980. It had been available to elites since at least the 1930s, when splits emerged within the growing anticolonial nationalist movement around the question of language (Carlier 1984; Chaker 1989; Ouerdane 1990). Nor can the prominence of April 1980 in cultural memory be considered solely a reaction to state violence against Kabyles. Events that were arguably more serious had already occurred. In 1974, for example, at an annual cherry festival in the town of Larba n At Iraten, the army reportedly killed three protesters when it was called in to subdue demonstrations that had erupted over the replacement of new Kabyle singers Ferhat Imazighen Imoula and Aït Menguellet with Arab singers (Ouerdane 1990: 185).[6] In 1980, by contrast, no one died.[7] The Cherry Festival incident, while clearly an important event in the history of Kabylia's relationship to the state, is not narrated in terms of the development of a new collective consciousness. What, then, was different about 1980? What enabled the cancellation of Mammeri's lecture to be retrospectively constituted as an originary moment—a moment with which most accounts of the Berber Spring (including this one) begin?

The events of April 1980 took on such importance because they occurred in a location where several rapidly expanding institutional networks converged: the university and, in particular, the University of Tizi Ouzou Hasnaoua, which had opened just over two years earlier.[8] Four sites draw my attention: the Arabization program implemented in the Algerian public schools; a small group of cultural collectives established by elites in Paris in the decade following independence; the modes of student governance being practiced at Algerian universities; and the international press and human rights organizations. My point of entry will be by way of the 1993 Tafsut celebration in the city of Tizi Ouzou, which I was fortunate to be able to attend. Whereas by 1993, the connections between these sites were so well established as to seem natural, I show how in 1980 they were drawn together conjuncturally. From this moment of commemoration, I work both crosswise and backward, tacking between the 1993 events and the social constituencies and circulatory pathways bound up with these events.

I begin with the Algerian public school system of the 1960s and 1970s, considering how the state's program to "Arabize" its population unwittingly facilitated the development of Amazigh identity in three ways. It provided Kabyles entering school in the 1960s and 1970s with a shared experience of their mother tongue as an object of repression and thus desire; it inculcated a homogenizing Arabophone linguistic ideology that provided a template for the development of Tamazight as a standardized code capable (at least in theory) of connecting speakers of different Berber varieties; and it furnished a ready-made network through which a discourse of Amazigh identity could travel clandestinely. I then move to the nascent Berber cultural associations in Paris during the 1960s and

1970s. Unlike later Paris-based associations, which were aligned primarily toward the diaspora community, these early associations were strongly oriented to Algeria, and Kabyles in Algeria participated in the production and dissemination of their projects and products. From there, I consider the Algerian university governance system, which provided a crucial public forum in which students could develop consensus among themselves and collaborate with adjacent constituencies. Even as activist Kabyle students contested the particular ideological orientations of the Algerian state, they drew on practices consistent with a mode of state-based governmentality that would enable them to collectively mobilize when Mammeri's lecture was canceled. Finally, I consider how Amazigh discourse was further amplified via the international press, where it was ultimately mapped onto another available network: human rights.

Arabization

April 20, 1993. I am standing with my video camera on a hill overlooking the entrance to the University of Tizi Ouzou, where hundreds of young men and a few women are beginning to congregate for their annual march through the city. Groups of demonstrators begin to form, with those at the front of each group holding large banners. One banner poses a question, in French, that Mammeri had asked years before: "If we are Arabs, we don't need to be Arabized. If we are not Arabs, why Arabize us?" As demonstrators begin to march, they chant, fists raised, in French and Tamazight: "We are not Arabs, Tamazight in the Schools" ("Nous ne sommes pas des arabes, Tamaziɣt di lakul").

Without Algeria's Arabization program, the Berber Spring would likely never have happened. For Algeria as for most ex-colonies, decolonization demanded "recovery" of the nation's language, for language was seen as a crucial dimension of national personality. The problem was that the linguistic situation in Algeria at the moment of decolonization was far from straightforward. During the long period of French colonization, the Arabic language, not surprisingly, was marginalized. A 1938 law had gone so far as to declare Arabic a foreign language in Algeria (Grandguillaume 1983: 96). Schooling of *les indigènes* (the indigenous population) took place primarily in French. School was not the only route to acquiring French-language skills. In regions of high emigration, including Kabylia, most men had at least a basic ability to speak French. Arabic and Berber, Algeria's indigenous languages, comprised a number of varieties. Varieties of Arabic changed from eastern to western regions of the country as well as between urban and rural areas of the same region (Grandguillaume 1983: 13; Taleb-Ibrahimi 1995). Berber varieties differed not only among geographically distant Berber groups (i.e., Shawi, Ibadites, Tuareg, Kabyles) but also within a region. Few Algerians were schooled in either classical or modern standard Arabic, which differed substantially from spoken varieties. This effectively made

"Tamazight in the Schools" reads this graffiti, which is scrawled across a wall in the city of Tizi Ouzou. 1993.

French, already the language of state administration, a lingua franca in many parts of the country.

When the Algerian government set out its ambitious program to "Arabize" the population in the years following independence, it was confronted with daunting challenges. Who was qualified to teach the language? What books could they use? How to handle the fact that the entire state and administrative bureaucracies operated only in French, including the administrations of the schools themselves? The Ministry of Education addressed the situation with a number of measures that appeared to many as arbitrary and disconnected from the country's sociolinguistic reality. Thousands of teachers were recruited from Egypt and Syria. They taught in modern standard Arabic, but they could not easily communicate in Algerian varieties of spoken Arabic even in predominantly Arabophone regions, let alone in Berberophone parts of the country. School texts were imported that were not adapted to Algeria's historical and demographic contexts. Even more problematic were the measures taken to sequence the implementation of Arabic in the schools. Recognizing that Arabic could not replace French overnight, the Ministry of Education worked out a complex plan whereby the schools were "Arabized" one or two grades at a time.[9] For students, this meant that the first few years of schooling were generally in Arabic and the rest were in French. Seemingly arbitrary dates were set for Arabizing new grade levels. In some schools only a third of the students in each grade were Arabized. Arabization concerned not only the schools but also the semiotics of public space, as overnight, French signs were replaced by Arabic ones and people awakened to an illegible world.

The position of Arabic in newly independent Algeria was clearly fragile, and Arabization was an understandable and no doubt necessary attempt to create a national population that shared at least one common code. Yet if Arabization was primarily intended to free the country from its reliance on the colonizer's language, it also created a growing sense of marginality among Kabyles. Consider Ammar's story.[10] Born in 1957, Ammar was enrolled in one of the first classes to begin school in the Algerian state system after independence. His memories of his early school years remained vivid when we talked in Montreal in March 2002. Speaking Kabyle was forbidden, Ammar explained, not only in the school itself but also anywhere in the school's vicinity. This prohibition was enforced through a nail that circulated from child to child in a perverse version of the game American children recognize as hot potato. When a child was heard speaking Kabyle, that child would receive the nail. To get rid of it, the child would have to catch someone else violating the rule and would pass the nail to them. This continued until the next morning in class, when the child left holding the nail would be punished—perhaps by being forced to kneel for four hours without a break or by being physically struck. Parents, too, got involved in the nail's travels, as one parent would accuse the other's child of giving their child the nail. The absurdity of this system was not lost on the students. One day, Ammar recalled, he was standing with a group of children in the school courtyard when the teacher approached. Usually, the approach of the teacher meant that the children would quickly switch into French or Arabic (French was permitted at the time). This time, though, one child decided to test the limits of the nail's power by trying to find out what counted as linguistic expression. Pointing to another child, he cried out, "Mister! He just laughed in Kabyle!" After a moment of stunned silence, the child who had the nail threw it to the ground, ending that particular episode without punishment. The nail provided Ammar with his first visceral experiences of linguistic marginalization: He literally held his sense of difference in his hand. He was only ten or eleven when he began to reject the status that the nail conferred. He recalled being approached by a student who told him that he had witnesses who would testify that Ammar had spoken in Kabyle on school property. He then tried to hand Ammar the nail, but Ammar refused to take it.

While Ammar's story is the most poignant of the tales I heard, a number of Kabyles described to me how they were punished—usually, slapped—for speaking Kabyle at school. It was these very students—the ones who began elementary school during the 1960s—who would become the university students of 1980. Yet even as the public schools helped to produce linguistic hierarchy, they also firmly instilled in these students a state-centered linguistic ideology in which language and national identity were viewed as inextricably linked. They provided a template for the understanding of a single written language (code) as linked to but subsuming a number of different spoken varieties ("dialects"). Finally, the public schools provided an incipient dissemination network through which a growing number of products oriented to Berber identity could travel clandestinely. What were those products? Who was producing them? How did they end up in the hands of students like Ammar?

Berber Cultural Organizations in the 1960s–1970s

April 20, 1993. I am driving with Said, son of my host family, to Tizi Ouzou to celebrate Tafsut. He told me that all of Kabylia would be on strike, but I am not prepared to find every café and restaurant closed—something that did not occur even on Fridays, the national day of rest. Said drops me off at the cultural center. Over the outside door hangs a sign, printed in Tamazight: Axxam n Yedles Mulud At Mɛammer *(House of Culture of Mouloud Mammeri). Above these words, the same message is conveyed in a set of symbols that I recognize as belonging to the Tifinagh alphabet developed by the Tuareg Berbers. I enter the cultural center and am surrounded by a series of displays: old pottery and tools, each with its name affixed; women's dresses hanging in the sunny windows; a plaster of paris model of a village, surrounded by posters explaining its synchronic and diachronic histories; and dried leaves from native plants, mounted on construction paper and labeled in French, English, Latin, and Berber. Although I am initially drawn to the displays themselves, I also begin to notice the ways these various exhibits are connected to their producers. Most displays have been put together by village cultural associations, as indicated by identifying devices ranging from large banners to small, hand-lettered signs. Banners with the acronym MCB (Mouvement Culturel Berbère, Berber Cultural Movement), the umbrella organization sponsoring the event, hang throughout the building. One exhibit displays mounted newspaper clippings, tracts, and flyers about the first Berber cultural organization, the Agraw Imazighen or Académie Berbère (Berber Academy).*

During the 1960s and 1970s, several Berber organizations formed in Paris that would provide important sites for the formulation and dissemination of discourses of Amazigh identity.[11] Unlike later associations in France, which would target primarily the growing diaspora community, these initial organizations were also oriented to Kabyles in Algeria. Borders between France and Algeria were porous during those years, and people moved back and forth readily. So although the associations were based in Paris for political, logistical, and legal reasons, there was considerable trans-Mediterranean traffic.

The first association, the Académie Berbère d'Echanges et de Recherches Culturelles (Berber Academy of Cultural Research and Exchange, ABERC), was founded in 1967 by a small group of Kabyle writers, artists, and intellectuals,

Outside the Mouloud Mammeri Cultural Center in Tizi Ouzou, a banner reads, "Until the Constitutionalization and Institutionalization of Tamaziɣt." The cultural center's sign is in Tamazight and Tifinagh. April 20, 1993.

including Mouloud Mammeri and Taos Amrouche, a novelist and singer who had already brought Kabyle folk songs to international audiences. The association sought to situate Berber culture through a discourse of universality and rights that emphasized the similarities between Berbers and other minorities (Slimani-Direche 1997: 92).[12] Largely the province of elites, ABERC appears to have had little popular impact. In 1969, one of its founders, Mohand Arab Bessaoud, took charge of the association, changed its name to Académie Berbère/ Agraw Imazighène (Berber Academy/Assembly of Imazighen, the Agraw), and reoriented it toward a specifically political struggle for Berber linguistic and cultural rights in Algeria.[13] Exclusivity replaced universality, as Bessaoud and the Agraw foregrounded the differences between Berbers and Arabs (and proclaimed the superiority of the former).[14] In Bessaoud's hands, the Agraw became a populist and activist organization whose primary base was comprised of immigrant workers. The Agraw directly targeted cultural and linguistic politics in Algeria, especially the Arabization program, through its journals *Iṭij* (Sun) and *Imazighene.*[15] It was the first organization to call explicitly for making Berber an official and national language (Slimani-Direche 1997: 112).

One way the Agraw's journals entered the country was in the luggage of returning travelers. Once there, they were typically passed from hand to hand. A university student might give a copy to a brother or cousin, who would carry it to school and pass it around; the journal might then leave with a different person, and so the process would continue—making the journal's trajectory unpredictable and virtually untraceable. Ammar recalls that he first saw the journal *Iṭij* when he was in primary school. A few years later, he happened to have an instructor sympathetic to the Berber cause who would pass journals to him and a few other students. Another time, Ammar recalls that he and his friends began giving journals to one of their teachers, with whom they would have long discussions about language and identity. At a local level, then, the journals acted centrifugally, serving as material artifacts around which discussions took place and small, informal groups formed. At a regional level, these nodes began to constitute a decentralized network that would be available to be mobilized in 1980.

Circulating journals produced by the Agraw Imazighen was hardly risk free. Being caught with an issue was cause for arrest. The poet Ben Mohamed, who wrote the text of the hit song *A vava inouva,* was brought in for questioning by the police only once, when he was (wrongly) accused of passing around the journal *Imazighene.* In the summer of 1976, some 200 youths were imprisoned and "intensively interrogated" (Chaker 1982: 390)—in other words, probably tortured—for being caught with an Agraw publication. But if the readership of its journals was restricted, the Agraw also introduced into circulation something that was equally controversial but easier to disseminate: the Tifinagh alphabet.[16] The Agraw turned this alphabet, which had originated with the Tuareg Berber population in the Sahara Desert, into a sign of Amazigh history and identity. Tifinagh also was invoked to dispute the Algerian government's claims that Berber had never been written and thus could not be considered a national language. Boualem, a founding member of the new Kabyle song group Yugurten, recalled how captivated he was when he first got a copy of the alphabet from someone at his school. Afraid to show it even at home, he carried it around in his sock, folded in quarters, and he furtively began transcribing in Tifinagh some of the traditional Kabyle poems he knew.

Boualem was one of only a handful of students who learned Tifinagh as a code. For most, it served to index a notion of Amazigh identity, along with whatever sense of fear, defiance, or desire that might entail. From the school, the alphabet moved to the street, where it took the form of public graffiti. Boualem recounted to me that, along with some friends, he scrawled a Tifinagh character on a wall and then ran away quickly, feeling, he said, as though he had committed a blasphemy. During the Berber Spring, Tifinagh letters were painted on the windows and the signs of public buildings (Chaker 1982: 397). One Tifinagh character is now a widely recognized symbol of Amazigh identity in Algeria, Morocco, and the diaspora, circulating on jewelry, T-shirts, posters, calendars, hats, and websites.[17]

Although an important initial site of encounter among activist Kabyles in Paris, the Agraw tended to promote an extremist and by many accounts racist (anti-Arab) discourse that was a poor candidate for widespread circulation. Its Manichean vision did not appeal to the growing numbers of university-educated Kabyles who had begun to join the Agraw's ranks. In 1972, some of these left the Agraw (which would continue to exist until 1976) and formed a new group, the Groupe d'Etudes Berbères (Berber Studies Group, GEB), at Vincennes University in Paris. Unlike the Agraw, which had been legally constituted as an autonomous association of foreigners in France under the French law of 1901,[18] the GEB had to formulate its identity and mission in relation to the particular demands and structure of the university system. In the spring of 1972, Vincennes University (no doubt responding to the 1968 student uprisings in Paris, where educational reform was high on the agenda) established what it called autonomous working groups (*groupes de travail autonomes*), through which students themselves, working collaboratively with an instructor, could develop their own research objectives and design a program to achieve them. Because this program bore credit, it had to be approved by a university pedagogical commission, budgeted, and accepted by a department. The GEB thus oriented itself to existing academic disciplines, organizing its offerings around the familiar terms of history, language, and civilization.[19] As part of its mission, the GEB also agreed to produce an ongoing journal, the *Bulletin d'études berbères* (Bulletin of Berber Studies), which circulated in Algeria in a manner similar to the publications of the Agraw.[20]

In 1978, forks appeared in the circulatory pathway forged by the GEB. Some members maintained a center at the university; they halted publication of the *Bulletin d'études berbères* and created the more academically oriented journal *Tisuraf* (Small Steps). Well-known academics including Pierre Bourdieu, Ernest Gellner, Abdelmalek Sayad, Germaine Tillion, and Lucette Valensi, to name just a few, joined its editorial board.[21] Other members sought to orient their work to a broader public. They formed the independent collective Imedyazen (The Poets), which published popular reading materials (comic books, children's books, novels), produced cassettes (most notably, those of the new Kabyle singer Ferhat Mehenni and his group Imazighen Imoula), and organized concerts and other cultural events. Imedyazen also produced and distributed the journal *Tisuraf,* although editorial control remained at the university. During the events of 1980, Imedyazen would serve as a crucial liaison with the foreign press as well as with human rights organizations.

To say that the first post-independence Berberist associations were created in Paris is not to say, of course, that there were no structured forums in Algeria during the 1960s and 1970s. Two key locations were the Kabyle radio station and the Kabyle language classes taught by Mouloud Mammeri at the University of Algiers from 1965 to 1973. More informal working groups were also constituted, as was the case at the University of Algiers in 1965, when three faculty members including Mammeri met together for several months (Redjala 1988: 73). One of these, Ramdane Redjala, would become a founding member of the GEB and its first instructor. Moreover, Kabyles in Algeria contributed articles to the *Bulletin d'études berbères* and actively promoted the journal's circulation. The fact remains, however, that the Algerian state made it difficult, to say the least, for explicit Berberist gatherings to take place. The ubiquitous threat posed by state intelligence agents (referred to as the SM or Sécurité Militaire) made cultural activists unwilling to meet formally or to talk with any but their most trusted allies.

By 1980, then, universities in both France and Algeria were already becoming crucial sites for the formulation and dissemination of a discourse of Amazigh identity. The university was also a place where new forms of social organization were emerging. Young men from different villages and regions were coming together in a state-centered location, where age- and lineage-based conventions of public speaking that prevailed in their villages of origin were no longer operative (cf. Chachoua 1996).

Governance

April 20, 1993. Demonstrators begin to gather at the university. The organizers of the march are everywhere. Fearful of police violence that might lead to a stampede, the organizers divide demonstrators into small groups of several dozen to around a hundred people. Every group is given a banner that bears a different slogan. I make out a few of them: "No Democracy without Tamazight," "April 20, Day against Repression." The groups wait at the university entrance until organizers signal them, one at a time, to begin the march, with each group separated from the others by as much as fifty feet. Three or four organizers accompany each group, walking backward so as to face the group they are responsible for. One organizer leads that group's chants. Because the march had not been authorized by the city, organizers periodically signal for their group to squat down, rehearsing what they would do if police—who stood sporadically around the edges of the march—began shooting into the crowd.

The few days surrounding April 20, 1980 were characterized by moments of spontaneous, uncontrolled, and violent outrage on the streets of Tizi Ouzou and surrounding towns. But the Berber Spring was not born in the streets. It was a coordinated and relatively organized affair that was made possible largely because of a state-sanctioned structure already in place: the university student governance system.[22] Students at the University of Tizi Ouzou appropriated this system, temporarily taking over the university itself, to compel the state's attention.[23]

As the 1964 Charter of Algiers suggests, the state sought to limit and contain the ways in which citizens could come together. Two forms of official organization were available to Algerian university students in the 1970s and early 1980s. One was the national student organization UNJA (Union Nationale de Jeunesse Algérien, National Union of Algerian Youth).[24] Long dominated by the communist sympathizers of PAGS (Parti de l'Avant-Garde Socialiste, Party of the Socialist Avant-Garde),[25] who were uninterested in the Berber cause, the UNJA

During a protest march through the city of Tizi Ouzou on April 20, 1993, organizers ask their groups to squat down in case police decide to fire on the crowd. The march had not been authorized by the government.

was also reportedly infiltrated by state intelligence agents of the SM (Sécurité Militaire) and thus was a risky place to contest state policy. Nevertheless, according to one of my interlocutors, the UNJA was sometimes used as a cover for Berber activities. The second organization available to students was the governance system. In 1980, this system would provide a decision-making body through which students could organize and orchestrate demonstrations, strikes, and other coordinated actions. It would also constitute a nodal point of interface with city and state officials, adjacent social constituencies, and the press.

The student governance system loosely mirrored the official organizational structure of the FLN itself. Just as at the state level, a general assembly provided a forum in which students could come together to discuss matters of concern. Smaller working committees and commissions could be created on an ad hoc basis to address specific issues. Students of similar political leanings might form a committee to advance their particular agenda within the context of the university. Thus, at the Cité Universitaire (student housing complex) of Ben Aknoun, on the outskirts of Algiers, culturally active Berber students controlled the management committee for many years prior to 1980, and were among those who helped to organize the 1980 movement (Chaker 1989: 30).

When, on March 10, 1980, Mammeri's lecture was canceled, students turned the governance structure into a dynamic and flexible organ of communication.[26] The cancellation itself was hardly newsworthy. It was not the first Berber cultural event to be shut down by the state, and the cancellation was not initially reported in the press. The incident did not spark immediate public outrage: No spontaneous street demonstrations broke out on March 10 itself. Instead, some of the thousand or so students who had gathered to hear the talk called a general assembly (GA) for the following morning. At that assembly, students put together a small demonstration, which took place just after the meeting. The state-based logic that went into the planning of this event is evident in its destinations, which included city hall and the FLN party's headquarters (Chaker 1982: 394).

Initially, no one beyond Tizi Ouzou seemed terribly interested in what was happening. City inhabitants did not join the protest march (although Rachid Chaker claims that they "tacitly approved" it; Chaker 1982: 395). In Algiers, some reportedly doubted the accuracy of the students' account or questioned Mammeri's motives. But as students met in general assemblies over the next several weeks, they developed internal consensus about subsequent steps and activated channels to the state via well-established public discourse conventions. At a GA on March 12, for example, they drafted an open letter to the president (that they would subsequently widely disseminate) in which they formulated their demands in terms clearly recognizable to the state, drawing on excerpts of the 1976 National Charter (Front de Libération Nationale 1976) to argue that, by the state's own logic, Berber should be considered a national language (see Chaker 1982: 395). On several occasions (March 15, March 29, April 19), students met in a GA to organize delegations to the president, which were received by his general secretary. The GA also tried to keep events from getting out of hand. Thus, on March 20, the GA decided to prevent high-school students from carrying out a planned march on Tizi Ouzou (Chaker 1982: 399). General assemblies could be flexibly called in relation to unfolding events. For instance, on April 6, the GA called for a strike so that students could participate en masse in a large April 7 demonstration planned for Algiers; on April 8, the GA voted to continue striking until students' demands were met.

General assemblies also provided a place of liaison where university students could coordinate with other groups. This was especially the case with university employees, who attended many general assemblies and would form working committees with students. Workers at the hospital of Tizi Ouzou and nearby factories (in particular, the SONELEC factory at Oued Aissi) were also periodically included. These groups worked together to organize widely observed regionwide strikes on April 16 and May 18–19. They also coordinated around major demonstrations, such as the one held on April 7 in Algiers. The events themselves began to be appropriated in relation to the agendas of adjacent groups and constituencies. Some of these included the opposition Socialist Forces Front (FFS) party, which as early as March 16 disseminated its own tract about the events in Algiers; a small women's movement protesting newly proposed changes to the Family Code, which joined in the April 7 march with its own banner ("La Parole aux Femmes"); and associations of doctors and lawyers (Chaker 1982: 421). While the interests of these various constituencies were not necessarily convergent, the groups did coordinate on more than one occasion, and the general assembly served as one forum where such coordination could be negotiated.

Other organizational structures also began to form as the situation heated up. Thus, in response to the increased presence of anti-riot police in the Tizi Ouzou region at the beginning of April, a small group of faculty and students met on April 4 to consider creating an Anti-Repression Committee (Chaker 1982: 403). A second preliminary meeting was held on April 6; a third was planned for April 7, following the march in Algiers, to evaluate the behavior of the police. The group's anticipation of violence was born out: On April 7, police blocked off routes so as to cut the demonstration in half. Some demonstrators were reportedly "savagely beaten" (Chaker 1982: 405) and a number were injured. More than 110 were brought in for questioning; 20 were jailed overnight; and several were detained longer. That night, the group met and called a general assembly for the following morning, at which the Anti-Repression Committee was formalized. Sixty-five members, split evenly among students, faculty, and university employees, were appointed, and the committee was subdivided into four working groups: Information and Coordination, Cultural Animation and Vigilance, Official Exterior Relations (i.e., district officials, police, state), and Nonofficial Exterior Relations (i.e., the press, other universities).

It is tempting in retrospect to portray the movement as expanding and intensifying as the days of the occupation wore on. This is not what happened. Indeed, if the police presence had not intensified, the occupation might eventually have worn itself out.[27] Tensions within the movement itself were increasing, especially between students and employees. On the night of April 10, only a few students remained at the university; most went home for the weekend. But when students returned on April 11, the police surrounded the university, refusing to let anyone enter without student identification. Anyone caught with a tract was arrested. On April 12, a concert by the political singer Ferhat that was to take place in the Kabyle town of Sidi Aich was canceled, and the singer was arrested. On April 14, Adelhak Bererhi, the Minister of Higher Education and Scientific Research, made an appearance at the GA in Tizi Ouzou, accompanied by labor union representatives. This appears to have troubled already tentative alliances among students and workers, once again slowing momentum. Only a few students remained to occupy the university on the night of April 14. The next day, however, police in unmarked cars surrounded the university and began harassing these who tried to enter. At a nearby SONELEC factory, state intelligence agents arrested a worker who was distributing tracts calling for a strike; in response, workers took an FLN Central Committee member and a SONELEC manager hostage. On April 16, a general strike paralyzed the Kabyle region. That night, Bererhi telegraphed an ultimatum to the mayor of Tizi Ouzou: If classes did not begin again by April 19, students would be prohibited from returning to the university and faculty would lose their jobs.[28] A televised speech by Algeria's then-President Chadli Ben Djedid condemned the student actions. Momentum once again seemed to dissipate. The next day, April 17, only 150 students and a handful of faculty remained at the university, and there were reportedly disputes among them. Yet on April 19, a "raucous" (Chaker 1982: 416) GA, attended by students, faculty, and hospital and factory workers, debated whether to send a joint delegation to the president and organized three working sessions for that afternoon: Student–Worker Unity, Democratic Freedoms, and Evolution of the Movement. After long committee meetings lasting in some cases until 3 o'clock in the morning, most students were in bed when, at 4:15 A.M., the police stormed the university dormitories, the hospital of Tizi Ouzou, and the nearby SONELEC factory.

The Press and Human Rights

April 20, 1993. Dozens of newspaper articles about the Berber Cultural Movement hang alongside dresses, posters, and photographs on the walls of the Mouloud Mammeri Cultural Center. Nearby, the Algerian Association of Amnesty International has set up a booth. Both remind me of my initial visit to the Kabyle region in 1990. I had just met Bachir, who as a child had imagined the Amazigh as a primitive savage. Bachir brought out an extensive collection of newspaper clippings on the Berber movement that he had been amassing since his release from prison in 1986. He had been picked up at a demonstration in support of the founders of the Algerian League of Human Rights, themselves jailed in 1985. There was no longer any doubt in Bachir's mind about what it meant to be Amazigh.

If the spring of 1980 became a pivotal moment in Kabyles' relationship to the state, it was also because students achieved extraordinary access to the media. First of all, students provided themselves with their own means of document production by seizing control of a university copy facility. This occurred in relation to a negative story about Mammeri that the state newspaper *El Moujahid* had printed on March 20. Mammeri had drafted a rebuttal, but the paper refused to run it. Students sought permission to reproduce Mammeri's text at the university, but were refused. In response, on April 5, students occupied a copy center, where their first act was to mimeograph thousands of copies of the forbidden text. Massively distributed in Tizi Ouzou and Algiers, this text was also reprinted in the French paper *Matin de Paris*. Later that week, students met in a GA and called for an unlimited strike as well as ongoing occupation of the copy center. This gave them the ability to mass-produce tracts, copies of correspondence sent to the president or the press, and calls for demonstrations or strikes. In effect, the students had gained access to their own press. The Anti-Repression Committee monitored events and provided an ongoing liaison to international news agencies. On April 9, the committee held its first press conference, which was attended by reporters from *Le Monde* and Agence France-Presse (AFP). The next day, reporters from the radio station France Inter and the Spanish press agency EFE were present. By April 13, the Associated Press was in attendance. Stories about the events would eventually run in the *International Herald Tribune, Newsweek, The Economist*, and the *Daily Telegraph*, among others.[29]

The state press sought to narrate the events as either a foreign plot or a regionalist secession movement, both designed to thwart the achievements of the Algerian revolution. The international press, in contrast, increasingly constituted the events through a discourse of human rights. The story began quietly. On March 13, the French newspaper *Libération* published a brief paragraph about the canceled lecture. Four days later, on March 17, *Le Monde* correspondent Daniel Junqua went to Tizi Ouzou and wrote the first of what became a series of articles on the nascent movement. The creation of the Anti-Repression Committee contributed to shaping the emerging movement in relation to human rights concerns. The committee's first tract, "Call for the Liberation of the Prisoners," was produced on April 8. A week later, the press itself became part of the human rights story: On April 15, the France Inter reporter (Alain Meynargues) recorded an interview with a faculty member and a student; Meynargues was subsequently arrested, his papers and tapes temporarily confiscated. Even as the Anti-Repression Committee continued to hold almost daily press conferences in Algeria, members of the Paris-based Imedyazen cooperative were bringing the events to the attention of human rights organizations including Amnesty International, the International League of Human Rights, the Association of Democratic Jurists, and Unesco. Imedyazen was also beginning to put together, and would subsequently publish, an archive of articles on the events that reached 400 pages (Imedyazen 1981b).[30]

It is not my purpose here to provide a daily account of the ensuing events. Suffice it to say that for the next six weeks, demonstrations, strikes, and periodic clashes with police continued, as did negotiations between student delegations and government officials. Twenty-four political prisoners who had been jailed in the days surrounding April 20 became a focal point around which opposition was organized. The GA and the working committees continued to constitute the primary venues where the demands of what was now being called the Berber Cultural Movement (Mouvement Culturel Berbère, MCB) were formulated and events coordinated. When students voted to end the strike and to resume classes at the University of Tizi Ouzou on May 26,[31] they also formed three permanent commissions around the issues of the release of prisoners, cultural animation, and the democratization of the university. This work continued at a month-long convention called the Seminar of Yakouren, an unprecedented event in Algeria's history, at which a 124-page platform was formulated, presented to the government, and later published in Paris (Imedyazen 1981a).[32] Soon thereafter, the journal *Tafsut* ("Spring") was launched at the University of Tizi Ouzou—the first ongoing Berber publication produced by Kabyles in Algeria.[33]

The Berber Spring consolidated the university as the central forum for the production of Amazigh discourse. It also served as a point of reference for younger students like Bachir, who used it as a way to develop a state-based form of identity as well as to demarcate themselves from their parents' generation. The Berber Spring did not, however, mobilize the population uniformly. Ammar

The University of Tizi Ouzou's Department of Amazigh Language and Culture opened in 1990, thanks in part to well-organized Kabyle activism throughout the 1980s. The department sign is in French, Arabic, and Tifinagh.

described how, on the night of April 20, he returned from Tizi Ouzou to his village and went door-to-door to garner support for a regionwide march on the city the following morning. He met resistance from many in his parents' generation, who had lived through one war and were not eager to start another. As Ammar put it, "We were fighting two battles: Le Pouvoir [the government] and our parents." The enterprise of pedagogy and persuasion begun by Ammar and others like him is ongoing.

April 20 may be best understood not as an explosion of a repressed population but as a nexus where new institutional arrangements, dissemination pathways, and discourse practices converged. It was surely no accident that the first generation to attend public school in independent Algeria—and the first generation to be greeted with the state's Arabization program—came of age in 1980. The public schools and universities also provided crucial dissemination networks and constituted locations where students could engage in new discourse practices. That the University of Tizi Ouzou had recently opened was also of paramount importance. Kabyle activists and scholars writing about April 1980 were profoundly aware of these factors and had, in many cases, personally participated in the events. If they cast April 20, 1980, in a ritual frame of repression, liminality, and reversal, it was obviously not for lack of awareness of the factors I discuss above. Indeed, it was largely out of the historical detail embedded in their writings that I developed this analysis. Why, then, might they have chosen on the whole to frame the events in ritual rather than conjunctural terms?

These indigenous writers have been profoundly attentive to the way discourse travels. When framed as a ritual of reversal, April 20 is far more available for recirculation, reinflection, and commemoration than it would be if it were framed as a historical conjuncture. As ritual, April 20 has become a repository for a sedimented history that Kabyles can tap into as they seek to lend weight to emergent concerns. Moreover, as ritual, April 20 can travel. Berber communities elsewhere appropriate the date to articulate concerns related to their own political contexts. As a translocal event, April 20 also provides a tangible point of reference around which Berber communities in North Africa and the diaspora can imagine a common Amazigh community (see Silverstein 2003). Thus, on April 20, 2002, a "planetary march" to protest the Algerian government's recent assassinations of Kabyle youth took place in Algeria, Belgium, the Canary Islands, Paris, Toulouse (France), Italy, Morocco, London, and Montreal.

On April 21, 1993, the day following the demonstration I witnessed, the Berber-friendly Algerian daily *Liberté* ran a half-page photograph on its front page, featuring six men holding a banner that read "Institutionalization and Constitutionalization of Amazigh Identity" (*Institutionalisation et Constitutionalisation de l'identité amaziɣ*).[34] Although in 1993, Amazigh identity had not been institutionally or constitutionally recognized by the state, the movement for Amazigh or Berber identity already had a long institutional history of its own. It was perhaps for this reason that the state did not grant permission for the 1993 demonstration. That it took place in Tizi Ouzou regardless is a testament to the movement's institutional strength. The state had good reason to be afraid.

The Berber Cultural Movement would not have been possible without a growing sense of a specifically Berber postcolonial cultural identity that had been developing throughout the previous decade. One of the key products through which Kabyles were constructing a newly self-reflexive vantage point on their own heritage during the 1970s was the music of the Kabyle singer Idir.

2   Refracting Berber Identities

In 1973, the song *A vava inouva*[1] ("Oh my father") galvanized the Algerian population. Composed by a young, unknown musician who called himself Idir ("to live"), from a text penned by poet Ben Mohamed, *A vava inouva* is built around the sung refrain of a story told by old women throughout Kabylia. Idir's song depicts a grandmother seated at the hearth, spinning tales far into the night as the snow falls outside. Idir harmonized the story's familiar refrain on an acoustic guitar, using an arpeggiated chord style associated with popular western folk stars such as Joan Baez or Bob Dylan. The song literally stopped Algerians in their tracks. A friend from the capital city of Algiers reported seeing people walk backward down a department store escalator to hear it playing over the ground-floor speakers. Nor did the song's allure stop at the Algerian borders. *A vava inouva* was the first Algerian hit in Europe and the first to be played on French national radio, and it made the news in such prestigious French publications as *Le Monde* (Humblot 1978). It reached me in the United States in 1980—well before I imagined that I would one day visit the village where the song was born—when an Argentine friend living in Paris sent me a cassette of some of the most popular tunes on the Parisian airwaves. More than twenty years after its release, the opening notes could still produce a roar. When I heard Idir play at the Zenith Hall in Paris in November 1996, he turned this song over to the immigrant crowd, strumming his trademark accompaniment as 7,500 spectators sang the refrain by heart.

A vava inouva's effect on Kabyle Berbers was electrifying. The song engendered simultaneously a sense of deep recognition and a feeling of novelty. For many of the older women storytellers whose repertoire inspired the song, *A vava inouva* mirrored back to them their own practices: "When they hear the song, they see themselves," as my language tutor put it.[2] For postwar generations raised in Kabylia, the song produced a new form of cultural memory. Many of my interlocutors would tell me of how the song evoked the evenings they spent as children listening to their grandmothers' tales, snow blocking the doors. For those raised in the diaspora, *A vava inouva* came to stand for the homeland, taking on the mantle of tradition that it purported to represent. The song also provided a subtle yet significant counterweight to the Algerian state's discourse, which positioned Berber culture as backward and at odds with the state's modernizing projects.

A vava inouva enabled Kabyles to see themselves from an entirely new vantage point. Songwriter Ben Mohamed called this new way of seeing an "internal perspective" or an "internal gaze" (*le regard intérieur*), informed by neither the East nor the West but by indigenous modes of knowledge. It is the construction of this "internal gaze" that most interests me. Developing a socio-semiotic history of *A vava inouva,* I argue that the song worked as both palimpsest and prism. On the one hand, the new song wrote over the older women's story in such a way as to enable the previous text to acquire new significance. Yet if the older text gained new visibility, it was also because *A vava inouva* worked in a refractive capacity. That is, it displayed the women's story through the lenses of distant products, styles, ideologies, and circulation networks in a way that made the story—and "Berber culture" more generally—interpretable in an entirely new manner (cf. Feld 1996). In short, the song's "internal gaze" was in fact a kind of bifocal vision, through which Berber culture was brought into new focus by being set in relation to distant geopolitical events and entities. This can be seen in four linked sites of discourse production and circulation to which the song was oriented: ethnographic projects, postcolonial rediscoveries of tradition, Algerian cultural politics, and an emerging market for what would come to be called world music.

Ethnographic Projects: An Encounter with Duvignaud

The Tunisian desert village of Shebika would seem an unlikely place to begin *A vava inouva*'s history. Seemingly bypassed by modernity, the village was falling apart when French sociologist Jean Duvignaud first visited it in 1960. Nondescript houses, their roofs collapsing, a cemetery with crumbling grave markers, a mosque, a saint's tomb, and a single storefront grocer bordered a small oasis. A sixty-pupil state-run school was the only sign of the village's links to an outside world. A decade later, speaking at the French Cultural Center in Algiers, Duvignaud described the six-year research project he undertook in Shebika, which had culminated in the making of an ethnographic film.[3] Ben Mohamed happened to be in attendance at the lecture. As Ben relates it, Duvignaud described how the film had helped Shebikans to transform the image they had of themselves. Before the film, most Shebikans reportedly had but one desire: to leave the village. But when they saw the ethnographer arrive in Shebika with a team of urban researchers, sophisticated recording equipment, and funds to pay villagers for their knowledge, they gradually began to view their lives through the ethnographer's lens. During his talk in Algiers, Duvignaud no doubt drew on his 1968 monograph *Change at Shebika*. In this work, Duvignaud claimed,

> [Our] investigation brought about a notable change in the village. Hitherto disdained objects, devalued acts and half-forgotten beliefs regained a sort of vitality from the very fact that a researcher recorded them in his notebook. . . . Through the repeated scrutiny to which we subjected him, the man of Shebika developed a new perspective of himself. . . . The man of Shebika *gave himself a name* in the larger context of the life of Tunisia when he discovered a language in which to give his new experience expression. (1970 [1968]: 296–298)

For Ben Mohamed, the talk sparked a desire to create a forum that, like Duvignaud's film, would serve as a mediated mirror, enabling Kabyles to develop a new perspective on their own traditions.[4] "Our system of reference," he realized, had been "either the East or the West, [but] we didn't have a way to look at ourselves, an internal gaze [*le regard intérieur*]" (Arnaud 1992: 166). At the time of the talk, the tune of *A vava inouva* was already in Ben's head; several weeks earlier, Idir had asked Ben to write verses for a melody that he had composed around the story's traditional refrain. Duvignaud's presentation was the catalyst Ben needed: He could train his poetic lens, he realized, on the Kabyle practice of storytelling itself. What he sought to put on display in the song would not be a particular story, however, but the process of cultural transmission. He would highlight locations where cultural knowledge was formulated and passed down.[5] By describing the setting in which stories were told, Ben also foregrounded the mundane, everyday practices that had theretofore been unremarked, reversing the usual figure-ground relationship, so that activities that had been taken for granted were now highlighted.

A focus on the mundane is also, of course, one of the hallmarks of ethnography. But Ben was not out simply to turn Kabyle practices into inert museum pieces. By rendering Kabyle practices cultural, he sought at the same time to make Kabyle culture political. Here, too, he was inspired by the Shebikan story. Seeing their lives on film had political impact for the Shebikans. As they came to identify and valorize their traditions, they became increasingly dissatisfied with the state's neglect of their village. When the Tunisian government announced plans to build an administrative center in the region, the villagers staged a quarry strike, refusing to mine until the government also agreed to repair their homes.[6] Duvignaud attributed this collective action—one in which "*Shebika played the role of Shebika*" (1970 [1968]: 297)—to the new consciousness villagers developed as a result of the research project. As he put it, "the attitudes aroused by repeated questioning led the village to the extreme political limit of self-affirmation" (1970 [1968]: 297–298). Ben Mohamed took this to heart. If Kabyles could develop a new desire for their culture, their ability to mobilize as a region might also be enhanced.

Of course, *A vava inouva* was hardly the first medium to display Kabyle traditions through an ethnographic lens. Kabylia had been a privileged location of ethnographic study for more than a century before the song's creators were born. Kabyles served as ethnographic subjects from the first military accounts of the 1840s to the work of Bourdieu and beyond. The "Berber village" had long been an object of ethnographic analysis. Kabyle poetry and stories had been collected and published since the 1860s by both French and Berber enthusiasts. Even the story that inspired *A vava inouva* had already appeared in print at least once (Amrouche 1979 [1966]). The ethnographic novels of Mouloud Feraoun, written in French and published during the 1950s, betrayed a related emphasis on the everyday (e.g., Feraoun 1954). On the whole, however, these works had been the province of intellectuals and relied on literacy in French. *A vava inouva*, in contrast, reached a mass audience in its own tongue through the compelling medium of music, and via dissemination technology that nearly all could access. As it popularized the ethnographic gaze, *A vava inouva* also transformed it, appropriating a cultural way of seeing in order to develop a vernacular modernity.

The Pan-African Festival

Ben Mohamed was not alone in the effort to develop a cultural way of seeing that could simultaneously provide a basis for political mobilization. Culture, long central to colonial projects, was also a site around which postcolonial predicaments were being articulated. Nowhere was this more apparent than at the First Pan-African Cultural Festival (Premier Festival Culturel Pan-Africain), which Ben and Idir both attended. Conceived around the argument that "culture, [once] an arm of domination, is now a weapon of liberation" (Société Nationale d'Edition et de Distribution 1969: 99; Révolution Démocratique Africaine 1970: 41),[7] the Pan-African Festival was anchored in the latest intellectual and artistic currents of the day. Neo-Marxist ideology was repeatedly invoked to shift the locus of cultural production from a privileged, European-educated elite to "the people."[8] Anthropological definitions of culture formulated by Malinowski, Sapir, Lévi-Strauss, and others were appropriated, if at times ambivalently,[9] both to attest to basic human similarities and to resituate under a universalizing rubric of "culture" a range of practices that had been labeled primitive or backward during the colonial era (Organisation de l'Unité Africaine 1969c). At stake was the need to develop modes of self-representation that would be free of the lingering traces of the colonial gaze. As a member of the Guinean delegation (the Pan-African Festival's gold-medal winner) put it: "The colonized must first take himself in hand, critically evaluate the effects of the influences he has been subjected to by the invader and which manifest in his behavior, in his way of thinking and acting, in his conceptions of the world and of society, in his way of relating to the values created by his own people" (Société Nationale d'Edition et de Distribution 1969: 99–100; Révolution Démocratique Africaine 1970: 41–42). The emergent self, a cultural tabula rasa, could then be inscribed with a new identity predicated on a "return to the source" (Cabral 1973), selectively appropriating its own heritage: "One cannot simply empty the colonized of the culture that has been imposed on him, that has intoxicated him, unless one proposes a culture that replaces it, in this case, his own culture, which implies an act of resurrection, of revalorizing and popularizing this culture" (Société Nationale d'Edition et de Distribution 1969: 100; Révolution Démocratique Africaine 1970: 42; see also Fanon 1963).

Produced in Algiers in 1969 by the Organization for African Unity (Organisation de l'Unité Africaine, or OUA),[10] the Pan-African Festival was organized as a kind of cultural olympics. It brought to Algiers some 5,000 contestants from thirty-five African nations who competed in areas including folk music, traditional instrumental music, ballet, classical song, modern music, theater, and cinema.[11] Running simultaneously was a symposium featuring speeches by eight African heads of state and prominent representatives from other African nations, the Soviet Union, North Vietnam, and the Palestinian liberation movement El-Fath. Intellectuals, writers, and artists were in attendance from twenty-four non-African nations, including most of the countries of Western and Eastern Europe as well as the Soviet Union, India, Japan, Latin America (Argentina, Uruguay, Brazil), the Caribbean (Cuba, Haiti, Jamaica), and North America.[12] Such luminaries as Albert Memmi, René DePestre, and Amilcar Alencastre were among the invited guests. Although by 1969 the essentializing premise of *négritude*—which posited a "black" civilization that erased historical and geographical specificities—was disputed by most speakers, its legacy was apparent. Musicians Archie Shepp and Nina Simone were invited to demonstrate relationships between African rhythms and America's jazz and soul traditions (Organisation de l'Unité Africaine 1969a). Also present from the United States were Maya Angelou, Stokely Carmichael (who had already written about Pan-Africanism), and a number of leaders of America's Black Panther movement, including Eldridge and Kathleen Cleaver.[13]

When the Pan-African Festival came to town, Ben Mohamed was twenty-five years old and working as a civil servant for the city of Algiers. Born on March 10, 1944 in the Kabyle region At Wasif (Les Ouacifs), Ben moved to Algiers in 1958, four years into the Algerian revolution. As was the case with many school-aged children at the time, Ben's formal education was interrupted by the war, so in 1969 he enrolled in night courses to prepare for a career in civil administration. Ben had been interested in poetry since 1952 when, at the age of eight, his father brought him to a local café to hear renowned singer Slimane Azem. Captivated, Ben spent hours poring over a mimeographed booklet of Slimane Azem's songs that his father purchased for him—Ben's first print-mediated encounter with Kabyle poetry. Two years later, in 1956, Ben met a Kabyle woman who had been resettled to his village because of the war; he recalls clinging to her skirts to listen to the poems she created. In 1958, Ben began composing his own poetry while working at the market stall his father owned. Fortuitously, the stall was located between a record merchant and a bookseller, giving Ben ready access to much of the latest cultural production. As he listened to the songs his market neighbor was playing, Ben found himself unhappy with the words. How, he wondered, could one sing about beauty—of a woman, of the Algerian countryside—while a war was raging? Taking melodies he liked, he began to compose new texts that reflected his experience of the violence that surrounded him.

The Pan-African Festival would profoundly mark Ben Mohamed. "It was there," he told me during a 1996 interview, "that I began to grasp what it meant to belong to a culture." For the first time in his life, Ben called in sick so he could participate in the events. Immersed in African cinema and theater,[14] Ben didn't have time to attend the dozens of talks on postcolonial culture, identity, and politics that were simultaneously taking place.[15] But when these texts were subsequently published (Société Nationale d'Edition et de Distribution 1969), Ben devoured them, connecting his own experience to writings by Joseph Ki-Zerbo (1969), Albert Memmi (1969), Amilcar Alencastre (1969), and René Depestre (1969). Ben found Nigerian writer Ki-Zerbo's remarks especially provocative:

Ki-Zerbo was interested not simply in celebrating the past but in reconstituting indigenous traditions via "one of the new semiotic mediums afforded by mass communication," so as to "return to the African people a reinvigorated and dynamic image of their own culture" (Ki-Zerbo 1969: 344). Ben began to imagine what it might mean to create a relationship to "traditional culture" that saw culture not as an objectified or static entity but as a source from which to create "cultural responses adequate to [the people's] constantly changing situation" (N.A. 1976: 38).[16]

While Ben was engaging with theorists of postcoloniality, Hamid Cheriet—a young Kabyle geology student, who would soon become better known by the stage name Idir—was crisscrossing the Algerian hinterlands in search of not stones, but songs. Born in 1948 in the Kabyle village At Lahcène (At Yenni), Idir moved to Algiers in 1963, where his family had been living since their house was requisitioned by the French army in 1960. (Idir had remained behind in Kabylia for the three intervening years, enrolled in a boarding school run by the Jesuits.) Idir, too, was powerfully moved by the Pan-African Festival events. When I spoke with him in 1996, he told me: "I saw other human dimensions. I saw sweaty, satiny, black skin, tremendous expressive power in the music. . . . I asked myself, what is this great power that has swept down on us, this great nation that has arrived with such unbelievably rich folklore?"[17] Idir was most struck by the "verticality" of the harmonies and rhythms, which contrasted with the more linear or horizontal melodic style of most Algerian music he knew: "I said to myself, but we too, we must have this dimension somewhere, hidden, we just need to draw it out." So it was that school vacations found him immersed in traditional music and poetry, learning new instruments and percussion styles, discovering the rhythms of his own nation: "the spaces, the sounds . . . that make us vibrate, through which we can forge a personality." Listening at the same time to the music of the Beatles, Cat Stevens, and Simon and Garfunkel, Idir got a French teaching assistant at the university to show him how to play chords on his guitar. Soon after, he began harmonizing the Kabyle melodies that he had heard since childhood.

Although the Pan-African Festival was instrumental in helping Ben and Idir develop a newly reflexive vantage point on Kabyle cultural practices, it also accentuated their sense of marginality within the Algerian nation. Both of them experienced a contradiction between the revolutionary spirit that was sweeping Africa, Latin America, and other parts of the Third World and Algeria's cultural politics. Idir elaborated: "I felt I was living a paradox. Excited to be part of a revolutionary generation, we felt a kinship with Che Guevara and embraced slogans about the people's legitimate rights to take their destiny into their own hands and freely express themselves. We lived in this Algeria that had succeeded in its revolution and was said to be the beacon of the Third World. But at the same time I felt a contradiction: How could a system that advocated freedom repress my maternal language, my Berber identity, lumping us all together into a single Arabo-Islamic mold?" (Ouazani and Hamdi 1992: 31–32).

Algeria's Cultural Politics: Modernity and Authenticity

Only once was Ben Mohamed brought in for questioning by the police. He had been accused of passing around a copy of *Imazighene,* the forbidden journal of the Paris-based Agraw Imazighen (Académie Berbère), and the police wanted to hear what he had to say. After the interrogation, one officer took Ben aside. What, he asked Ben, was so political about *A vava inouva*? After all, the text of *A vava inouva* is hardly subversive. The song is based on a motif similar to that found in Little Red Riding Hood, where a wolf tricks a young girl by masquerading as her grandmother. Here, it is the girl's grandfather who lives alone in a hut in the woods. His granddaughter brings him food daily, gaining admission to the hut only when she repeats a particular phrase and jingles her bracelets. An ogre overhears this exchange and one day imitates the young girl, eats the grandfather, and awaits her arrival. Not deceived, she goes for help and the villagers burn down the hut, with the ogre inside.[18] Why was a song based on this tale revolutionary? Why had it produced such a frenzy?

A vava inouva's relationship to Algeria's cultural ideology was slippery. Both the song and the state were working within a "problem space" (Scott 1999)[19] governed by two linked terms: modernity and authenticity (cf. Bendix 1997; Bigenho 2002; Ivy 1995; Schein 1999). These terms were triangulated in various ways in relation to Algeria's Arab, Berber, and French histories. The same product or practice could be understood differently depending on how one positioned it. From one angle, *A vava inouva* articulated closely with the state's project to "modernize traditions": It took part of a folktale, surrounded it with new verses and music, and disseminated it via the mass media. As it did so, however, the song refashioned the links between authenticity and modernity so as to produce a dynamic and potentially subversive new synthesis.

Triangulating Difference: The Politics of Language

Language was a key site around which Algerians debated the relationship between modernity and authenticity. The national charter mapped out a state fashioned along familiar Jacobin lines, with nation, language, religion, and cultural personality seen as mutually reinforcing emanations of a singular spirit. The credo "Islam is my religion, Arabic is my language, Algeria is my fatherland"—initially articulated by Shaykh Ben Badis, leader of the anticolonial nationalist Etoile Nord-Africaine (ENA) party in the 1930s—was inscribed in the first Algerian Constitution, which proclaimed Islam the religion of state and declared Arabic the "national and official language of state" (Front de Libération Nationale 1964c: 9).

In practice, the varieties of Arabic spoken by most Algerians diverged substantially from the pan-Arab code, Modern Standard Arabic, which the state sought to impose. Those who had been to school—including virtually the entire elite—had been educated in French. The "language war" (Lakoff 2000) in Algeria initially concerned how the linguistic labor between French and Arabic would be divided. Some argued for an ongoing role for French while others contended that only through radical Arabization could Algeria truly free itself of its colonial past. Arabic, in the latter view, was the sole language capable of serving as a vehicle for the authentic Algerian personality. This view predominated at the state's first colloquium on culture, organized in 1968 by the ruling National Liberation Front (Front de Libération Nationale), where party representative Mohamed Chérif Messadia proclaimed that "to count on a foreign language to express the national personality is like trying to transmit electrical current through wood" (Messadia 1967: 38).[20] The FLN's leading light Taleb-Ibrahimi would go so far as to invoke the expertise of linguists in support of this position, citing one linguist's claim that "speaking another language isn't speaking one's thoughts in other words, it's thinking differently, and thus, thinking something else" (Taleb-Ibrahimi 1981 [1972]: 215; cf. Handler 1988: 160). (That Taleb-Ibrahimi prepared these remarks in French and published them in France's *Le monde diplomatique* did not appear to have troubled him.)

Whether Arabic could serve as a language of modernity was more contentious. Some saw French as oriented toward the future and Arabic as backward-looking, unable to express modern concepts or technical terms. Although this position was rarely advanced in the national press, it can be deciphered from the insistent and occasionally defensive rhetoric of its opponents. One report, for instance, condemned those "who judge the Arabic language incapable of being set against other languages" and contended that "it is no longer acceptable . . . to discuss the question of whether or not this language can express a particular situation, a particular concept, a particular problematic" (Front de Libération Nationale 1971: 20, 29). (The same report reminded French-language proponents that at one time, French itself had been found wanting, as German was seen as the only European language able to handle philosophy.) Advocates of French were accused of being divorced from their culture, thus inauthentic: "The man who is steeped in French culture found himself [after independence] cut off from his intellectual heritage. . . . [H]e did not see in Arab culture anything but a culture of the past that could not aspire to translate the current of modern ideas" (N.A. 1968: 39).

The relationship between Berber and Arabic was triangulated against this Arabic-French matrix. With regard to the state's claims that Arabic was the sole authentic Algerian language, Berber advocates contended that only the Berber language was truly native to North Africa; Arabic, like French, had been imposed by a conquering population. As for the politics of modernity, Berber was located vis-à-vis Arabic in the same way that Arabic was positioned with regards to French: Berber was said to lack the ability to express modern concepts and technical terms. Further, Berber was seen not as a rule-governed code but as a dialect that lacked even its own alphabet and grammar. This perceived deficiency was mapped onto the character of Kabyle populations, whose ways of speaking became a sign of their apparent lack of culture. Kabyles viscerally experienced their difference on the streets of Algiers. "I remember [the first time] my uncle brought me to Algiers," related the singer Ferhat. "There were two Kabyles on the street in front of me, speaking in Kabyle in low voices. A third one heard them and cried out [a greeting in Kabyle] and everyone in the street turned around to get a glimpse of this 'Martian.' . . . And I remember that even in my village, when people were going to Algiers, others would say, 'You're going to Algiers but you don't speak Arabic? Then you shouldn't go.'"[21] My host told of how, during his first stay in Algiers as a child, Arabic-speaking children would taunt him in the street, crying out, "Kabyle, Kabyle" (*aqbayli*). His feeling of humiliation, he recalled, led him to remain inside.

Because the association of Berbers with backwardness was linked to the claim that Berber was not a rule-governed language but a dialect that could not be written, studied, or employed as a modern communication tool, Berber linguists and scholars began to develop grammars and dictionaries. They also began to employ more systematically the newer term of reference for the code itself: "Berber" was increasingly replaced with the more prestigious "Tamazight." Just as Modern Standard Arabic was thought to stand above the many varieties or "dialects" of Arabic spoken throughout the Arab world, so could Tamazight, they thought, provide a standardized code that would link the Maghreb's various Berber populations. Under the cover of Mouloud Mammeri's Berber-language classes, held since 1965 at the University of Algiers, a group of young cultural activists began to develop neologisms as well as mathematic and scientific terminology.[22] The government halted the class in 1973, but not before it had trained dozens of young Kabyles, including Ben Mohamed and Idir, to read and write their native tongue.

For Berber activists, to argue against the state by demonstrating that Berber/ Tamazight could indeed serve as a language of modernity was to fall into another kind of trap. For references to Berbers in official discourse were few and far between. The Arabic-French controversy dominated language debates. It was as if by not talking about Berber, the state could imagine that it was not a factor (see Irvine and Gal 2000). Anyone who opposed Arabization was thus assumed to be pro-French. This had the unfortunate consequence of leaving Berber advocates open to accusations of being at best influenced by foreign forces and at worst by imperialist and antirevolutionary forces (see Chaker 1989: 80; Mahé 2001: 478–479; Ouerdane 1990: 175). For the state, anyone who sought to acknowledge the differences between Berber-speaking and Arabic-speaking populations could only be a neocolonialist *provocateur* threatening the unitary nationalist spirit of the new nation.

Folklore

Folklore provided virtually the only window through which Berber cultural production was tolerated. The emergence of a nationalistic folklore may have constituted a way for Algeria to set itself apart from the primitiveness of "undifferentiated culture" by claiming a rich and diverse cultural heritage that was simultaneously an authenticating marker of a true nation-state (Herzfeld 1987: 53, 77–78; cf. Askew 2002). Local folk traditions were also considered proof that 130 years of French rule had not penetrated the nation's soul (cf. Chatterjee 1993). Folklore was not simply to be preserved in static form, however, but to be modernized so as to constitute the basis of a revolutionary national culture. This was made explicit at the state's first National Colloquium on Algerian Music, held in 1964, where participants discussed ways of "reappropriating the national heritage, pruning the dead branches, extracting the waste, purifying it, and, finally, imprinting it with dynamic movement" (Front de Libération Nationale 1964b: 19). This articulated eerily with what Ben and Idir hoped to accomplish in *A vava inouva*. Discussions of state-sponsored musical events published in the Algerian press could apply equally well to some of their songs. Both projects, for instance, sought to "adapt . . . 'traditional' music to our national reality" and "enrich . . . it by modernizing it" (A.M. 1973). Both were interested in "shortening long poems, lightening up slow rhythms and tempos, in order to avoid the monotony that comes from long poems and heavy melodies" (Taleb-Ibrahimi 1973).[23] Both relied on gaining an understanding of local traditions as a basis for innovation: "Once the repertoires inherited from the past have been established, once each person has been sufficiently imbued with the specific traits of our culture, only at that point is he permitted to innovate by drawing on everything our era offers" (Mekhlef 1969: 12–13). Moreover, both located women as closer to the source tradition. The 1964 colloquium went so far as to advocate going "into the households, since music, the tunes, the words, are held by Kabyle women" (Front de Libération Nationale 1964b: 68). For "the Kabyle man, isolated in his mountains, turned inward to his valleys and forests" (Front de Libération Nationale 1964b: 65), had to contend with the colonial "intrusion," and was thus led away from music and poetry; it was up to the Kabyle woman (somehow miraculously isolated from the upheavals wrought by colonialism, immigration, and war) "to carry the flame of the music and to perpetuate its existence" (Front de Libération Nationale 1964b: 65). In a similar manner, Idir and Ben looked to women as sources: Idir traveled to villages to record women's songs, and Ben worked from tapes a friend's grandmother made for him.

If Idir's and the state's approaches to traditional music were rhetorically similar, in practice they diverged considerably. The state's approach to Kabyle music foregrounded its authenticity at the expense of its modernity. At the 1964 National Colloquium on Algerian Music, Kabyle music was one of five genres considered, alongside Bedouin, Andalusian (classical), shaabi (popular), and modern. Reports by the commissions investigating classical, shaabi, and Bedouin musics were scientific in tone. They focused on documenting each genre's style and articulated specific proposals for preservation and transmission, such as creating a recording archive, notating melodies and texts, teaching solfeggio, and making use of a range of dissemination media. The Kabyle report, in contrast, was saturated with indexical links between the music and "the character of the mountain dweller" (Front de Libération Nationale 1964b: 64) and is worth quoting at some length:

> The population of Kabyle expression, subjected to the varied and multiple contingencies inherent in the life of a peasantry attached to the land, to its existence in the midst of harsh and thankless nature, has revealed itself a poet expressing— with a naturalness stripped of all artifice—the state of its spirit, its character, its impressions, its hopes, its disappointments, in short, of the reality that it lives and the ideal that it aspires to; withdrawn into itself and living in a fierce, not to say hostile, nature, its physical and moral isolation lead it to a continuous introspection that it cannot compromise. (Front de Libération Nationale 1964b: 64)

The phrase "population of Kabyle expression" itself indexes the controversial status of Berbers in relation to the state. Not only did it replace the term "Kabyle people," which met strong objections in the initial report (Front de Libération Nationale 1964b: 67–68), but the phrase also awkwardly sidestepped the word "language." Moreover, whereas other reports emphasized how to ensure the future of the genre in question via particular pedagogical methods, Kabyle poetry and music were considered not learned but instinctual:

> The virile and warlike instinct of the mountain dweller, his sharp sense of freedom, his expansive nature that breathes, despite misery and deprivation, the joy of living. All that expresses itself in an ardent poetry, in musical airs vibrant with enthusiasm and overflowing with sentiments that are often naïve but always full of sincere exaltation. (Front de Libération Nationale 1964b: 65)

If the Kabyle report differed from the others in its focus on population rather than pedagogy, in at least one respect it was similar. The reports all articulated the need to collect, transform, and disseminate Algeria's musical traditions. Samples of every Algerian folk genre were to be gathered by teams of researchers sent on a "cultural pilgrimage" into the countryside; the samples would be inventoried, classified, standardized, transcribed, and then taught as part of a uniform national curriculum (Front de Libération Nationale 1964b: 57; see also Déjeux 1975, 1982). Some would be purged of foreign influence; others would be newly illuminated via techniques that would foreground "previously hidden treasures that colonialism prevented us from knowing" (Front de Libération Nationale 1964b: 68); still others could serve as source material for a modern Algerian music suitable for sampling abroad.

Festivalization

The call to develop a national Algerian music resulted in a panoply of cultural festivals.[24] Held every one to three years, the festivals generally took place in Algiers during the month of Ramadan. Their impact extended well beyond the nation's capital, however, because of their pyramidal structure. To earn a spot on the national stage, a group or singer would first compete in a series of local and regional tryouts (also organized as festivals). Once a group reached the national level, it was again judged and prizes were awarded. National festivals could involve hundreds and sometimes thousands of performers. The 1978 Festival of Popular Music and Song, for instance, reportedly involved some 20,000 participants, including 7,300 groups and 5,000 individual artists or singers (Merdaci 1978).[25]

Festivals were important sites in which the links between authenticity and modernity were ideologically forged. Groups were encouraged to forage into the presumed cultural past in order to "harvest" popular oral literature at risk of becoming simply the "forgotten flowers on our ancestors' graves" (Bendimered 1969: 12). Establishing authenticity was so integral to the state's festival program that it was often a primary criterion for judgment and evaluation. The first of three evaluation criteria at the First National Festival of Music and Popular Song, held in 1969, was "authenticity of the work presented" (Bendimered 1969: 12). Authenticity and modernity (or related terms) were frequent festival slogans: "Authenticity and Opening" (*authenticité et ouverture*) and "Inventory and Creativity" (*inventoire et créativité*) were among the festival themes around the time of *A vava inouva*'s release. Echoing Pan-African Festival rhetoric, displays of authenticity were described as awakening a primordial identity that had been obscured during colonialism: "Day after day, the striking force of a word [*verbe*] in freedom shook us, awakening echoes that a genetic atavism had recorded in us unawares. The concentric circles of these intense rediscoveries permeated our reflexes conditioned by the West, transforming them into wet firecrackers" (Mekhlef 1969: 12).

National festivals were supplemented locally by "culture weeks" and "culture days," organized in most cities and towns by the state-built Houses of Culture (Maisons de la Culture).[26] Many festivals were recorded and archived at the National Institute of Music (Institut National de Musique, INM) and Algerian Television and Radio (Radio-Télévision Algérienne, RTA), becoming the very Algerian traditions that they were supposed to represent. The proliferation of days, weeks, and months of "culture" led to sardonic protests that there wasn't enough "culture" to fill the time allotted. As journalist Djamel Benzaghou noted, "A town shouldn't be forced to organize a whole week of culture if it can fill only one day" (Benzaghou 1977: 13). "'Culture' isn't a few days in a year or a year in a lifetime," noted another (N.A. 1981). As the novelty of festivals wore off or as they became stifled by ideological rhetoric, they began to be critiqued and satirized. For instance, a cartoon by the satirist Slim in the weekly *Algérie actualité* depicts what looks like a hapless state employee reading this proclamation (Slim 1981):

> Notice: The inhabitants of Oued-Hallouf are notified that throughout the town, between March 9 and March 13, there will be culture. After this date, any individual found possessing culture will be required to return it to the proper authorities.

Berber culture was ambivalently positioned with regards to the politics of authenticity and modernity. On the one hand, Kabylia was known for its rich folklore; indeed, Algeria's most celebrated national folklore festival was held annually in the Kabyle city Tizi Ouzou. Berber music or dance that was understood to be "passed down through the ages" was unproblematic. Yet if authenticity could come from the Kabyles, modernity was bestowed only by the state. In an especially crass illustration of this polarization, at the 1978 Folklore Festival in Tizi Ouzou, one Kabyle group staged a typical olive-picking ritual as a group from the Arab city of Mostaganem sang and danced about the agricultural revolution (Blidi 1978).

When Idir and Ben Mohamed were coming of age in Algiers, authenticity and modernity were in the air even as Berber culture was increasingly being consigned to the past. Idir and Ben selectively engaged the state's own discourse, but they turned it to different ends. They sought to appropriate folk traditions to develop a forward-looking, contemporary vision of Berber identity. Between 1970 and 1972, Idir embarked on his own cultural pilgrimages into the Algerian hinterlands. Traveling from Kabylia to the Aures mountains, from Constantine to Oran, he collected songs and learned local rhythms, instruments, and musical styles. After one such journey, he composed the melody of *A vava inouva*, building it around the sung refrain of the story told by old women throughout Kabylia. He asked Ben Mohamed to write new verses.

The Story, Made New

Ben Mohamed's text worked to create a new lens through which Berbers could situate their heritage in simultaneous relation to authenticity and modernity. By inserting a fragment of a women's story into a contemporary song about the storytelling process, Ben and Idir created a kind of bifocal vision: The distance achieved by the new artistic medium paradoxically brought Berber culture closer. Textually, this worked through a process that Bakhtin called "stylization" (Bakhtin 1981: 362–363). Stylization refers to the representational process of constructing an artistic image of another's language. It juxtaposes two consciousnesses: the one that represents (the stylizer) and the one that is represented (the stylized). As Bakhtin notes, against the backdrop of the contemporaneity of the stylizer and his audience, what is represented, or stylized, acquires new meaning and significance.

Consider first the refrain.[27] The refrain of *A vava inouva* is nearly identical to that found in the traditional story. The text closely resembles one that I recorded in Idir's natal village of At Yenni in November 1993. Idir's refrain also loosely follows the melodic and rhythmic contours of the older story-refrain. The story-refrain lent itself to stylization because it was already detachable: In the story, the refrain stands out because it is sung while the rest of the tale is narrated. Moreover, since the story-refrain is repeated, a periodically recurring element that punctuates the story's unfolding, it can operate metonymically to stand for the larger story. Because the refrain carries a history of its use (Bauman and Briggs 1990; Silverstein and Urban 1996), it also serves to index the story-telling context in general.

Idir's song *A vava inouva* turned the loom into a symbol of Kabyle culture.

Refrain, A Vava Inouva

Ţxil-ik lli-yi-n tebburt a baba-inu ba.	I beseech you, open the door for me, father.
Ççen-ççen tizebgatin-im a yelli ɣṛiba.	Jingle your bracelets, oh my daughter Ghriba.
Ugʷadeɣ lweḥc l_lɣaba a baba-inu ba.	I'm afraid of the monster in the forest, father.
Ugʷadeɣ ula d nekkini a yelli ɣṛiba.	I, too, am afraid, oh my daughter Ghriba.

The refrain employs grammatical forms (direct address, first person, and imperative) that would ordinarily draw the listener's attention to the predicament of the speakers (the father and his daughter Ghriba)—who are, after all, trying to fool a monster via their secret code of jingling bracelets. Yet in the context of the surrounding verses, the father and daughter are rendered inert. The two verses, cast entirely in the third person, make it clear that storytelling is to be evoked as cultural memory. The situationally specific meaning or moral typically associated with the particular story is erased. Verse one describes a typical storytelling scene familiar to anyone who grew up in Kabylia. It portrays the grandmother spinning her tale, surrounded by family members engaged in age-old activities: the daughter-in-law weaves at her loom (a quintessential symbol of Kabyle culture); the son worries about where the next meal will come from; the grandfather, cloaked in the traditional burnous, sits in a corner; the children gather around the grandmother. Verse two situates the scene as part of a broader cyclical pattern in which Kabyle life unfolds. It evokes the passage from fall to winter by employing a key symbol of each: a screen for drying figs in the fall (*idenyen,* plural of *adni*) is replaced by a log of holly oak (*aqejmur n tesaft*), used to build hot fires in the winter. As porridge steams in the pot, the whole family comes together to listen to the story.

In relation to the new verses, the refrain becomes a "narrated event" that is drawn into a second "event of narration" (Lee 1997; cf. Silverstein 1993). This second event governs the way the refrain is interpreted. The verses make it clear that storytelling is to be evoked as cultural memory; the situationally specific meaning or moral typically associated with a particular story is erased. This is accomplished through a distinct linguistic style that revolves around an idyllic chronotope, or a way of representing time and space through what Bakhtin (1981: 224ff) called "folkloric time." Representation in folkloric time is limited to only a few of life's basic realities, which are portrayed as equally valid and in close proximity. Human life is conjoined with the life of nature; labor is un-mechanized; and life activities are intertwined with agricultural cycles. Time and space stand in a unique relationship, such that a unity of place makes possible a cyclical blurring of temporal and generational boundaries.

The verses of *A vava inouva* develop around an idyllic chronotope. They describe not unique historical individuals but a set of complementary gender and generational roles that succeed each other through the ages. The old-style Kabyle Berber house (evoked metonymically by the word *tasga,* referring to the inner wall) provides a unity of place within which the generations come together, cut off by the snow from the surrounding world. Metaphorical evocations of the seasons further reinforce the sense of cyclicality. The habitual present tense characterizes the verses, fixing the actors in place: They endlessly repeat the gendered and generational roles to which they are assigned. The refrain resonates into these idyllic images, losing its performative meaning within the particular story as it comes to represent the storytelling process.

The internal gaze that Idir's song develops also takes shape through the two subject positions around which the song is organized. A self-conscious consumer of cultural heritage who views the scene from the outside surrounds an embedded consciousness, that of the old woman storyteller, who is possessed by culture, condemned to repeat endlessly the habits of tradition. Although her words are brought forward, she is not. Her words are quoted by a new voice that allows none of the initial intent to leak through (Bakhtin 1984: 185–204; cf. Lee 1997). What is relevant is not what the old woman is teaching but that cultural knowledge existed and was passed on. By quoting the story refrain within a text characterized by a different linguistic style, Idir's song creates a contemporary window through which the traditional process of storytelling is put on display. Storytelling itself has become the subject of song, the subject of a new metanarrative about the way cultural knowledge is communicated.

By depicting the process of storytelling in a new artistic medium, *A vava inouva* both assumes and transforms the very role of cultural transmission that it purports to describe. A new cultural actor looks at his society from a novel vantage point: that of simultaneously standing within and outside, looking in and looking back. This vantage point, however, is also constructed in relation to an external market. For the new song draws its performative potency not from the embedded genre of women's tales but from the new performance and dissemination context (Briggs and Bauman 1992: 159). In other words, when listeners hear the song, they are not suspended in the story, raptly attentive to the grandmother's next words. Rather, they are simultaneously looking back at the process of storytelling and across at the other listeners, who are not the family members sitting around the grandmother but all of Kabylia, Algeria, and the international community—especially France, the former colonial power.

Circulation

The perception of newness that greeted *A vava inouva* was generated not only through the song text but also through the medium in which the song was produced, the pathways across which it traveled, and the technologies that made such travel possible (cf. Feld 1996; Manuel 1993; Shannon 2003; Urban 2001). Perhaps more than anything else, the song's new musical idiom generated a space in which Berber traditions such as storytelling were seen as if in translation. It was not that Berbers heard the text itself in a foreign tongue, but that the music was so clearly associated with a western folk-rock style that it opened a wide interpretive space—an "intertextual gap," in Briggs and Bauman's (1992) terms—within which the traditional story was recontextualized, coming to stand for Berber culture. If representing the story as "culture" was a key aspect of the internal gaze, the music itself and the circuits through which the song moved helped to produce Berber heritage as an object of desire.

A vava inouva was initially played in Algeria on what is popularly referred to as the Kabyle radio station (officially, the Chaîne Nationale 2 or the Second National Station)—one of three state-run stations (Arab, Kabyle, and International). Both Ben and Idir were familiar faces at the station. Ben began making guest appearances on Kabyle radio shows in 1966. Three years later he was offered his own program, called *L'émission du matin* (The Morning Show), and he set out to develop a way of speaking that would resonate with a wide Kabyle audience. Invoking a mental image of his mother as his interlocutor, he incorporated traditional poetry, proverbs, and stories into what became a highly successful repartee. In a later show, *Journey into the World of Poets and Poetry* (Voyage dans le monde des poètes et de la poésie), he went further, translating poems and songs from around the world into Kabyle both to demonstrate that the Berber language could be a vehicle for universality and to borrow the voices of foreign poets (such as Pablo Neruda, Vladimir Mayakovsky, Louis Aragon, Nazim Hikmat, Jacques Prévert, and Mahmud Darwish, among others) in order to raise political issues that censorship prevented him from addressing directly. All told, Ben was involved in hosting or producing nearly a dozen shows between 1969 and 1982, despite the radio's anti-Berberist politics, which saw his shows canceled every six to nine months. Idir (then called Hamid) also frequented the station, although not in an official capacity. He made his radio debut in 1972 with the song *Ers-ed ay Iḍes* (Come, O Sleep), and he sang *A vava inouva* on the air before it was officially released.

A vava inouva was first recorded as a 45 with the local firm Oasis.[28] The song reached the French producer Chappell, who negotiated with Idir to produce an album and with Pathé-Marconi, a subsidiary of the multinational recording industry giant EMI, to distribute it. First, however, Idir was required to complete the obligatory two years of military service in Algeria, so not until 1976 was the album released, under the title of its hit tune, *A vava inouva*.[29] That Idir was picked up by Pathé/EMI suggests that his music already had the potential for widespread appeal, for it was simply not profitable for the "Big Five" recording companies to target markets viewed as exclusively ethnic (Wallis and Malm 1984: 89).[30]

When *A vava inouva* reached the European market, it joined a stream of similar musical products that were beginning to appear in the early to mid-1970s in both Western and Third World nations. Hundreds of local bands from Chile to Sweden, from Wales to Tanzania, were beginning to articulate concerns with identity and authenticity, singing in their own languages and blending indigenous melodies and instruments with acoustic guitars.[31] Western artists, too, were beginning to incorporate the musics of "elsewhere"—Simon and Garfunkel, for instance, recorded the Andean-inspired *El Condor Pasa* in 1970. The emerging market for what would come to be called world music no doubt provided a niche for *A vava inouva* once it reached the French airwaves. Getting airplay in France, however, was no small matter for a relatively unknown Algerian singer. Algerian artists were regularly played on stations such as RFI (Radio France Internationale), which was oriented to Maghrebi audiences, but until Idir no Algerian singer had been heard on a station geared to French audiences. A well-timed call from producer Chappell would change that. In 1975, during then–French president Valéry Giscard d'Estaing's historic visit to Algeria (the first by a French head of state since Algerian independence), Chappell arranged for *A vava inouva* to be played on France Inter, making it the first Algerian song to be broadcast on French national radio. From there, the song took off, becoming the first Algerian hit among European listeners and selling some 200,000 copies by 1978 (Humblot 1978: 15). The song was translated into over a dozen languages and taken up by groups around the world.[32] It greeted me in Paris when I arrived to begin my fieldwork: The French woman renting me a room had left it on my desk, as a clear icon of Berber culture. Its success ricocheted back to Algeria. As the first Algerian song to resonate outside the North African community, *A vava inouva* produced a sense of pride among Algerians, and par-

When this Kabyle man took up the guitar, the first song he tried to play was Idir's *A vava inouva*.

ticularly among the Kabyle population. "For the first time in its history," noted journalist Abdelkrim Djaad, "Algerian song had earned a place in the so-called advanced countries, where third-world cultures had been viewed as sub-cultures" (Djaad 1979: 22–23).

Acclaim in Europe was not the only reason for Idir's success in Algeria: Algerians also had to have the means to hear the song. *A vava inouva* came out just as radios and cassette players were becoming accessible to Algerians. Both the nature of the song and the technology through which it circulated helped to organize new spaces of reception, which may also have contributed to the song's sense of novelty. Radios began to appear in some villages just before the Algerian revolution, in the late 1940s or early 1950s. Not until the war, however, did listening to the radio become part of the fabric of social life. Even then, radio listening was a highly public and gendered affair, as men would congregate in a village café to hear the news. It would have been considered highly inappropriate to listen to the radio in mixed-gender company, but the problem was not usually posed because most households did not own radios until after the war. Record players, too, were uncommon; the first one to arrive in my home village came with an immigrant in the mid-1930s, but phonogram technology was never adopted by the majority of the population. Algeria had begun constructing a state-run record production facility in the early 1970s, but because equipment was ordered from the United States, the facility was not up and running until 1975 (A.B.A. 1984). Replacement parts also had to be imported from the United States; at one point record production reportedly stopped for two years because of a lack of parts. As a result, 2.5 million cassettes were sold for every record (A.B.A. 1984; see also Benaziez 1979). Cassettes appear to have entered the market in Algeria in 1972 (Moussaoui 1980b).

The increasing presence of radios and cassette players in the home allowed for the possibility of new reception practices that were not organized by age or gender. Before Idir, only one Kabyle singer had begun to pry open a new space in which family members could listen to music together—Slimane Azem, who was known for song texts that were primarily political and without sexual innuendo (see Azem 1984; Mahfoufi 2002; Nacib 2002). *A vava inouva* significantly expanded that space. Inspired by Kabyle traditions, the song was perceived as innocuous; indeed, the song itself describes mixed-gender listening to old women's stories, which was already an accepted practice. Focused around identity issues, Idir's music does not evoke the controversial domain of love or desire. Moreover, many of Idir's songs blur previously gendered repertoires. Before Idir, it was inconceivable that a male singer would publicly perform women's traditional songs. Idir not only appropriated these songs but also imitated a female style of vocal ornamentation. An older immigrant woman from Idir's natal village At Yenni told me that when she listened to Idir "it was as if we were hearing our mother, our grandmother who sang, even if it was a man. We didn't think, 'it's a man singing,' it isn't the voice of Idir in our ears . . . it reminds me of what I have lived, I put Idir aside."[33] This is not to say that the song revolutionized listening practices across Kabylia. To this day, there are regions and families where listening remains a largely gendered affair. However, those households that now listen together invariably locate the moment of change with either Slimane Azem or, especially, with Idir.

A vava inouva's international acclaim, musical styles, and new forms of reception helped to counter prevailing images of Berbers as backward or outside modernity. One Kabyle woman, a high school student in Algiers in the late 1970s, told me about the local impact of Idir's first appearance on national television, which occurred only after he had released two hit albums in France. "You should see the Kabyle singers they usually showed," she said. "They were all old men singing some awful religious thing, their false teeth rising and falling every time they opened their mouths." The next day in school, her Arabophone classmates would tease her: "Is that the best you Berbers can do?" But when Idir appeared, it was a different story. She knew the event would be momentous when, for the first time ever, her father called the whole family together around the television. Her exhilaration at hearing innovative and contemporary Kabyle music was shared by her classmates. More than thirty years later, Algeria is still singing *A vava inouva*. For those born after the song's first release, it has become an emblem of Berber identity, a sign of the rich heritage, legitimacy, and modernity of Kabyle culture.

"No culture without cultures," writes Jean-Loup Amselle (2001: 14). The conditions of possibility for developing an "internal perspective" on Berber culture were from the beginning planetary in scope. *A vava inouva* created a new vision of vernacular modernity by setting Berber traditions in relation to ethnographic, nationalist, and postcolonial discourses as well as world markets. These orientations were superposed to produce a prismatic effect. As they were layered into the women's story it became interpretable from novel vantage points. This effect was enabled by the medium of recorded song and the circulatory pathways through which it was propelled. As *A vava inouva* moved through the world,[34] it refracted its travels back to Kabyles in Algeria, who could then see themselves anew through distant eyes.

Even as *A vava inouva* engaged with ethnographic and nationalist discourses, it also exceeded them. The song drew on an ethnographically informed "poetics of detachment" (Kirshenblatt-Gimblett 1998: 18) to put the women's story on display, but it centered this process in indigenous hands a decade before the "reflexive turn" in anthropology had heightened awareness of the power dynamics of ethnographic representation (Clifford 1983; Clifford and Marcus 1986; Marcus and Fischer 1986). Similarly, the song blended Kabyle and western melodies, instruments, and styles to create a form of "world music" well before the term became popular in the West, suggesting that the phenomenon of world music was as much a Third World as a Western creation. With regards to the state, on the surface, *A vava inouva* seemed consonant with Algeria's articulated intention to "modernize traditions," but it configured "authenticity" and "modernity" into a new synthesis that the state could neither understand nor control. Whereas the state used authoritative discourse to demand unconditional allegiance, casting itself as the indivisible and indisputable "word of the fathers" (Bakhtin 1981: 342–343), *A vava inouva,* through its overlapping orientations to a range of ideas and styles, products and places, used an internally persuasive, dialogical discourse that invited reflection, "awaken[ing] new and independent words, . . . organiz[ing] masses of our words from within" (Bakhtin 1981: 345). As the song traveled from village to vinyl, it recreated the practice of village storytelling, and "Berber culture" more generally, as an object of desire that invited new forms of reflection and identification.

Idir and Ben Mohamed's quest for indigenous poems and songs that could serve as vehicles for a new vision of Berber identity was predicated on the assumption that an authentic "Berber culture" could be located in Kabyle village traditions. In singling out the village as a key locus of tradition and culture, Idir and Ben were not alone. For more than a century, the Kabyle village had served to inspire colonial agents and ethnographers as well as cultural activists.

3   The Mythical Village

To make known the village is to make known the whole society.

—Hanoteau and Letourneux, *La Kabylie et les coutumes kabyles* (Kabylia
and Kabyle Customs), 1872–73

One sometimes wonders whether the anthropologist is perhaps the only one
who is not involved in this constant movement from and to the village.

—Peter Van der Veer, *Nation and Migration*, 1995

One of the most striking displays at the April 20, 1993 cultural exhibit in Tizi
Ouzou was a model of the Kabyle village Taksebt. Placed on a large table in the
middle of its own room and made of plaster of paris, the village was perched
atop a mountain, the whole structure measuring perhaps a foot-and-a-half high
by two-and-a-half feet long and wide. At the mountain's crest, a smattering of
tiny brown houses were situated on several intersecting roads. Along the bottom, next to a key indicating that the model had been designed on a 1:1000 scale,
were the names of the model's three creators: M. Hamel, M. Hammami, and
K. Mouloud. Taped to the walls of the room in which the model sat were some
two dozen posters detailing, in French, the village's synchronic and diachronic
histories. Aside from four cardinal directions written on the sides of the model,
the mountaintop village sat alone on a bright blue board, utterly removed from
its geopolitical surrounds.

The Berber village has been "good to think" across three discursive traditions—colonial, anthropological, and activist—for well over a century. It has
been exhibited, miniaturized, staged. It has been cast as an originary locus of
cultural identity, visited by singers like Idir for inspiration, and made into a
backdrop for diaspora performances and videos. Detached from social process,
the village has been turned into a figure of culture that bears witness to a collective Berber heritage. In contrast, the contemporary village, when assessed
against this romanticized figure, is increasingly critiqued for its loss of traditional lifeways and values. Like a holograph, the village appears to change according to the viewer's perspective. It can be alternately idealized or disparaged
depending on the angle from which it is viewed. At the same time, neither position is possible by itself: Idealization and critique are interdependent.

Three locations have been heavily surrounded by a discourse of tradition and
loss: the "Berber House," the men's assembly or *tajma^cat,* and the wedding.
Through an ethnographic account of the ways these sites operate in one Kabyle
village whose population is split between Kabylia and Paris, I suggest that the

sites have been turned into repositories of tradition precisely because, through them, the ongoing trans-Mediterranean circulation that characterizes the village is potentially the most visible. By conferring on these three sites a mantle of tradition, the destabilizing dialectic between presence and absence that pervades the village can be temporarily arrested and managed.

The Holographic Village: From Contemporary Activists to Colonial Agents

During the heady post-independence years of the 1960s, preserving village traditions was not a project that most Kabyles could have articulated. To the contrary: As my interlocutors recalled it, during that period they were seeking to "modernize" their lifeways by, for instance, discarding their wooden dishes in favor of new plastic ware, abandoning their pottery water jugs for jerry cans, or replacing handcrafted silver and enamel jewelry with imported, gold-filled necklaces, earrings, and pins. Thirty years later, with the revalorization of tradition instantiated in the music of Idir and promoted by the Berber Cultural Movement, a language of preservation had come to seem natural. Young Kabyle activists regularly mined their own villages and homes in search of old pottery, tools, and clothing to display at the cultural exhibits that were beginning to take place across the region. Their interest provoked their parents and grandparents to look at old artifacts with new eyes. I vividly recall one gnarled older woman showing me with pride a number of jugs and wooden dishes—labeled and carefully stored in her basement—that she had lent to the cultural association in her village for display. Nor were artifacts the only things being revalorized. In a 1992 exhibit that I visited in Algiers, Kabyles turned themselves into signs of culture, reenacting such traditional practices as weaving or churning butter in a living diorama of village life. Similarly, in a 1994 concert by new Kabyle singer Lounis Aït Menguellet in Paris, the stage itself was laid out like a typical village, with men situated at the tajmaᶜat, or village assembly, and women at the well, a painted mountain backdrop behind them. A highlight of the performance was a staged reconstruction of a traditional village wedding.

At the same time, today's village is talked about in disparaging terms. In countless conversations, Kabyles contrasted contemporary village life to what they imagined to be a "real" or "authentic" village located in the distant past. My fieldnotes are full of my interlocutors' running comparisons between "now" (*tura*) and "then" (*zik*), with contemporary practices almost invariably seen as lacking. Even the poet Ben Mohamed, whose texts are stocked with images of traditional culture, told me in 1996 that since he left his village nearly forty years earlier, he had never spent more than two nights there. "For a long time," he said, "I asked myself [why it was that] as soon as I arrived, I wanted to leave. ... It was only with time that I came to understand that I wanted to preserve my image of the village that I knew before. The new village scares me."

Activists were hardly the first to view the Berber village through the twin lenses of nostalgia and loss. By the late nineteenth century, the village had already seduced a generation of French colonial administrators. They saw in the village a romanticized reflection of Europe's own rural past, while fashioning the Kabyles as a peasantry of small landowners who would assimilate easily into the colonial state (cf. Williams 1973). Consider the comments of Emile Masqueray, director of the Ecole des Lettres (School of Letters) in Algiers in the 1880s and a leading proponent of the Kabyle Myth (which located Kabyles as being closer to the French than Arabs were): "Sedentary, [the Kabyles] built villages similar to our own, in which they held regular assemblies and organized small republics. All around, they created gardens, planted trees, worked the fields, and separated their lands with borders: thus, they knew the pleasures and the responsibilities of individual property. Confined within narrow valleys or taking refuge on inaccessible slopes, they communicated very little with the rest of the world" (Masqueray 1983 [1886]: 15). Nor were indigenous activists alone in depicting the village as an enclosed, self-contained universe. A mere decade after the French had militarily subdued the Kabyle region, and at a time when intraregional, tribally based affiliations were still very much in play, Colonel Adolphe Hanoteau had already singled out the village as the primary frame for Kabyle society: "To make known the village," he wrote, "is to make known the whole society" (Hanoteau and Letourneux 1872–73, 2:7). Hanoteau located the village within a series of concentric circles that never intersected with the colonial state: above the village were the tribe (*lɛaṛc*) and the confederation (*taqbilt*); below it were various patrilineal groups (called *taxerrubt, adrum,* or *tɛarift*) (Hanoteau and Letourneux 1872–73, 2:4–7). Almost a century later, Pierre Bourdieu, while completing his military service in the Algerian colony, would describe virtually the same system, adding the house (*axxam*), the site of the smallest patrilineal group, as the "smallest cell" (1958: 11) and the core of the whole structure. If for Hanoteau the village was the key to the Kabyle universe, Bourdieu similarly distilled the village to what he took to be its essence, the Berber House: "a microcosm organized by the same oppositions and the same homologies which order the whole universe" (Bourdieu 1979 [1970]: 143).

Despite the hundred years that separated them, both Hanoteau and Bourdieu shared two linked presumptions. First, both maintained that a society could be represented metonymically through its smallest unit; they differed only on what that unit was. Second, both removed that unit from history, constituting it as a fixed center around which everything else could revolve. In the century between the two came a series of works that drew on related assumptions about the Kabyle village even as they advanced competing intellectual and political interests and agendas.[1] To this day, the Berber village continues to cast its spell, now echoing in the anthropological literature as a troubled figure of precolonial difference against which Western modernity can be defined.[2]

At the same time, the romanticized figure of the traditional village, structurally removed from wider historical, political, or economic currents, has served as a foil against which the evils of colonialism, war, and immigration could be measured. Accounts of rupture and fragmentation, of disappearance and loss, are all dependent on the image of a prior village that comes undone through its contact with an outside world (e.g., Khellil 1979; Lacoste-DuJardin 1976; Miyaji 1976; Sayad 1977). Bourdieu worked this dialectic in reverse: His now-famous accounts of an idealized precolonial Kabylia (Bourdieu 1977, 1990) were preceded by, and conceptually dependent on, the thesis of breakdown outlined in his extraordinary but little-known study of the resettlement villages built by the French army during the Algerian revolution (Bourdieu and Sayad 1964; see Goodman 2003, Silverstein 2004a). To Bourdieu and his coauthor Abdelmalek Sayad, such camps produced an irrevocable break with the "morphological bases" (Bourdieu and Sayad 1964: 117) of society, causing a "pathological acceleration of cultural change" (35). The hapless Kabyle was caught between the two worlds: "[He] has of the modern economic system . . . a necessarily mutilated vision, such that he can perceive only decontextualized scraps; of the traditional system, what remains is only scattered fragments. . . . [T]hrough lack of ability to speak the two cultural languages well enough to keep them separate, he is condemned to the interferences and contradictions that constituted a *sabir culturel* [cultural jargon]" (167–168).

In colonial, anthropological, and activist discourse, then, the Kabyle village has been construed through a holographic lens in which wholeness and rupture alternate depending on one's angle of vision. At the core of both portrayals is a view of the village as a fixed, originary entity that exists—or that once existed—outside time and history. Focusing on the village I call Amkan (a pseudonym meaning "place"),[3] where I lived among both Algerian and Parisian populations from 1992 to 1994, I approach the Kabyle village not through a bifurcated frame but as an organization of circulation. A sense of village belonging must be continually enacted through movement itself, as people, products, corpses, and car parts travel unevenly through trans-Mediterranean space. In proposing an approach to the Kabyle village as both object of representation and locus of circulation, this chapter is situated in relation to such works as Michael Gilsenan's account of a Lebanese village as a spatially configured network of relationships (Gilsenan 1982), Susan Slyomovics's study of the Palestinian village Ein Houd/ Ein Hod as an "object of memory" constituted differently by Arabs and Jews (Slyomovics 1998), and Katherine Hoffman's analysis of a Moroccan Anti-Atlas village (*tamazirt*) as discursively constituted in relation to gendered practices of moving and dwelling (Hoffman 2003).

The three sites that draw my attention as locations where movement is managed—the house, the men's village assembly, and the wedding—are also sites of what Michael Herzfeld (1997) calls "structural nostalgia," in which idealized visions of the past compete with critical evaluations of the present.[4] These locations are being characterized through nostalgia and loss precisely because it is around them that the instability at the village core is the most pronounced and potentially the most threatening.

Departures

The population of the village of Amkan spans the Mediterranean. In Algeria, the village is located in the heart of the *wilaya* (department) of Tizi Ouzou about ninety miles east of Algiers. It is marked by the absence of more than two-thirds of its population, who reside in Paris. Amkan is subdivided into four named sections; most of my work (in both Algeria and Paris) was conducted with the residents of one section, which I call Tamkant (a pseudonym meaning "little place"). Of approximately 1,420 inhabitants counted as belonging to Tamkant in 1994,[5] only 28.2 percent (400) resided there year-round; approximately 54.2 percent (770) lived in France, 10.6 percent (150) in Algiers, 5.2 percent (75) in other Algerian cities and towns, and .6 percent (8) in Canada. Yet while technically those who consider themselves to be "from" the village are dispersed among a number of cities and towns on three continents, most locate the village in relation to only two geographic locations: Kabylia and Paris. I use the term "village" or "trans-Mediterranean village" to refer to the community that is formed across and between these two sites, which share related organizational structures, linked economies, and ongoing circulation of people and products. I specify one or the other side of this community with the term "Algerian village" or "Parisian village" (or a variant thereof).

Despite Masqueray's idealized portrayal, he was one of the first to acknowledge that Kabyle villages were probably never self-sufficient. He described the relative emptiness of the village, as most men had left to work for "the Jews of Algiers" or in "the province of Constantine" (Masqueray 1983 [1886]: 100). In the twentieth century, two wider processes accelerated this emptying out: Kabyle immigration to France, and the postcolonial development policies of the Algerian state.

Immigration

The first men left Amkan for France in the 1910s, part of an initial wave of Kabyle emigrants, who—for reasons relating to the region's agricultural challenges (rugged terrain, uneven rainfall), the colonial confiscation of its more productive lands, the relative ease of travel between Kabylia and France, and the greater familiarity of Kabyles with the French language—arrived in the metropolis a generation earlier than Algerians from other regions (Khellil 1979; Mahé 2001; Sayad 1977). France welcomed this influx of manual labor, which supported the Fordist assembly-line production increasingly required by its factories. Renault, Citroen, Begsay (sugar), and Magie (soup) were among the first employers of men from Amkan; once one man was hired, he would find work at the same site for his brothers and cousins. From the Kabyle perspective, this early emigration served to bolster the village economy, then primarily agricultural, by furnishing an influx of cash to meet household needs or to finance a

The French automaker Renault was a major employer of men from Amkan.
This plant is located on the western edge of Paris.

special project (e.g., a livestock or seed purchase, a wedding, house construction). Emigration was considered temporary. One or two representatives—
always male—from each family would journey to Paris after the annual harvest
and return in time for the spring planting. Alternatively, families might send a
few men at a time for a period of several years. Upon their return, brothers or
cousins would replace them, thus assuring both enough men to work the family
fields and a steady flow of money from the metropolis to the village. From early
on, then, the Kabyle village developed an ongoing presence in France that was
directly linked to the shifting economic and manpower needs of both the
Kabyle region and the French metropole.

By the 1940s, the nature of emigration began to change, as World War II intensified the flow of North Africans to the metropolis. Called to serve in the
French army, many remained after the war, when jobs in reconstruction were
plentiful. Although immigrants still viewed their situation as temporary, some
of them began to reinvest a portion of their earnings in France, purchasing cafés
and hotels. In 1948, members of one of Tamkant's largest patrilineages bought
the first village hotel, and it became a revolving-door rooming house for the
groups of men that would migrate regularly between Amkan and Paris. This
hotel was soon joined by others in the same neighborhood, marking Amkan's
place on the map of the Kabyle region that was emerging on the Parisian soil,
as immigrants from a particular region would lay claim to entire blocks of the

French capital.[6] Between the end of World War II and the 1960s, France's needs for manual labor continued unabated; during this period, almost every able-bodied Algerian man spent at least a few years in France, and Amkan was no exception. This second generation of immigrants differed, however, in that most came equipped with at least a primary school education, and some plied a trade such as mechanic, technician, or carpenter. In the late 1950s, the first women from Amkan accompanied their husbands to Paris, but they remained the exception.

Just after Algerian independence (1962), some emigrants returned to Algeria, with hopes of making a fresh start in the newly independent nation. During the 1960s, internal migration to Algiers and other cities began to outpace European emigration in many parts of Algeria. In the Kabyle region, families whose homes and lands had been destroyed during the Algerian revolution often chose to go to Algiers rather than return to villages where they had lost everything. Amkan, however, had remained largely intact during the war, and its men continued to seek work in France while in most cases leaving their wives and families in Algeria.

Once Algeria was no longer juridically part of France, laws and conventions began to be put in place that would directly shape the form future immigration could take. While the Evian Accords[7] guaranteed the free circulation of Algerians in France upon presentation of an Algerian identity card, conventions governing employment of Algerians in France underwent continuous transformations and refinements (see Talha 1989). By 1974, faced with recession and growing unemployment, France passed legislation that considerably tightened immigration policy.[8] Soon after, Algeria followed suit, claiming that it wanted to retain its own work force. The number of Amkan members living in France continued to rise, however, as a result of another French law, known as the Family Regroupment Act (*Regroupement familiale*), which permitted immigrants with steady jobs and adequate housing to bring their families to France as legal residents. Because of this Act, the total number of immigrants from Amkan living in France more than doubled, rising from 901 in June 1973 to 2,174 in June 1994.[9] As wives and children began arriving, immigration lost its temporary character. Men left the old hotels and began to invest in private housing, scattering to various Parisian suburbs. The children of these immigrants enrolled in the French school system, and many are now graduating with professional degrees and training. Members of the third generation include doctors, lawyers, professors, and computer scientists. Young immigrant women have also begun earning professional degrees and joining the work force. Commerce continues to be a mainstay of the immigrant economy, however. As well as enhancing the family's status in both sides of the village, owning a café, restaurant, or hotel provides a steady income for the owners and a regular source of employment for other village members. Amkan immigrants now own well over 100 cafés, restaurants, and hotels in the Parisian region.

In the 1990s, new immigration became extremely difficult due to factors such as Algeria's civil conflict, growing anti-immigrant sentiment in France, and

France's own double-digit unemployment. The Family Regroupment Act was not renewed. With the 1992 expiration of the Evian Accords, a visa requirement was imposed on Algerians. Since the acceleration of Algerian civil strife in 1993, obtaining even a tourist visa has become exceedingly difficult. While Algerian university students may apply to pursue advanced degrees in France, they may no longer enter the French job market after they finish their studies. The only way for an Algerian to permanently settle in France today is to purchase a café, restaurant, or other business, or to marry a French citizen or permanent resident.

Development

If emigration was initially motivated in part because of the difficulty of making a living from the land in Kabylia, it was perpetuated after the Algerian revolution in relation to Algeria's development politics. Until the revolution, virtually all families in Amkan worked the land to some degree. Wheat and barley crops, used to make the dietary staple couscous, were harvested each year, along with potatoes, onions, garlic, and a variety of vegetables. During the war, most agricultural activity in Amkan came to a halt. A French army patrol stationed in the village carefully controlled all comings and goings to the outlying fields, automatically suspecting villagers of carrying food to the Algerian fighters.[10] A scorched-earth policy destroyed forests, fields, and livestock throughout the region (see Bourdieu and Sayad 1964).

Following the war, agricultural practices resumed. However, the new socialist state's development priorities favored industry over agriculture and, within the agricultural sector, large-scale, state-controlled programs over local initiatives. The state's limited efforts to promote local farming involved "modernizing" it by sending tractors, threshing machines, and other equipment to rural areas. My host Lounes recalled that beginning in 1965, the state (via the SAP, Service Agricole Polyvalent or Comprehensive Agricultural Service) would send a combine harvester (*moissonneuse-batteuse*) to the region for three months each year to help with the grain harvests. One year, the harvester failed to arrive, and the crops perished in the fields. After that, grain crops were abandoned. "It was as if people could no longer imagine harvesting without modern machinery," commented Lounes, adding, "We lost the desire and the knowledge to do things by hand" (personal interview, Tamkant, August 4, 1993).

The state also monopolized distribution and sales channels, making it difficult for anyone but members of the ruling National Liberation Front (FLN) to obtain materials necessary for agricultural production.[11] Produce could be sold only through state-controlled cooperatives, whose fixed, often subsidized, prices prevented local farmers from making a profit. By the early 1970s, villagers had begun to purchase grain from state-run stores rather than grow it themselves. Today, no one in Amkan supports a family exclusively from the land. At most, families supplement their needs by planting a modest vegetable garden, raising livestock (cattle, goats, sheep, chickens), and harvesting olives to make olive oil, a dietary staple. This work generally falls to women.

The state's discouragement of private agriculture helped to reshape Amkan into the bedroom community that it has now become. Aside from a handful of men employed in village shops or hired as day laborers on local construction sites, most men who live year-round in the village commute to jobs in factories, schools, banks, or administrative offices in the region. A handful of young women also work in neighboring towns. The experience of leaving the village begins at an early age. Starting in the sixth grade, children board a bus each morning for a twenty-minute ride to regional middle and high schools.

In the late 1980s and early 1990s, Algeria's efforts to decentralize its economy and promote a measure of private enterprise[12] began to create new opportunities in villages like Amkan. One man started his own wholesale thermometer business from his home; another launched a housing construction company. Large fields in the region have again been planted by local entrepreneurs, who are now permitted to own equipment and sell their produce at competitive prices. For most individuals, however, finding work still entails leaving the village. With Algeria's skyrocketing unemployment, even that no longer guarantees a job. In my host family alone, three university-educated individuals in their twenties all sat idle for several years in the mid-1990s, unable to find work in their fields.

If today's village is largely configured in relation to national and transnational processes such as development and immigration, these processes are experienced on both sides of the village as continuous departures and arrivals, absences and presences. The "village" must be continuously produced through the negotiation of presence and absence, belonging and exclusion. One place where village affiliation is constituted in relation to the constant movement of its inhabitants is in the house.

The Berber House

The Berber House is one of anthropology's most enduring ethnographic objects. More than thirty years ago, in a contribution to a volume devoted to Claude Lévi-Strauss, Pierre Bourdieu developed an analysis of the Berber House that has by now traveled far and wide (Bourdieu 1979 [1970]).[13] As Bourdieu described it, the Berber House worked as a hall of mirrors in which each part of the house was reflected in and refracted by other domains of social life. The house, he thought, constituted "a microcosm organized by the same oppositions and the same homologies which order the whole universe" (Bourdieu 1979 [1970]: 143). The layout of the house and the disposition of objects within it were articulated through structural relations of similarity and opposition (e.g., male:female :: dry:wet :: light:dark :: outside:inside) that also organized time (the seasons, the agricultural calendar, the day, the human life cycle), space (the house, the objects within it, the village layout), human activities (cooking, weaving), and the group itself. Thus, for instance, Bourdieu saw the way the center beam of the house rested on its pillars as analogous to the sexual union: Both

participated in shaping an orientation to the world as a set of opposing mascu-
line and feminine energies that periodically were brought into contact with each
other (1979 [1970]: 52).[14]

Since its publication in 1970, Bourdieu's study has produced another hall of
mirrors, this one anthropological. Traveling through citations from one work to
another, the Berber House has been made to constitute a foil against which a
new kind of ordering and disciplining of space seems to emerge in sharp relief.
Timothy Mitchell, while expressing "reservations" (Mitchell 1988: 49) about the
danger of setting up a precolonial Other as the opposite of ourselves, drew on
Bourdieu's description of the Berber House to lay the foundation for his discussion of an alternative semiotic order in which things were connected through
relations of sameness or sympathy, antipathy or disagreement. According to
Mitchell, no separate code of representation existed apart from the things themselves; space, objects, and human activities were dynamically interconnected in
a "vibration of echoes and repetitions" (Mitchell 1988: 61), constituting a Foucaultian realm of resemblance. In a related enterprise, John Pemberton prefaced
his analysis of Javanese precolonial history by repeating verbatim Mitchell's
"reservations" that scholars were setting up a "precapitalist totality . . . to satisfy
our yearning for a lost age of innocence" (Pemberton 1994: 17, citing Mitchell
1988: 49). While the house itself is absent from Pemberton's discussion, its pe-
numbra lingers.

If the Berber House has fueled the anthropological imagination, it has also
become a key symbolic location for the representation of Berber identity among
contemporary Berber activists seeking to carve out a place for their history, language, and cultural traditions within the Arabo-Islamic Algerian state. Berbers,
too, have turned the house into a text, constituting it as a representation of their
heritage. This is especially apparent in a coffee-table book (Abouda 1985) in
which photographs present the house as what Susan Stewart calls a distressed
genre—that is, the house has been "pried from a context of function and placed
within a context of self-referentiality" (Stewart 1994 [1991]: 74). The photographs contain almost no traces of social life. The occasional Kabyles who do
appear have been turned into signs of older lifeways—in fact, some of their images also appear on postcards. The political Kabyle singer Lounis Aït Menguellet
drew on related images of emptied-out houses meant to evoke memories of an
older Kabylia in his music video (Aït Menguellet 1994), which was shot in Paris
and marketed to diaspora communities across Europe and North Africa (see
chapter 8).

"Your House Speaks for You"

The house is crucially important to the social organization of Amkan,
but not for the reasons Bourdieu described. Rather than constituting a site
where the society's "generative schemes" converge, the house produces presence
despite the physical absence of its inhabitants. The majority of houses, mapped

A Kabyle village in 1993. Most of these houses were constructed after Algerian independence (1962), using cement and other modern building materials. Note the edge of the rooftop terrace on the right.

first onto blueprints and contingent upon budgets, are constructed of stone or cement built around a sturdy frame of iron rods anchored in a concrete foundation. The more prestigious ones are characterized by multiple stories connected with indoor staircases, individual rooms off central hallways, built-in closets, tile floors, and an abundance of glass windows with European-style wooden shutters. Contrary to Bourdieu's Berber House, described as inwardly structured to keep outsiders at bay (standing as "female" or "private," Bourdieu argued, in relation to the rest of the village, which was "male" or "public"), the most envied modern homes feature large, open terraces with spectacular mountain views. In addition to a separate living room, several bedrooms, a modern bathroom, and a kitchen, new houses contain a range of appliances and luxury items. Most are equipped with a refrigerator, sink, gas stove, and cupboards holding plates, glasses, serving dishes, and silverware. The more prosperous families might also have wall units housing a color television, a stereo system, china, books, and a VCR.

Building a house is a way of enacting one's presence and standing in the village even when one is absent. Most emigrants maintain a residence in the village although they are physically present for perhaps a month—at best, several months—out of the year. In the words of my host Lounes, "When you're not in the village, there's only your house to speak for you." The importance of a house is also attested by the sometimes extreme sacrifices made in Paris to be able to construct in Kabylia. Lounes's brother-in-law is a case in point. He housed his wife and four children in a tiny apartment in Paris while building a large house in Amkan. Only years later did the family purchase an apartment in France. This family is hardly alone. It is almost a truism that immigrant families often occupy substandard housing, crowded into only a few rooms lacking modern amenities, while building large dwellings in their natal villages. A house is more than a way for immigrants to display to those back home their success in France; more importantly, it marks their presence in the village during their long absences. It also allows them to maintain, as Abdelmalek Sayad noted, a fiction of return (Sayad 1977: 64) and thus a means of continuing to forge ties to their natal village.

Houses can also be sites where relationships are maintained, and where debts are sometimes accrued, between permanent inhabitants and immigrants. In many immigrant families, one member may remain in Algeria to occupy the house and perpetuate the family's presence. Other immigrants give their keys to a relative, who looks after and may even sleep in the house while they are away. Immigrants may also hire carpenters, masons, or day laborers who live year-round in the Algerian village, forging economic relationships around the maintenance of their homes that sometimes turn into long-term debts. In one case I learned of, a contractor made and installed several doors and windows but never submitted a bill. Each time the immigrant owner ran into him in the village, the owner would ask for the bill: "Soon, soon," the contractor would reply. Ten years passed like this, during which time the immigrant remained in the contractor's debt.

Finally, the house itself can occasionally become a target of social sanctions. In one extreme case, a village man was caught running a prostitution ring from his home on the outskirts of Amkan. The man was first put into "quarantine" by the village assembly—that is, no one could look at, speak to, talk to, or do business with him. Some felt, however, that the man had brought such dishonor to the village that a stronger punishment was called for. Under the cover of darkness, a small group went out and burned his house to the ground. Here, physically removing the house was a way to restore the village's good standing in the eyes of the surrounding community.

Mobility and Morality

The house also serves as a locus of social morality. Early in my stay in Amkan, I took a wrong turn and ended up in unfamiliar territory. I felt conspicuous and out of place, as if I were trespassing. My feelings were not off base. In Amkan as in most Kabyle villages, houses tend to be situated within a territorial map loosely organized through the patrilineage or *adrum*. Four patrilineages, further divided into fourteen subpatrilineages, constitute the village section Tamkant. Three are "Kabyle" (*leqbayel*) patrilineages, while one patrilineage (that of my hosts) is comprised of marabouts (*imrabḍen*). Much as

Bourdieu described it (1962 [1958]: 15), the overall contours of the patrilineages tend to be spatially reproduced in the arrangement of houses, with families
of particular subpatrilineages usually located in close proximity. Well-trodden
dirt paths connect each patrilineage to Xamsa Iberdan (my pseudonym for this
place, meaning "five paths"), a public square at the center of Tamkant where
young men hang out, a grocer sells his wares, and cars periodically come and
go. Forking off these main paths are others leading to residential quarters associated with particular subpatrilineages and used primarily by inhabitants, visiting family members, and others with good reason to be there; it was onto one
of these that I had stumbled.

A moral economy organized by lineage, age, and gender is inscribed onto the
soil not via an inherent structuralist logic but through the daily choices men
and women make about where, when, how, and with whom to move through
village space (cf. Maggi 2001). An unmarried young woman who travels alone
outside her immediate group of households opens herself to scrutiny, for she
risks being suspected of seeking out the attentions of a man, perhaps simply by
passing his house or, worse, by delivering a note for him to his sister or niece.
Such a woman would be evaluated as lacking shame or modesty (*ur tseth' ara*)
(cf. Abu-Lughod 1986). At stake is *lherma,* or the respect that a household enjoys
within the village. Fadhma, a twenty-five-year-old emigrant, represents a case
in point. She arrived in Amkan in the summer of 1992 wearing a short, sleeve-
less, hot-pink dress. When she informed her older brother that she was not going to change her clothes to walk to the village grocery store, she provoked a
tirade. "Your behavior involves everyone" ("*tu impliques tout le monde*"[15]), he
reminded her; scowling, she went to don her long *taksiwt,* the white dress that
most women of Amkan wear in the Algerian village. It does not take a pink dress
to violate propriety. Young women know that their own ability to find a husband
depends on their good reputation, so they avoid putting themselves into situations where they could be critiqued. Fatima, an eighteen-year-old year-round
Tamkant resident, told me that when her invalid mother would ask her to go to
the grocer at the center of Amkan (located in a different village section) to buy,
say, tomatoes, she would often walk to the edge of the adrum and wait until
enough time had passed, then return to her house, telling her mother that the
tomatoes were sold out. Expected gender behaviors are also inflected by a woman's emigration status. Emigrant women already tend to be viewed as looser, so
they have to redouble their efforts while in the Algerian village if they want to
be seen as respectable. Zahra, an emigrant friend whom I met with in cafés all
over Paris, rarely walked the three minutes from her house to mine during her
summer vacation in Tamkant because she had to pass through the public square
Xamsa Iberdan and be seen by the group of men who typically socialized there.
When she did come for visits, it was always with a sister or cousin, as women
traveling in pairs or groups diffuse suspicion. Women who lived in the village
year-round, in contrast, would traverse the square without hesitation.

While men can circulate with greater ease, they are not free to go just anywhere. They would not, for instance, enter the private paths leading to residen-

tial quarters of another adrum, particularly in a different village section, without good reason. Nor are women the only ones whose behavior is sanctioned. A man suspected of paying a woman inappropriate attentions risks being fined by the village assembly or even physically attacked by the woman's relatives. I experienced this firsthand when I received a series of sexually suggestive, anonymous notes. I showed them to a male friend in my host family, and it was all I could do to persuade him not to lie in wait that night and ambush the man he suspected of writing them.

The village, then, is constructed as a locus of social morality through the ways inhabitants circulate within it. At the same time, the village as a moral community transcends its geographic limits. If word of the potentially controversial actions of an emigrant living abroad—especially a woman—reaches the ears of her relatives in the Algerian village, their reputations and standing may suffer. Running commentary generated through telephone calls and by frequent visits in both directions ensures that anonymity, even in a cosmopolitan city such as Paris, is difficult to achieve. Several of my immigrant female friends would jokingly use the phrase "*di taddart i telliḍ*"—"you are in the village"—to describe their feeling that in Paris, they might run into someone from Amkan at any moment, and therefore that they tended to dress and behave accordingly. This feeling was brought home to me one evening as I was strolling down the Champs-Elysées with an immigrant friend. She told me that she felt uncomfortable when men looked at her; she imagined them thinking, "Oh, so you're the kind of girl who can go out at night." For her as for many others, the "village" had become a pervasive moral presence, a "mentality" or mindset that could inform her actions and behaviors even when she was physically distant.

If houses on the Algerian side of Amkan are laid out in relation to lineage, this is only one of a broader field of spatial relationships in which the household participates. A paved state road bifurcates the village and is lined by a number of locally owned businesses, including several storefront groceries, two bakeries, two cafés, a mill for processing olive oil, two woodworking shops, a blacksmith, a jeweler, a stationery shop, a minimally equipped health center, and an elementary school. A post office houses the only public telephone. In addition to this modest commercial center, which can be frequented by anyone in the village (with the caveats described above), each village section contains several grocery stores, generally used primarily by the section's inhabitants. The village is also home to four mosques, one in each section, and two saints' tombs (*taqubbeṯṯ*, from Arabic *qubba*), one of which reportedly houses the ancestor of the marabout lineages of Tamkant.

Amkan is also well connected to the surrounding region via automobile and public transportation. During my stay, forty cars were counted in Tamkant, an average of one car for every ten to twelve inhabitants. This figure does not include the steady stream of vehicles arriving with emigrants each summer. In 1993, one extended emigrant family alone drove to the village from the ferry in Algiers in four cars, including a Mercedes. Several emigrant families keep one car in the village year-round for summer use. For those lacking access to a car, state and private (since 1989) buses travel several times a day between Amkan, Tizi Ouzou, and Algiers. Smaller passenger vans, all privately operated, connect Amkan with surrounding towns and villages. Amkan is also connected via the airwaves. In addition to receiving the single Algerian state television channel, many households capture European programming via satellite dish. Collectively purchased by contributing village members in the early 1990s, the dish is perched atop the highest local landmark—the village mosque. A second satellite dish, bought by an individual for his family's private use, sits on the roof of his eighteen-room house.

Finally, many households in Amkan today are in close relationship with at least one household in Paris, usually that of a brother, an uncle, or another relative. This trans-Mediterranean connection can supply year-round Amkan residents with periodic influxes of French goods, and until the rise of civil strife in the early 1990s, assurances of occasional visits to France, as a close relative in France could furnish the housing certificate required for a tourist visa (such certificates are still generated but have little force).

In sum, when viewed in relation to the circulation of its inhabitants, the village appears not as a stable structure at the core of the life process but rather in a permanent state of temporariness and flux. While the house may be located within something like a model of concentric circles moving from house to patrilineage to village section, lines of connection also extend from the house to the workplace, to the surrounding region, and frequently to one or more houses in Paris. The house is not a center where "generative schemes" converge but a point of departure and arrival. Finally, the house is not a silent, inward-facing structure; rather, it "speaks" to the community—it is a primary marker of presence in the Algerian village despite the physical absence of its owners, and it is a marker of status for all Amkan residents.

Village Assemblies

The tajmaᶜat or men's assembly is another celebrated institution in Kabyle society.[16] As a place where men come together regularly to manage village affairs through discussion and debate, the tajmaᶜat has occupied a privileged place on the ethnographic map since the earliest days of French colonization. Seen by French military ethnographers as a kind of primitive democracy, it was taken as the primary indicator of Kabyles' similarity to Europeans and their readiness for assimilation into the metropole. In the 1870s, the local bodies of law (lqanun) developed by men's assemblies were collected and codified by French colonel Adolphe Hanoteau and jurist Aristide Letourneux along the lines of the Napoleonic Code (Hanoteau and Letourneux 1872–73). This volume briefly became the law of the land in Kabylia (Ageron 1960: 334; Mahé 2001: 204), a mandate that further worked to triangulate Berbers and Arabs in relation to France. Even after French civil law was established throughout the region, decisions of the tajmaᶜat continued to hold sway in most village matters.

In the past, the small stone benches under the archway were one place men congregated to discuss village affairs. Today, the tajmaᶜat is usually held in modern meeting rooms. Note the Amazigh graffiti on the wall.

Within activist circles, the tajmaᶜat occupies an ambivalent position. On the one hand, it is regularly invoked as evidence of the region's inherently democratic and secular spirit. As such, it took on special valence during the early 1990s in relation to Algeria's attempt to establish a multiparty democracy, as Kabyles pointed to the tajmaᶜat as an indicator of the fact that they, in contradistinction to Arab Algerians, were already versed in democratic practices. It is also constituted as a sign of Berber heritage—recall that it was featured on the set of a Paris-based concert. Layered into this nostalgic valorization of the tajmaᶜat, however, is a harsh critique by younger men, who disparage what they perceive as the factionalism and cronyism of their elders. Older men, too, can wax nostalgic about the tajmaᶜat, but for different reasons. They mourn the loss of traditional ways of speaking[17] and are critical of what appears to them as a lack of respect for the old ways.

If the tajmaᶜat is alternately constituted as a locus of nostalgia or a target of critique, it is perhaps precisely because through the tajmaᶜat, the instability at the village core is potentially at its most visible. For the tajmaᶜat constitutes one of the primary forums where presence, absence, and belonging are negotiated out of the flux and movement through which the village is constituted. The tajmaᶜat is designed to track and manage the very temporariness of presence in both sides of the village. It also works to generate a sense of belonging through the possibility of exclusion.

The tajmaᶜat is above all an affair of men. I never attended a tajmaᶜat meeting in Algeria. In Paris, I was graciously invited to one meeting (at which the men were reportedly on their best behavior). My account is drawn primarily, then, from my discussions with men who attended the tajmaᶜat as well as from the ways in which its decisions circulated outside of the formal meetings. On the Algerian side of Amkan, the tajmaᶜat is organized by village section. Each of the four sections has its own tajmaᶜat, which usually meets weekly. The tajmaᶜat is overseen by a small village committee (called *Comité du Village* or *imɣaren n taddart*), which includes a president, a treasurer, and one or two members from each adrum or patrilineage. The presidents of the four village section committees may also meet together to discuss whole-village affairs. The tajmaᶜat deals primarily with three kinds of issues: maintenance of collectively owned village properties, discussion of intra-village problems or propositions, and interpersonal conflicts between village members.

Attending the weekly tajmaᶜat meeting is one of the primary ways presence in the Algerian village is performed. The first article of Tamkant's *qanun* makes this explicit: "Presence is obligatory for all men over 18, including emigrants. Absence is excused only with a valid reason. All non-excused absences will be subject to a penalty of 50 dinars."[18] The qanun further specifies that all men present in the village must participate in collective work sessions to accomplish such tasks as repairing cemetery walls, laying drainage pipes for the disposal of wastewater, clearing brush, or widening public paths. Work sessions can occur as often as every week when weather permits. These sessions are increasingly resented, and a few villages have begun to introduce paid labor (by village youth) in place of obligatory work, but this practice has not been adopted in Tamkant. Instead, in response to increasing numbers of men opting to pay the fine rather than attend the session, in 1993 the village section president quadrupled the fine for nonattendance of work sessions, from 50 to 200 dinars (a day's pay for a day laborer) (cf. Mahé 2001: 489).

The tajmaᶜat has the power to raise monies for special village projects by levying a small head-tax—a procedure that simultaneously keeps track of who is in the village.[19] The tax is applicable to every resident, from newborns to the aged and infirm, and is paid by the head of each household. The tajmaᶜat also marks belonging by defining deviance. It levies fines for behaviors viewed as inappropriate and, in extreme cases, administers the ultimate sanction: It "banishes" an individual or family from the village by putting them in "quarantine" (*kksen-t i tufiq*, "they remove him from the community"; in French, *bannir quelqu'un du village*), which excludes them from all village economic and social activities and forbids others from acknowledging their presence in any way. A quarantined or "banished" individual may not even buy a few groceries in a local store. Quarantine extends to death. During my stay in the village, the tajmaᶜat refused to allow the village religious leader (*ccix*; in Arabic, *shaykh*) to conduct funeral rites for an individual who had been in quarantine for many years because he was an alcoholic who brought prostitutes to his home (a shaykh was recruited from outside), although his burial in the village cemetery was permitted.[20]

The tajmaᶜat can also work to make less visible the sometimes extreme economic differences among residents. One way this operates, of course, is through the head tax, which takes no account of income levels. While on the one hand the tax perpetuates economic inequality, it also enables the fiction to be maintained that all contribute equally to village affairs. Another place where the tajmaᶜat intervened to level status differences was at funerals. In 1992, the tajmaᶜat in Tamkant came under the leadership of younger, activist men, and one of their first acts was to convince the assembly that the village should pay for the communal meal that takes place following a death. This ensured that funerals could no longer be sites for ostentatious displays of wealth.[21]

On the Parisian side of Amkan, immigrants have created a separate administrative organization, also called tajmaᶜat. The Algerian tajmaᶜat structure is not simply reproduced in the diaspora, however, nor can the Parisian one be described as a "pale copy" of the Algerian original, as Abdelmalek Sayad suggested (1977: 77). Rather, it is transformed in important ways, becoming a new structure that adopts a shared semantics as a way of imagining connections to its Algerian counterpart. The Paris-based village committee, also called Comité du Village or imɣaren n taddart, functions at the village rather than the village section level. Five representatives, one from each of the four village sections plus one from the marabouts, serve on the committee; in Paris, it is these committee meetings that are referred to as tajmaᶜat.[22] Within a village section, each adrum or patrilineage also selects a representative, who both reports to the representative of his village section and transmits the decisions of the larger village committee to sub-adrum representatives. These individuals in turn serve as liaisons with the heads of household in their group. In theory, the structure works like a pyramid. To reach a decision, each village section representative must persuade representatives at the adrum level, who in turn convince the sub-adrum representatives, who must then rally the households they represent.

The primary responsibility of the Paris-based tajmaᶜat organization is now to organize repatriation of the dead, a practice begun in 1946.[23] When a death occurs, every villager present in Paris at the time of the death (whether as a permanent resident or a tourist, and including children) is responsible for making a contribution, which stood at 10 francs (about 2 dollars) in 1994. With over 2,000 people in Paris, the village can quickly raise around 20,000 francs ($4,000 in 1994), which covers the full cost of repatriation—funeral home expenses, proper preparation of the corpse at the Great Mosque of Paris, purchase of a coffin conforming to international standards, air travel, an ambulance to carry the corpse from Algiers to the village, and one round-trip plane ticket for a family member to accompany the corpse.[24] As the Paris qanun makes explicit, when a death occurs, the family of the deceased must immediately report the death to the committee. Should someone make their own arrangements for repatriation, the costs would not be covered.

Payment of repatriation dues is one of the primary areas of tension among Parisian villagers. Disputes arise frequently around who is to be considered part of the Parisian village for accounting purposes. Each adrum and sub-adrum representative is responsible for collecting the appropriate sum from all the families in his group; failing this, he must pay the sum out of his own pocket—a not uncommon occurrence. At minimum, the representative's task is to inform those under his jurisdiction of an impending collection, but his job can also entail mediating disputes among family members. Some disputes arise over how many individuals a family must pay for. When relatives from Amkan visit from Algeria, they, too, are required to pay, and accusations can fly concerning whether a particular individual was or was not in France at the time of the death in question. Sometimes people are accused of attempting to hide arrivals, advance departures, or delay the declaration of births in an attempt to avoid payment. Sub-adrum and adrum representatives often become embroiled in such disputes, which can echo all the way to the final tajmaᶜat meeting, producing heated arguments among village section representatives about how many individuals each is responsible for. Payment or nonpayment of repatriation dues also serves as a way to define deviance and (occasionally) to produce exclusion. For instance, if a man has long been paying for a brother who refuses to participate, the day may well come when he's had enough. Unacceptable behavior by one family member, such as excessive use of alcohol or drugs, could also trigger refusal to pay for that individual.

The initial collection of money takes place at designated cafés—several for each village section and one for the marabouts—that are owned by individuals from that section. Payment must take place in cash and in person, not by check —a process that also serves to maintain face-to-face contact. When my host Lounes, for instance, traveled across Paris to the designated café to pay his dues, he would often spend several hours talking with the owner, a distant cousin. Late payment is fined at 20 francs. From the café, the section representative brings the payments, still in cash, to the tajmaᶜat meeting. The money travels together with a list of residents, as article 6 of the Paris qanun specifies: "At every meeting a detailed list of members must be presented. Each head of household must give a list to the head of his sublineage. Each sublineage head must give his list as well as the money [he collected] to his village section representative (if he fails to do so he will be fined 50 francs). Each village section representative must present his complete list to his four colleagues [on the village committee], otherwise he will have a fine of 50 francs."[25] The money is carefully counted and recorded, by village section, in a handwritten ledger, which effectively serves as an ongoing, if irregular, census of Amkan residents in Paris. The importance accorded the village committee meeting is indexed by a fine: If a representative is even a few minutes late, he is automatically fined 50 francs.

The meeting I attended in June 1994 was held in a tiny office of a dilapidated hotel—owned by an Amkan family since 1948—in the Stalingrad section of Paris. It began with a handshake all around. The five men then sat down around an old desk. Each one in turn presented his list and handed over the money for his village section to the treasurer, who counted it carefully before entering the sum into his ledger. Each representative then signed the ledger. Because I was present (I was later told), there was little discussion of the accuracy of the numbers, but that was reportedly unusual. At that meeting, 2,174 Amkan residents were counted as being in France. Because two deaths had recently occurred, each resident had contributed 20 francs, bringing the total collected that day to 43,480 francs ($8,700). In the past, such a sum would have been kept in cash by the treasurer. The treasurer in 1994 told me that when he was first appointed, he had reluctantly continued that practice, keeping the money under his bed until one day when it got wet and he had to iron all the bills. At that point, he opened a bank account and presented it to the committee as a fait accompli; the interest the account earned quelled any mistrust they may have had about keeping the money in one individual's name.

Because by June 1994 I had spent nearly two years in the village, on both sides, I wanted to contribute to the collection, and had paid my 20 francs to my head of household. This threw off the committee; they weren't sure where to record my contribution. I was surprised, for I couldn't see that an extra 20 francs (about 4 dollars) would make much difference one way or another. As for the tally of residents, the total fluctuated each time anyways. Whether Tamkant had 641 or 642 people that day didn't seem especially significant to me. The committee, though, saw it differently. Did my contribution entail further implications? Would I be able to claim rights in the system? I began to understand that my presence mattered precisely because this was a site where belonging to the village was managed, and I upset this careful accounting. The committee ended up listing my contribution as a gift to the village.

Yet the repatriation system is not inflexible. It both defines who is considered to be "in the village" and allows for a measure of fluidity. An individual who does not wish to be buried in Algeria may opt out of the system by written request, and he is duly "removed" from the village; to date, this is rare. Occasionally, a village member who has not paid his dues for a substantial period, and who has failed to respond to repeated entreaties, can be "removed" from the village by a unanimous tajmaᶜat decision. To be reinstated, the individual must petition the committee, present apologies for lack of participation, cover all back dues, and pay a sizable fine (around 1,500 francs or $300 in 1994). Generally, women who marry into the village from outside are included in the repatriation system of Amkan, while those who leave the village by marriage are not. In a few cases, however, an Amkan woman and her non-Amkan husband have been incorporated into Amkan's repatriation system (thus becoming "part of the village") by special arrangement;[26] here, a financial gift to the village is required. Perhaps, then, I could have "joined" the village, but it would have required the invitation of my host family and the committee as well as a significant gift, a commitment to maintaining relationships, and ongoing future contributions.

In addition to organizing repatriation, the Paris-based committee also raises money for projects to improve the Algerian village infrastructure. Generally, this is at the request of the Algeria-based committee, which sends a letter (not via the mails but in the hands of a returning immigrant) detailing a specific project and reminding immigrants—sometimes pointedly—of their obligation to provide support since they do not participate in the collective work sessions. Such projects are handled by village section, not by the village as a whole, because "otherwise," as one representative said, "we'd never agree on anything."

The tajmaꜤat organizations in both Algeria and Paris are being challenged by new, youth-dominated cultural associations that seek to revalorize certain village practices while reforming others. I consider these associations in some detail below; suffice it to say here that they represent a compelling point at which interests that are at once subnational and transnational interpenetrate with and help to shape village-based initiatives.

Weddings

When I arrived in Amkan in August of 1992, I was told that I had come at a good time. The weddings were about to begin, and I would be able to witness Kabyle "traditions" firsthand. Perhaps more than any other site, the wedding (*tameɣra*) is perceived as a repository of tradition by Kabyles from both sides of Amkan. Because they are perceived as traditional, weddings were events where I was able to videotape more easily than I could elsewhere. In fact, those Amkan residents who can afford it will videotape their own weddings; the videos may travel with emigrants to Paris, where family members who did not make the summer trip to Algeria can view them. I was looking forward to watching my tapes with my host family, hoping that they would spark rich commentary about performance practices. What I got instead was a list of names. "That's Unisa, daughter of Mohamed. There's Khalida. Farid. Abdullah, brother-in-law of Rachid." This would go on for ten, fifteen, thirty minutes, and gradually I gave up on hearing anything more. Only later did I realize that the practice of naming was itself the point, a way of taking note of who was at the wedding and a means of recognizing people that they may not have seen for a year or more.

The wedding or, more specifically, the evening dance known as the *urar*, is the only place where almost everyone present in the village shows up at the same time. Any Tamkant man who marries—whether he is a year-round resident or an emigrant, and whether the "legal" ceremony took place in Algeria or in France—may choose to celebrate the wedding through a tameɣra, a three-day festival held in Tamkant itself.[27] Indeed, most people I talked to considered this the "real" wedding. My host's son Said, for instance, was legally married in the eyes of the state months before he held his tameɣra; not until after the tameɣra did his new wife come to live with him in Tamkant. Likewise, an emigrant may officially marry in Paris—especially if residency papers are involved—and stage a tameɣra in Tamkant the following summer. One extended family flew dozens of its members to Algeria for just two weeks to stage a double wedding in Tamkant, even though, for one of the couples, both bride and groom resided permanently in France. That said, not every emigrant chooses to hold his

tameɣra on the Algerian side of the village. Weddings in Paris are usually celebrated in village-owned cafés.[28] They do not, however, have the same cachet as
those held in the Algerian village, and they generally do not involve the whole
village section.

Although weddings in Algeria are talked about in terms of tradition, they
have been significantly reconfigured in relation to the growing dialectic between
presence and absence that characterizes the village. Specifically, the timing, location, and organization of the wedding are all shifting in ways that maximize
presence. When Lounes and Jejjiga were married in the spring of 1966, the gathering was held in a private household and was attended primarily by members
of each subpatrilineage. At that time, weddings could occur at any point during
the year. Several decades earlier, most weddings were reportedly held in relation
to the agricultural cycle, occurring after the fall harvest. The days on which
weddings are held have also changed. In earlier decades, the days were reportedly chosen in relation to beliefs that certain days of the week were inherently
more propitious than others; those days that were so selected varied by region
(Laoust-Chantréaux 1990: 191, 192; cf. Laoust 1993: 72, 101; Westermark 1914:
86–88). Today, in contrast, Amkan weddings take place almost exclusively in July
and August, becoming a key site where links between year-round and emigrant
populations can be generated and maintained. Moreover, all weddings begin on
Wednesday evening and last through Friday morning—the Algerian weekend.
This permits the presence of the increasing number of villagers who spend the
workweek in Algiers or other Algerian cities.

The wedding is also being spatially reconfigured to enable the entire village
section to attend. Samira, the twentysomething daughter of my hosts Lounes
and Jejjiga, recalled that when she was a child, weddings were held in private
homes; at her uncle's wedding, held in the courtyard of the family house, only
the subpatrilineages of the bride and groom, plus a few close neighbors, were
invited. Today, just a few events in the three-day wedding are limited to close
family members. Said's wedding was a case in point. A gathering in his house
on the opening afternoon, for instance, was attended primarily by members
of his mother's and father's subpatrilineages. A luncheon hosted by his bride
Jamila's household involved members of her immediate family and Said's subpatrilineage, with each family represented by one or two invited guests. Ordinarily, trips by the bride to the saint's tomb and the well in her new village, as
well as a ceremony in which a belt is fastened around her waist by a man in
the groom's family, would likewise be attended primarily by members of the
groom's own adrum (these did not take place at Said's wedding because the
couple left early on Friday for a honeymoon in France). Two events, however,
have been reconfigured to encourage—and in one case, require—the presence
of virtually everyone in the village section: the *urar* or wedding dance, held on
two consecutive evenings from dusk until the wee hours of the morning; and
the procession to pick up the bride.

An Amkan urar today is held in one of five open public squares, located in
each village section (four village sections plus a small marabout section). In

A young woman rides a rented bus to pick up the bride. The procession, which went from the groom's village to the bride's village, also included dozens of private automobiles.

Tamkant, the urar takes place in Xamsa Iberdan, the public square at the convergence of five paths that was formerly used as the *annar,* the space where grain was laid out and sorted after the harvest. Moving the wedding to this space accommodates the far larger crowd that is becoming the norm today. Virtually the entire village section attends the wedding; indeed, failure to show up risks damaging future relations. While most Kabyles I talked to enjoyed the urar, a few admitted to attending out of a sense of obligation. If they did not put in an appearance, they knew that there would be repercussions. Yet attendance is not automatic. Families must be personally invited on the morning of the first day of the wedding by a female member of the groom's household, who goes from door to door crying out "*aruḥen ɣer tameɣra-nneɣ*"—"come to our wedding."[29] Invitations, then, provide what may be the only face-to-face contact between families who see each other just in the summer.

While the urar can involve as many as 500 people, the way guests are arranged in space enhances individual visibility. At the center of the urar, a small patch of earth is left open for a dance space. Women sit on tiny stools they bring with them on one side of this space and men stand along the other side, the whole forming a jagged circle. The side on which the women sit slopes down toward the center, forming an auditorium-like arrangement where almost every face can be seen. It is harder to see the men at a glance, but they are visible in other ways. For instance, during a brief ceremony in which henna is applied to the groom's hand, most men come forward and present a monetary gift to the groom. In addition, most women—and some men—choose to dance, making themselves easily visible to the entire crowd. Indeed, dance is virtually required of members of those subpatrilineages closest to the groom's family; failure to dance can be perceived as a snub. "I dance for you, you dance for me," as one friend put it.[30]

The village section also displays its presence when the bride is brought back to the groom's house. It used to be, Said told me, that only the groom's immediate family would go to get the bride, but in the early 1990s it became increasing popular in Amkan to send as many people as possible. For Said's 1993 wedding, his mother counted fifty-one cars plus a full-sized rented school bus, all of which drove, horns honking, the seven miles to the bride's house. This procession, reportedly the largest ever seen in Amkan, was eclipsed only several weeks later by a still larger one. Such a display would hardly be possible outside of the summer months, with most emigrants in France. Said's sister Samira took pride in these processions, seeing them as a way for her village to display itself to surrounding communities.

The temporal and spatial organization of the wedding are not neutral frames, then, but are helping to actively constitute the village community. The wedding is emerging as a site where Tamkant members come together as a village in a new way, where those absent for much of the year can display their presence, and where residents from both sides of the Mediterranean jointly participate in a shared event that helps to generate a sense of village affinity and belonging.

If the wedding is described by both emigrants and year-round residents as a favored site where "traditions" are still visible—and, for at least some emigrants, as a return to their roots (*ressourcement*)—in the same breath, the urar, like the tajmaᶜat, is described as a site from which "traditions" are disappearing rapidly. References to "*zik*" ("then") abound in discussions of the tameɣra and the urar. That weddings constitute especially charged sites where tradition is being situated should come as no surprise: They are already spatially and temporally set off from daily life and marked by indexicalities that link them to a long series of related events extending far into the past. This makes weddings a privileged locus of memory, for they generate expectations of regularity and repetition against which transformations in village life are perceived and commented on. At the same time, weddings are among the sites where tradition is most explicitly challenged. The very cultural enthusiasts who seek to preserve their heritage are beginning to pry open the urar, using the wedding space to develop new kinds of performances that critique what they perceive as the old-fashioned customs or "mentalities" (mindsets) governing the social organization of the village and the family. In wedding performances, a notion of tradition thus operates in complex and sometimes disemic (Herzfeld 1987)[31] ways. On the one hand, it demarcates an emerging realm of privileged cultural capital that is thought to be disappearing; on the other, it serves as an almost pejorative evaluation of behaviors and "mentalities" increasingly perceived—at least by some—as "behind the times."

How can one best understand the tidy representations of the village in relation to the hard-to-track and sometimes unruly movements through it? An idealized image of the village as a site of tradition has taken hold precisely in those places of greatest instability and anxiety, where the dialectic between presence and absence must continuously be monitored and managed. The Berber House has been memorialized in coffee-table books even as it is torn down in Kabylia to make way for modern houses whose residents are absent for much of the year. The tajmaᶜat, romanticized as a site of indigenous democracy, in practice can involve a handful of men who spend hours vigorously debating who is in which part of the village at a given moment. The wedding, cast by Kabyles as the place where their traditions are most visible, is at the same time continually changing its form so as to provide at least one space where year-round residents and emigrants can recognize each other—both figuratively and literally. It is perhaps this village—the village in motion—that scared Ben Mohamed away from his natal home for forty years.

Ben is not the only one troubled by the village in motion. It also unsettles the familiar rural-urban dichotomy on which much of social theory has rested. This perspective locates change and movement far from rural villages, which are left only to react to what has transpired elsewhere (see Ferguson 1997; Williams 1973). Singling out the village, and particular institutions within it, as sites of tradition obscures the very ways in which the village itself works as an organization of continuous movement. Yet, as with the Berber Spring, trans-Mediterranean circulation does not lend itself easily to the discursive representation of identity, particularly on a playing field saturated by nationalist ideology. Casting the village in terms of tradition, with its attendant sentiments of nostalgia and loss, has far greater political and affective currency.

As long as texts are taken to be signs of identity, it should come as no surprise that colonial agents, anthropologists, and indigenous activists alike have sought to turn the village into a kind of text from which traditions can be read. Detached from social process, the house, the assembly, and the wedding can circulate as figures of culture that bear witness to a collective Berber heritage. Over the past century, Kabyle poetry, proverbs, and legends associated with village-based oral traditions have also been turned into source texts that contribute to the making of contemporary Berber identity.

Part Two.   *Texts*

4 Collecting Poems

"What arms were found on you?"
"Books."

—Kabyle prisoner of conscience during a trial, *Tafsut* 4 (March 1982)

Collecting poems and proverbs, songs and stories, hardly seems like a political act. Yet for more than a century, indigenous texts have served as lenses through which Berber identity and difference have been construed. They have been put to the service of almost every military, political, or ethnographic initiative toward or by Berbers since the conquest of Kabylia in 1857, from civilizing missions to ethnographic enterprises to the development of nationalist and subnationalist aspirations. Ben Mohamed and Idir were able to imagine that a village story about a monster in the forest might be a place in which Kabyles could see their own reflection, in part because oral texts (as anthropologists call them today) had already served to showcase Berber culture for well over a century.

The movement of so-called oral texts into new ideological spheres was made possible because of a deeply rooted belief in their purity and authenticity. In order for oral texts to be taken as signs of a collective Berber identity, they had to be understood as immutable objects whose essence traveled with them as they moved from performance to print. Collections of Berber poems and songs produced from the 1860s to the 1980s all share the premise that oral texts carry what has been variously termed the Berber soul, spirit, or (in contemporary parlance) identity. This spirit could not be altered, collectors thought, by the supposedly neutral practices of collection, writing, or translation. Indeed, oral texts were thought to move directly from producer's breath to collector's pen, untainted by either the producer's conscious awareness or the collector's touch (Herzfeld 1996). Since oral texts were assumed to originate in their producers, the ways in which collectors participated in their construction could be easily camouflaged. The focus, in other words, was directed to the text itself as a preexisting cultural object, and not to the complex strategies through which it was recontextualized or recreated. Oral texts have thus been powerful and persuasive naturalizing devices. Through sophisticated rhetorical strategies that make the texts seem authentic, the broader interests that first motivated their collection are masked.

A collector's claim that poems provide transparent reflections of an underlying native spirit is the very place where an investigation into the construction of difference should begin. Such a claim erases from the text the performance of the poet and the situation of collection. It also obscures the ways indigenous

These tables of books about Berbers, most dating from the period of French colonialism, were a popular display at the April 20 Cultural Exhibit in Tizi Ouzou in 1993. Today, Kabyles search these books for signs of their history.

texts have been implicated in the development of wider social and political agendas. These include the French pacification and civilizing missions of the mid-nineteenth century, European liberalism, nationalism, and postcolonial identity. Analyzing the entextualizing practices—that is, the framing essays, genre labels, titles, annotation practices, and translation strategies through which oral poetry has been rendered in print—can bring these agendas into focus. My interest lies not with the poetic text qua text but rather with the ways Berber poetry collections serve as repositories of social history and as locations where branching interconnections can be precisely tracked.

Understood in this way, the history of Berber poetry collection tells a story of the Kabyle-French relationship. Despite significant differences among them, the poetry collections—including those produced by Kabyles—are remarkable for their orientation toward the metropole. Indeed, the French presence was woven into the collections themselves—not just in the explicit ideological discourse found in framing essays or introductions but also through the entextualizing practices outlined above. In foregrounding the Kabyle-French relationship, the volumes tacitly worked to divorce Berber and Arab poetic traditions from each other. This helped to set the stage for subsequent triangulations in which Berbers and Arabs could be linked only in hierarchical relationship to a third term, "French." Yet the fate of texts written to serve colonial agendas is not stable (Goodman 2002b). That the poetry collections were produced with particular objectives in mind is no guarantee that they will not be read against the grain. While my focus lies with the initial collectors, I also acknowledge the possibility of later appropriations—starting from the fact that all of the collections I discuss have now been reissued, in most cases by Berber presses for Kabyle audiences eager to reclaim their own heritage. A history of poetry collection also opens new perspectives on the uses of oral texts in Idir's music, illuminating the ways in which Idir and Ben Mohamed both drew on and broke with earlier entextualization processes.

Civilizing Mission: Colonel Adolphe Hanoteau

French Colonel Adolphe Hanoteau (1814–1897) had a mission. As part of the pacification program France was carrying out in its newly conquered territory of Kabylia, Hanoteau sought to find out what the natives in this recalcitrant Algerian Berber region were thinking. The result was a nearly 500-page collection of more than fifty poems and songs through which, the colonel maintained, the Berber spirit could be unveiled.[1] *Poésies populaires de la Kabylie du Jurjura* (Popular Poems of Kabylia of the Djurdjura [Mountains]) was published in 1867, just ten years after the conquest of Kabylia. The seal on the book's cover announced its mission: Two cherubs surround an oval capped by a crown, with an eagle at its center and the letter "N" (for Napoleon) on the bottom. Framing the eagle, and curving up the sides of the seal, are four words: Administration, Law, Science, and Art. The spirit guiding the colonial missions of Hanoteau's day—the heyday of France's *mission civilisatrice*—could not be more clearly depicted. Administrative, legal, scientific, and cultural knowledge had become as important to the colonizing enterprise as military force.

Over the course of Hanoteau's long military career,[2] he became an expert in all four areas inscribed on the seal. He was a commanding officer in the Bureaux Arabes (Offices for Indigenous Affairs); wrote prizewinning grammars of the Kabyle and Tuareg languages (Hanoteau 1858, 1860); and coauthored a three-volume study of Kabyle laws and customs (Hanoteau and Letourneux 1872–73), which became one of the most frequently cited works on the region (Lorcin 1995: 114). Born in 1814, Hanoteau was part of a new generation of officers trained under a military philosophy that wedded social reform, science, and conquest. He was a graduate of the prestigious Ecole Polytechnique, one of France's "grandes écoles" and its leading engineering school. By the time Hanoteau entered the school in 1832,[3] it had become a hotbed of Saint Simonian philosophy. Hanoteau would go on to attend the Ecole d'Application de Metz, also strongly influenced by Saint Simonian ideas, which sought to hasten the demise of feudal systems, establishing in their place a new society in which what counted was ability rather than birthright. Such a society, to be based on the rational logics of science and industry, would be guided by "superior men" charged with not only spearheading reforms in Europe but also bringing European values to the far corners of the globe (Lorcin 1995: 134). Saint Simonian paternalism fit well with colonial objectives, for despite its emphasis on individual achievement, this philosophy of reform was at heart deeply hierarchical. Societies were evaluated not on their own terms but in relation to how well they measured up to the new criteria, with Europe as the implied standard.

Hanoteau was one of a number of officers trained at the Ecole Polytechnique who would carry out proto-ethnographic studies of the Kabyle region.[4] The lens through which these Saint Simonian army men viewed Kabylia was comparative: Where were the similarities and differences between Kabyle and French societies, and how hard would it be to close the gaps? Most military ethnography was published with the express encouragement of the army and circulated through military networks (Lorcin 1995: 103). Hanoteau's poetry volume was another matter. While the colonel's personnel dossier contains numerous references to his study of law, silence surrounds his work on poetry (Gouvernement Général de l'Algérie n.d.). According to a letter exchange between Hanoteau and the Ministry of War in 1865 (and housed not in his personnel dossier but in the ministerial archives), the colonel requested permission to publish the poems and was initially refused. The Ministry feared that circulation of the poetry could fuel unrest in the region. In May 1865, the Ministry apparently granted permission, but it took Hanoteau another five months and several more letters until, on October 21, 1865, the Ministry issued an official memo to the effect that the poems could be published. The Ministry's permission came with strict conditions: Hanoteau could publish the work only if no mention was made of the fact that the Ministry had authorized publication, either in the title, the text, or any subsequent announcements or articles (Fonds Ministériels n.d.). If Hanoteau was going to publish Kabyle poems, it had to appear to be at his own initiative.[5]

Why was Hanoteau collecting poetry to begin with? Whom was he collecting it for? Why was its publication so important to him that he pursued the matter with the Ministry of War? In his introduction to the volume, Hanoteau claimed to be gathering native poems "to furnish original texts to those wanting to study the Berber language, and to make known the populations who speak this language, not by the appreciations—always subject to error—of a foreigner, but through the *works of the spirit*" (1867: i; emphasis added). Hanoteau was convinced that poetry offered direct, unmediated access to the soul of a people. Such poetry could be especially useful to the French because, in the colonel's view, the population was unaware of what their poems revealed. In their poetry, Hanoteau contended, the Kabyles believed themselves "sheltered from our curiosity . . . depict[ing] themselves naively and unselfconsciously" (1867: i). He went on to outline two ways in which these unconscious revelations could be useful. First, they could allow the French to glean insight into native perceptions of the colonial presence and serve as a benchmark against which progress in the pacifying mission could be measured—especially valuable since the natives had "no sense of history" (1867: vi). Second, Hanoteau looked to the poems to assess the level of the population's primitiveness, which would in turn justify the colonizer's presence. From the colonel's Saint Simonian vantage point, literature provided "the most accurate expression of [a people's] intellectual and moral development" (Hanoteau 1867: i).

These twin goals of the civilizing mission were made to seem natural through the classificatory device of genre, as each goal was allocated its own genre of poems. Part 1 contains "historical or political poems" in which "the expeditions of our colonizers, the acts of our administration are presented from the Kabyle point of view . . . a kind of counterpart to our bulletins" (Hanoteau 1867: xi). Part 3 is said to contain "women's poems and poems about women"; in fact, it includes any poem related to marriage, magic, or sexuality, whether authored by men or women. Despite its mixed authorship, part 3's topics were indexed to women and used to assess the degree to which the Kabyles would require civilizing. Between these well-defined sections lie the poems that would not fit neatly into Hanoteau's classificatory rubric, grouped in part 2 as "poems of different genres."

Despite Hanoteau's claim that poetry was unmediated, the way he entextualized the poems—that is, the way he ordered, annotated, and presented them on the page—makes salient the mediating categories through which he viewed Kabyle society. Part 1 is a linear account of conquest: a fourteen-poem sequence begins with the fall of Algiers in 1830 and ends with the 1857 surrender of Kabylia.[6] Hanoteau titled each poem in part 1 so as to locate it as a stage of the military struggle: "Capture of Algiers," "Expedition of Maréchal Bugeaud," "Insurrection of 1856," "Campaign of 1857." Via such titles, which resemble European newspaper headlines, Hanoteau wrote the colonizer into the Kabyle poem itself. The newspaper effect was enhanced by graphical layout. The poem's title is the largest type on the page; a subtitle beneath it gives further specifics (dates and places); under the subtitle is the poet's name, in very small type (see Goodman 2002b for an example). Hanoteau provided no further information about the poets; they were incidental to his story and largely irrelevant in the context of his ideology, which held that poetry was not the positioned product of a historically situated individual but the manifestation of a "spirit" flowing through its bardic animator (cf. Herzfeld 1996). After the poet's name, Hanoteau configured the poetic text in three ways. He first transcribed the Kabyle poem in Arabic characters, and then in Roman characters; finally, he provided a French translation.[7] He annotated the French version of the poem with an extensive subtext of footnotes, some of which continued the tale of French conquest by qualifying lines of verse that lauded indigenous resistance and disparaged the French. For example, one poem ends with the line, "Our men brought destruction to him [the enemy, i.e., the French], he, too, is taking flight"; Hanoteau added a note saying, "It is unnecessary to say that the French troops did not run away; it was simply a poetic fiction intended to gratify the listeners" (Hanoteau 1867: 121 n. 1). Such footnotes provide an explicit frame that no doubt worked to orient the poetic text to a French public receptive to a story of surrender: Kabyles were portrayed as unequal and sometimes foolish adversaries in relation to the superior French military.

The hierarchical lens put in place with the "political or historical" poems was amplified in the "women's" section (part 3). It was there, for Hanoteau, that the gaps between Kabyle and French society were the most salient. Opening part 3 is a long essay decrying the status of Kabyle women, which Hanoteau considered "among the most miserable, a testimony to the degree to which this society is lacking in civilization" (Hanoteau 1867: 287). The poems Hanoteau glossed as relating to women, however, turn out to be any texts touching on marriage, desire, or sexuality—even if they were authored by men.[8] By confining women to these domains, Hanoteau ignored his own evidence. One of the poems in the "political or historical" section, "Lament for Dahman-ou-Meçal,"[9] was sung by women following the firing-squad execution of a Kabyle man named Dahman after he had shot and wounded a French lieutenant. The poem accused the French of executing Dahman in front of his mother. In small type below, Hanoteau rewrote the story, claiming that Dahman's execution was carried out appropriately. The colonel's sense of outrage in the face of what he perceived as native fanaticism and overdramatization ("Dahman . . . was simply a fanatic indignant to see Christians dirty his village with their presence," 155) leaked into the otherwise descriptive tone of the account. Hanoteau was so caught up in setting the record straight that he did not appear to realize that through this genre (which he correctly termed *adekker*), women had a forum to comment on political affairs.

As Hanoteau's comments on Dahman's execution indicate, religious practice was another area that came under French scrutiny. Because Kabyle society was governed by secular ("customary") rather than Islamic law, some French assumed that Kabyles were less attached to Islam and thus more readily assimilable into France. A few went so far as to claim that Kabyles had formerly been Christian and would return to Christianity under the proper tutelage (Ageron 1960: 317). As would become apparent in his 1872 work, Hanoteau did not share these assumptions: Kabyles could be every bit as fanatical as Arabs (Hanoteau and Letourneux 1872–73, 1:310–314). The colonel's views entered the poetry collection through footnotes and translation practices. For instance, in a poem entitled "Insurrection of 1856," Hanoteau replaced a term that he considered untranslatable (*imedjd'ab*, which refers, according to Hanoteau's footnote, to a person engaging in a form of ecstatic experience apparently inaccessible to the French) with *Aissaoua*, the proper name of the famous Sufi brotherhood with which many French were already familiar: "Since the Aissaoua and its practices are known to everyone who has visited Algeria, I used it to replace the word 'imedjd'ab,' *which cannot be translated into French*" (Hanoteau 1867: 115–116 n. 2, emphasis added). Here, *Aissaoua* was detached from its primary referent and was made to index a cultural difference that bordered on the incommensurable.[10]

The body constituted another site where the Kabyles' distance from the French could be measured, for a people's "moral hygiene" (Lorcin 1995: 125) was taken as a further indicator of its civilizational status. Here, too, Hanoteau's translation practices marked out the areas that he found especially problematic. Some terms were not translated into French but were glossed in Latin—not because there was no French equivalent but because Hanoteau himself would have blushed to repeat them before a "civilized" audience (1867: 430–433; cf. Clancy-Smith 1996: 215). The attentive reader of Hanoteau could also discover that the Kabyles never washed their clothes and didn't take them off until they disintegrated (1867: 26 n. 3; 398–399 n. 2); that when the French captured native women, they "gave them new clothes, of which they were in dire need" (1867: 29 n. 4); that the Berbers practiced exorcism of demons, believing that they were the cause of illness (1867: 415–416 n. 2); or that the Kabyles thought women without men were vulnerable to fleas (1867: 428 n. 1). The work's subtle embedding of intimate details about bodies and beliefs showed readers not (only) who the Kabyles were but also who the French were not. Such commentary suggests that the civilizing mission Hanoteau purported to be describing may have done as much to construct the "civilizer" as the other way around (see Stoler and Cooper 1997).

In sum, Hanoteau's claim that poetry revealed an unmediated native spirit masks the important ways in which the poetry collection worked to construct the Kabyles in relation to Saint Simonian ideals of rationality and progress. The way Hanoteau entextualized the poems also targeted an emerging French bourgeoisie receptive to the suggestion that its nation's conquests rested on humanizing principles, not brute force. By imagining their nation as a provider of clothing to women "in dire need," Hanoteau's readers could comfortably justify their capture in the first place. Yet the fact remains that Hanoteau's poetry collection was among the first works of its day to be composed primarily of indigenous texts. That such texts held the potential for alternative, potentially subversive readings was not lost on the Ministry of War. Nor is it lost on contemporary Berber activists. Mouloud Mammeri was among those who would draw on the Hanoteau collection, reading it against the grain to reconnect Kabyles with their history.

Liberalism: Si Ammar Ben Saïd Boulifa

Not all Kabyles looked favorably on Hanoteau's collection. Thirty-five years after its publication, Kabyle schoolteacher and Berber language instructor Si Ammar Ben Saïd Boulifa (1865–1931) responded to Hanoteau's work with a poetry collection of his own. Boulifa's 1904 *Recueil de poésies kabyles* (Collection of Kabyle Poetry), the first poetry volume published by a Kabyle, sought to return the interpretation of poetry to indigenous hands. Boulifa concurred with the colonel that poetry was indeed a reflection of a people's degree of civilization and a sign of its spirit: "In songs . . . [the Kabyle] betrays himself; there . . . he paints himself just as he is. . . . It's through the cry of the heart . . . that the poet communicates the character and spirit of the people as a whole" (Boulifa 1990 [1904]: 58). He felt, however, that Hanoteau had not chosen his poets well: Most poems were by secondary poets whose works were of questionable literary value (Boulifa 1990: 45). If poems reflected a people's civilizational status, Hanoteau should have ensured that the poetry he chose represented the best of what the Kabyles could do. Boulifa sought to counter this by publishing the works of Si Mohand, one of the region's most renowned and provocative bards best known for his love poetry (see Feraoun 1960; Mammeri 1969). Boulifa was also deeply disturbed by Hanoteau's views on the status of Kabyle women. Simply put, Boulifa thought that the colonel got it wrong, and he intended to set the record straight.

Boulifa was already in a mediating position. Born to a marabout family of modest means and orphaned early in life, he was sent by a maternal uncle to the first French school in Greater Kabylia.[11] Boulifa subsequently taught in various capacities, initially in primary school and subsequently at secondary school (Ecole Normale) and at the University of Algiers (Chaker 2001a).[12] By Boulifa's day, the concerns of the colonial enterprise were shifting from pacification to a liberalist focus on who was to be included in a republican democracy (see Mehta 1997; Bauman and Briggs 2003). In other words, if, as liberalist ideology contended, all men [sic] were created equal, which among them had acquired the moral and educational qualifications to be full participants in the republican project? Although Berberophile officers had long considered Kabyles the likeliest candidates for assimilation into France, this opinion was largely academic while the colony was under military rule. With the 1871 establishment of a civilian government in Algeria, the Kabyle Myth took on legal valence, culminating in a short-lived (and ultimately, failed) attempt to establish institutional structures that would move the Kabyles closer to the French while simultaneously accentuating Kabyle-Arab differences (Ageron 1960: 350; see also Ageron 1976). For a brief period (1880–1885) this triangulating, "divide-and-rule" philosophy became state policy, and the school was a primary site where it was implemented. The initial plan, as announced in 1880 by French Minister of Public Instruction Jules Ferry, was to build fifteen schools in the Kabyle region of Fort Napoléon (this was eventually reduced to four) (Ageron 1960: 342). One of the masterminds behind Ferry's plan was Camille Sabatier, administrator and judge in the Kabyle region, who would go so far as to attribute the Kabyle *qanun* (customary law) to European influence: "The unknown Lycurgus who dictated the Kabyle *kanouns* was neither of the family of Mohammed nor of Moses, but of that of Montesquieu and Condorcet. More than the skull shape of the mountain Kabyles, this work bore the seal of our [the French] race" (cited in Lorcin 1995: 159–160 [Lorcin's translation]; see also Ageron 1960: 323). Another mastermind was Emile Masqueray, director of the Ecole de Lettres in Algiers, who also looked to law to justify increasing educational opportunities for Kabyles: "A Kabyle law is for us an infinitely precious instrument; the more we use it, the more a trench (*fossé*) is dug (*se creuse*) between Arab Muslims and those whom they conquered [i.e., Berbers]" (cited in Ageron 1960: 323). For Masqueray, all that was needed to make the region French was to teach Kabyles the language (Ageron 1960: 342), and he strongly endorsed the Ferry plan. Given Boulifa's own position as one of the first indigenous teachers in Kabylia, it is likely that he knew Sabatier and Masqueray personally; as his poetry collection makes apparent, he certainly viewed their work favorably.

Boulifa came of age during the heyday of the Kabyle Myth, and in some ways he perpetuated its terms. In the essay that introduces his poetry collection, Boulifa sought to demonstrate Kabylia's inherent democratic spirit by linking Berber institutions and practices to the classical civilizations of antiquity. He described Kabyles as "borrowing . . . from Roman law its spirit" (Boulifa 1990 [1904]: 47); as being "at the sides of the Greeks, Romans, Persians, and Arabs" (Boulifa 1990 [1904]: 47, citing medieval chronicler Ibn Khaldun); and as displaying a "purely secular" character (Boulifa 1990 [1904]: 51). Citing works on Kabylia by authors from Strabo and Sallust to Sabatier and Masqueray, he contended that since ancient times, his society had operated on democratic and egalitarian principles. Yet if the Kabyle Myth took Kabyles to be more readily assimilable into France, it had long been haunted by the position of women, for it was there that the exclusionary argument could be made most forcefully (see Clancy-Smith 1996; Daumas 1912). Boulifa took the extraordinary step of extending the democratic mantle to Kabyle women, to wit: "The basis of Berber society rests, today as in the past, on equality and individual freedom, *without distinction of rank or sex. . . .* Animated by the most democratic spirit, the Kabyles do not forget that individual liberty is the most sacred thing" (Boulifa 1990 [1904]: 52, 56, emphasis added).

If in his introductory essay Boulifa presented Berber society in unabashedly liberalist terms, the way he entextualized the poems suggests an underside that stood in uneasy tension with the lofty republican principles to which he professed allegiance. Boulifa's primary corpus contains 108 poems of Si Mohand, followed by a second corpus of 161 poems of a similar genre whose authorship Boulifa could not "authenticate,"[13] and a brief third section consisting of one poem that critiqued the French administration. The poems are annotated by nearly four hundred footnotes, addressed to an educated French readership and containing detailed social and religious histories, reflections on the colonial presence, and evaluations of Kabyle practices. The footnotes depict not a "purely secular" (Boulifa 1990: 51, citing Sabatier) society but one structured through saint veneration and religious orders and punctuated by prayer and religious holy days. They describe not a society "without distinction of rank or sex" (Boulifa 1990: 52) but a stratified and heterogeneous mix of black slaves, Ibadites, and Jews, as well as a hierarchy of maraboutic lineages, some more noble than others. They emphasize not transcendent principles but the minutiae of everyday life: how to make clove necklaces, apply kohl to the eyes, smoke kif, or concoct a hashish mixture. The footnotes also supply detailed etymologies revealing that the Berber spirit to be read in poetry, far from pure or unmediated, was shaped by the region's Roman, Arab, Spanish, and French histories.

When it comes to women, Boulifa's notes are contradictory. At one point Boulifa commented on a love poem, arguing that the poet depicted men and women as equal partners in love (1990: 196 n. 240) and using this alleged equality to counter Hanoteau's claim that in Kabylia, woman was seen as only "an object of luxury, a being made solely to satisfy men's desire" (Boulifa 1990 [1904]: 196 n. 240, citing Hanoteau). Boulifa also attempted to reinterpret what might be considered problematic treatment of women by casting Berber society in evo-lutionary terms in relation to Europe's own past. Kabyle women were no worse off than, say, women in eighteenth-century France or imperial Russia (Boulifa 1990: 49). But most footnotes on women describe them as beautiful but distant, provokers of unrequited love and desire. For example: "It was for [Saadia] that the poet sought to commit the worst sins—drinking alcohol, smoking tobacco—in order to calm his tormented heart that could do nothing but beg for Saadia" (Boulifa 1990 [1904]: 195 n. 236). When women refuse the poet's love they are described as loose, even prostitutes (1990: 188 n. 169).

In sum, both Boulifa and Hanoteau located oral poetry outside the social or-der in an unmediated, unreflective, transparent realm where the people's "spirit" could emerge unfettered. Attention to the way they entextualized the poems, however, shows how their collections worked to construct specific ideological agendas. If Hanoteau looked to poetry to help him justify a need for pacificat-ion, Boulifa used it to depict Kabyle society through a liberalist lens that would set it on equal footing with Europe. His professed adherence to the liberalist principles of freedom, equality, and rationality rested, however, on a palpable tension surrounding what—through liberalist eyes—would constitute basic in-equalities and exclusions at the heart of his own society. These exclusions leak out, disorganized and almost unreadable, in footnotes, where the split between the lofty and the local is underscored, where descriptions of the dense web of social habits and practices, of the complex interactions between religion, race, and gender, challenge the liberalist ideals that Boulifa's framing essay so care-fully erects.

Literature, Folklore, and Nationalism: Jean and Taos Amrouche

For brother and sister Jean Amrouche (1906–1962) and Taos Amrouche (1913–1976), collecting poetry became a way to position Berber culture on a par with European culture, not in terms of the liberalist criteria of freedom and equality but through the categories of literature and folklore. At the same time, collecting poems began to define a new kind of otherness located within the self. Jean and Taos Amrouche situated poetry in relation to a sense of frag-mented duality within their own psyches, a state of internal otherness at the core of their being: "I am a cultural hybrid; cultural hybrids are monsters," Jean would say (Faigre 1985: 134). For them, Berber poems—especially the songs of their mother—were a means of transcending exile to reach a state of cul-tural and spiritual wholeness (which they could imagine only through its ab-sence; see Ivy 1995). This move was not idiosyncratic but part of a broader anti-colonial nationalist current emerging during the 1930s and 1940s, in which "folk" productions—particularly those of women—were increasingly associated with an "inner" or "spiritual" domain of "culture" considered impervious to colonial penetration (Chatterjee 1993).

Algerian Berber Christians by birth, Jean and Taos were raised primarily in Tunisia, where they received a classical French education. They accentuate some of the contradictions that came to characterize French-educated native elites throughout Africa. Jean was a teacher of French literature, a French-language poet, and a literary critic; Taos was a singer and one of the first Algerian female French-language novelists. Both served as radio hosts in Tunisia, Algeria, and Paris, where Jean produced a series of dialogues with prominent European literary figures (see Héron 2000) and Taos developed several shows, including one in Kabyle entitled "Let Us Remember Our Country."[14] Situated within an avant-garde intellectual milieu peopled primarily by Europeans, Jean developed a lifelong friendship with André Gide, had regular correspondence with Paul Claudel and François Mauriac, and occasional interchanges with Charles de Gaulle (see Amrouche 1994); Taos was well-acquainted with classical musicians Yehudi Menuhin and Olivier Messiaen, among others. Both collected, published, and recorded the songs of their mother as a means of simultaneously orienting themselves to and demarcating themselves from the European culture with which they were surrounded.

Jean

In an introduction to *Chants berbères de Kabylie* (Berber Songs from Kabylia), his 1939 collection of the poems sung by his mother, Jean Amrouche mapped the doctrine of man's fall from grace onto his own experience of exile, imagining a lost paradise where body and soul were at one with nature and the cosmos. He endowed the songs of his mother and his forebears with the power to reconnect him with the ancestral land and restore him to a state in which duality was absent, to an "ineffable origin, a Wholeness from which we are cruelly separated" (J. Amrouche 1988 [1939]: 36). At one pole, Jean conflated the notions of mother, nature, childhood, and innocence to produce an epiphany that he associated with Christian divinity. At the other, he linked European culture and civilization to exile, fragmentation, and duality.

If through poems Jean sought a return to a state of unmediated wholeness, he effected this return through highly mediated techniques that revealed the ambiguities of his own positioning in relation to both Kabyle and French societies. For even as he associated Kabyle poems with an unmediated natural realm, he simultaneously attempted to place them in a classificatory hierarchy of genres in which literature was associated with "high culture" and characterized by original expressions of universal, humanist themes, while folklore was seen as "low culture," particularistic and unoriginal. Seeking to demonstrate that Kabyle poems were comparable to Europe's "high culture," he invoked similarities with the works of Charles Baudelaire, Victor Hugo, Paul Claudel, Arthur Rimbaud, Paul Verlaine, and Giuseppe Ungaretti.

Translation strategies and genre attributions also served to configure the poems as literature rather than folklore. For the first time, the Berber text was erased. To constitute literature, the poems were made to stand on their own in French. On a visual level, the absence of Berber makes the book indistinguishable from any other volume of original French poetry. This is reinforced by the generic framing of the collection. Jean grouped the poems into sections titled with such familiar European headings as Love, Satire, or Exile (the latter section dedicated to André Gide). Further, as in European books of poetry (and unlike earlier Berber collections), no footnotes interject sociological or linguistic commentary, which tends to orient the poems as items of folk culture through which an indigenous population can be "understood." Erasure of the Berber text also starkly reveals Jean's own apparent adherence to a key premise that was an integral part of a more widespread European linguistic ideology: that the essence of a poem resided in a realm of pure signifieds, outside its concrete realizations not only in individual performance but also in the signifiers associated with a specific language. To reach this realm, Jean first detached a poem or song from the discourse of the individuals who recited it (here, his mother) and claimed that it constituted a shared item of Berber culture (see Urban 1996); he then extracted it from a particular language and situated it in a transcultural realm of universality, where it was thought to belong to "humanity." (Of course, the belief that some languages [i.e., French] were universal while others were not was also part of the broader language ideology informing Jean's approach.) At times, one wonders whether Jean felt that the universalist themes he saw in the poems were better captured by French than Berber: "To express an idea or a sentiment, or more precisely, that constellation of sentiment and thought that animates [the poems], [the poets] do not call upon an abundance of forms, but on a brief suite of images and symbols. There is no formal link between these images, no term of comparison. No doubt the [Berber] language itself did not put at their disposition a very developed grammatical apparatus" (J. Amrouche 1988 [1939]: 31–32).

Attending to Jean's French translations of the poems reveals, however, not a universal spirit but particular, culturally specific modalities of interpretation that can be understood in relation to Greg Urban's discussion of transduction: the transformations that occur when carrying over one instance of discourse to a new context with intent to replicate the original discourse (Urban 1996). Working between Jean's French texts and the Berber texts that were restored in a later edition (J. Amrouche 1988 [1939]) reveals that—in an attempt to replicate the spirit of his mother's poems—he erased Berber metapragmatic conventions (the set of culturally based understandings about how to interpret language) and substituted French ones. For example, one poem in the "Love" section (122–123) describes a lizard on a wall following a lovely young girl, burning desire filling its silent eyes. The French poem opens with an added line that injects a first-person narrator whose presence must be inferred in the Berber text: "If only I could become a lizard" ("*J'aimerais lézard devenir . . .* "). The entire French poem is then voiced in the first person, culminating with lines that would violate communicative norms associated with cultural standards of modesty if so voiced in Kabyle: "I will kiss your tiny mouth, I will awaken you if you sleep." In contrast, the Berber text voices the poem in the third person, desire distanced from the speaker through its displacement onto the lizard: "He will kiss her tiny mouth, he will awaken her if she sleeps." Whereas a Berber speaker would understand that the poet's desire was voiced in the third person, Jean apparently feared that a love poem in the third person would be unconvincing to a French reader, so he translated Berber metapragmatic understandings into French through voicing and semantics. Such a move has crucial implications for any claim that the poems represent an unmediated realm of Berber culture, for the Other—here, the French reader—is embedded in the texts themselves. These poems are not the same as the ones Jean's mother sang to him but have been saturated by and ultimately rewritten through the conventions and expectations of another cultural universe.

Even as he oriented the poems to the conventions of French literature, Jean continued to claim that they were direct expressions of the divine that entered the world through the words of those seen as most in harmony with the cosmos—"peasants," especially peasant women. The poets, for Jean, were mere conduits, unaware of what flowed through their poems: "It is certain that Kabyle peasants . . . never dreamed for a minute . . . that they were singing the great pain of man expelled from Paradise" (J. Amrouche 1988 [1939]: 36). Song and poetry were not learned, acquired, or the product of conscious reflection, but rather "unstudied," "instinctive," and "effortless," emanating from a "Spirit of childhood" (l'Esprit d'enfance) through which divinity manifests in the world (J. Amrouche 1988 [1939]: 44–45). In order for this spirit to shine forth, the interpreter (his mother) was effaced: "Her [his mother's] voice is present only to the degree that it is necessary for the birthing of the melody on the sea of silence. . . . The listener is put into direct contact with the beauty of the music and the naked richness of the words. The message is transmitted to him without the voice that's singing or the interpreter denaturing it by refracting it" (J. Amrouche 1988 [1939]: 55). Likewise, his mother's style of singing was "not the result of study, [was] not created from without but [was] formed instinctively and from the interior" (J. Amrouche 1988 [1939]: 59); her voice contained an "angelic naiveté" (J. Amrouche 1988 [1939]: 58). And the melodies were "untranscribable," conforming "not to any canons but to the requirements of the heart, the ear, and the spirit" (J. Amrouche 1988 [1939]: 52; see also 38, 51). Echoes of Hanoteau? Kabyle poetry—even for an educated poet—was still taken to be unselfconscious and unreflexive.

In sum, if Jean were convinced that his mother's poetry could help him to recover a lost sense of oneness, to transcend the uncomfortable hybridity he experienced as a Tunisia-raised Christian Berber Algerian writing in French, he could reach this state of communion only through the very European categories from which he sought escape. Further, by locating his mother in direct relationship to the cosmos, he precluded the possibility that her experience might also be hybrid. Her own complex subjectivity is utterly negated by Jean, for whom his mother's poems evoked only his own lack of wholeness. In his eyes, his mother had a single culture; he did not.[15]

Taos Amrouche also situated herself as a "hyphen between East and West."[16] On one side, she claimed to be but a "repository" for an age-old oral tradition. Her mother's songs, which Taos recorded on six albums and performed throughout Europe, simply passed through her, she claimed, as they had already flowed through countless prior generations since the dawn of time.[17] So as not to "disrupt the purity" of this age-old tradition, she refused to study solfeggio or vocal technique.[18] But while claiming that "pure tradition" flowed through her in unmediated fashion from a preexisting realm of orality, she configured the songs in complex relation to European folklore, nationalism, and the performance practices associated with "universal" classical music genres.

Taos displayed less tension than her brother Jean in categorizing her mother's songs as folklore because she associated folklore with the prestigious scientific and nationalist projects of accumulating and classifying historical, linguistic, and cultural knowledge. The conviction that there was inherent value in classifying the songs of her ancestors was shaped in part by the nationalist notion that a public domain containing items of shared cultural heritage should be filled with Berber stock. She grouped the songs her mother may have sung for a variety of occasions into an authoritative corpus of "95 prototypes," had them transcribed, and registered them in her name at the French copyright agency Société des Auteurs, Compositeurs, et Editeurs de Musique (Society of Authors, Composers, and Editors of Music, SACEM), where they acquired a new legal status.[19]

The scientific, classificatory discourse through which Taos situated her mother's songs also drew authority from the emerging disciplines of folklore, ethnomusicology, and anthropology, which erected such criteria as age, authenticity, or demonstrable kinship with other folk specimens as evidential tests to which specimens should be subjected in order to discern their cultural worth. These legitimating criteria permeate Taos's comments about the corpus. Kabyle songs, she reported, were considered by "expert musicologists" to be "among the most authentic and venerable messages in the world"; these specialists situated the poems far back in time—"thousands of years, perhaps even to ancient Egypt."[20] This association of age, authenticity, and scientific value was already present at the time of Taos's first public performance, at the 1939 First Congress of Moroccan Music, where she reported that linguists and other "people of science" were interested in "what was authentic" in her songs.[21]

Taos also oriented the songs to the requirements of scholarly and nationalist projects for a local folklore by situating them as oral. She did so in part via the techniques through which her recordings were presented. The recorded songs, whose texts appeared in print (French translation only) in either Jean's 1939 work or her own 1966 collection,[22] were often given French titles that identified each song with a broad universal theme: "Song of Exile" (*Chant d'exil*), "Love Song" (*Chant d'amour*), "Meditation Song" (*Chant de méditation*). The French translation of the songs followed. The presence of the Berber language, however, was primarily oral—although Taos sang in Berber, no Kabyle text was furnished. On her albums, Berber print appears only in a discussion of six musical genres or styles identified in the liner notes, which describe not the universal themes suggested by the French titles, but discrete melodic and rhythmic features; the notes also briefly discuss the kinds of occasions at which a song would be sung. Each song is linked to a Berber style, listed parenthetically after the title. The style indication is generally the only Berber text on the album jacket; furthermore, after her first recording, the styles are never explained but simply appear under the (French) song title, authenticating devices that mark a song as "folk."

In her performance practices, Taos displayed a more ambivalent relation to the folklore project. While she appeared at major international folk festivals, Taos traveled primarily in a classical music circuit. Her performance venues included the prestigious Théâtre de la Ville in Paris and prominent cathedrals and concert halls throughout Europe, where she cast herself as a cultural ambassador, a mediator between East and West: "I sing with the knowledge that these are *great works of art,* and I sing because I bear witness, and because I would like to awaken both the East and the West, obtain an awakening of consciousness both among North Africans and among Westerners, and particularly the French."[23] Although she claimed that her vocal style was instinctive and unaltered by learned techniques, her singing sounds far more operatic than folk to most listeners; her songs are unrecognizable to many Kabyles, while some Westerners compare them with Gregorian chant.[24] In short, while Taos may have attempted to replicate the Berber texts, she took significant liberties with the music—the very substance that was supposedly unselfconsciously flowing through her.

After Algerian independence, Taos's songs were increasingly situated as signs of a precolonial, pan-African identity, as evidenced by Senegalese President Léopold Sédar Senghor's comment, following her appearance at the 1966 First World Festival of Negro Arts in Dakar, that "what interested me the most was the unity of African civilization to which the songs bear witness."[25] In Algeria, however, her work also began to be associated with the problematic rise of Berber subnational consciousness. By 1969, she was barred from representing the Algerian nation at the First Pan-African Cultural Festival.

In sum, the Amrouches' claims that poems index a realm of cultural and spiritual wholeness were complicated by techniques that speak to the profound contradictions and dualities that characterize Jean's and Taos's experiences as expatriate intellectuals during a time when anticolonial nationalism was on the rise throughout the colonized world. Their work began to situate poetry as a cultural resource in which expatriates could find renewal; as elsewhere, culture was increasingly gendered female and associated with women's expressive forms. The Amrouches' relationship to poetry collection also suggests the emergence of a new kind of otherness located within the self and characterized by a fantasy of cultural wholeness that was imaginable only because it was already lost.

Postcolonial Identity: Mouloud Mammeri

In 1988, the poetry collection of Jean Amrouche was one of the first works to be reissued—with "restored" Kabyle texts—by French publisher L'Harmattan in collaboration with Mouloud Mammeri and Awal ("The Word"), the Berber press Mammeri had launched in Paris several years earlier. That the Kabyle texts were restored—incompletely, at that[26]—nearly a half-century after the work's initial publication speaks in part, of course, to the ideological climate of 1980s Algeria, where the state politics of unanimity was increasingly losing ground to a pluralistic, highly contentious, and soon to be violent struggle over the country's cultural, linguistic, and political futures. Yet the reedition of Amrouche's text also highlights the ways in which the self can become newly visible through the lens of the Other, for it was the poems *in translation* that called forth the Berber "originals" (cf. Venuti 1992). With Mammeri's own *Poèmes kabyles anciens* (Old Kabyle poems)—the work said to have launched the Berber Spring—this refractive process of doubling back to the self from the Other's vantage point (the very move described by Duvignaud) would take on new dimensions.

Poèmes kabyles anciens speaks a double language. On the one hand, it is aligned toward Europe and, in particular, toward ethnological science, with which Mammeri had a long and vexed relationship. In an important break with the works of his predecessors, Mammeri sought to extricate Berber poetry from an ahistorical, essentialized domain, which he recognized as a fabrication of colonial ethnology. At the same time, by attempting to convey the poetry's phenomenological dimensions, the work invites a contemporary Kabyle audience to experience the poems as living documents. Through the poems, Mammeri thought, Kabyles could immerse themselves in their history in order to reclaim a new future. Yet in seeking to recapture for Kabyles the immediacy of live performance, Mammeri perpetuated notions about a supposedly authentic realm of oral poetry, seeing his written collection as a necessary but impure reconstitution of this body of oral lore.

With a background in literary studies, Mammeri (1917–1989) was not formally trained as an anthropologist, but he was well versed in the ethnographic literature. From 1969 to 1980, Mammeri directed Algeria's major ethnological research center, the Centre de Recherches Archéologiques, Préhistoriques, et Ethnologiques (Center for Archeological, Prehistoric, and Ethnological Research, CRAPE), following the departure of the center's French director (Mammeri 1989: 17). Established in 1956 by the French, CRAPE was initially oriented to prehistory and physical anthropology (Mammeri 1989). Mammeri significantly expanded the center's ethnographic reach, and a growing number of Algerian students began to research their own cultural traditions under his direction. Mammeri himself carried out long-term projects on Kabyle and Tuareg poetry (Mammeri 1969, 1980, 1985). Committed to developing the Berber language as a modern instrument of communication, Mammeri continued work on a transcription system in the Roman alphabet, produced the first grammar of Kabyle Berber that was written entirely in Kabyle (Mammeri 1976), and supervised a team of students who produced *Amawal,* the dictionary of Tamazight neologisms (Azar 1990; see also Achab 1996). Under Mammeri's leadership, CRAPE became one of the few centers where the study of Berber language and culture was tolerated. This would not last: In 1980, Mammeri was asked to leave the center because of his role (and that of his students) in the Berber Spring (Colonna 2003).

From an early age, Mammeri viewed Berber poetry through a dual lens. On the one hand, poetry was part of his own lived experience. He grew up listening to the poems of his father, a renowned poetry specialist (*amusnaw*) in the village of Taourirt Mimoun (At Yenni). Yet Mammeri soon began to relate Kabyle poetry to foreign poetic traditions. At age eleven, he moved with his family to Morocco, where he began a classical education, continued four years later in Algiers. Inspired by his study of Greek and Latin, Mammeri began writing down the Berber poems he heard: "I felt that writing Berber verse was like Homer, who had composed the Iliad and the Odyssey" (Yacine 1990: 76). Mammeri's comparative perspective was also fueled by his father and uncle, who could recite verse in Arabic and French as well as Kabyle Berber. His father, Mammeri recalled, knew Waterloo,[27] but "didn't consider Victor Hugo and Waterloo any different from [Kabyle poet] Youssef ou Qaci" (Yacine 1990: 77).[28]

Mammeri's ambivalent position as native ethnographer structures *Poèmes kabyles anciens.* In a French-language essay that opens the volume, Mammeri wrote both against and through ethnography and its colonial precursors.[29] Scathingly condemning the way ethnology turned living poems into "dead objects" of analysis, he described the way native populations were objectified through their poetry as an act of violence:

> Ethnological peoples can serve to enlighten men, the true, civilized ones, about the times of their savage past. . . . It is we who have demarcated the off-limit Indian reserve, where provisional humanities continue to die while elsewhere unfold the highly rational games of the true civilization. . . . Freedom, the power to act on a collective destiny, was the weighty privilege of the Western man; the others were never more than the unconscious protagonists of a preexisting harmony. . . . Our poems were dead objects, mere arguments in the conceptual edifice erected by the West both to confine us and to understand itself. . . . But as subjects of this so-called objectivity we were in complete disarray. It wasn't just our skin or our sentiments that were attacked, it was our reason. . . . It is to reverse this process that I wrote this book, in the hopes of preparing the grounds for more radical projects, so that one day the culture of my ancestors will fly with its own wings. (Mammeri 1980: 14, 15, 47)

For Mammeri, the problem was not just that a few anthropologists were incompetent, but that the entire ethnographic enterprise was flawed: "How else could one explain that, on the basis of excerpts from sound, reliable, detailed documents, one could generate conclusions so foreign to the reality that they were supposed to represent?" (1980: 13). "The new science," he concluded, "in operating on the field of our intimacy, violated it, menaced it in its very being. . . . After having made use of diverse methods, drawn from the arsenal of the prestigious knowledge that dazzled us, it quickly became apparent that the only method that stood any chance of success was to reverse the perspective that western science had [taken up] against us" (Mammeri 1980: 14–15).

Much of Mammeri's sixty-page introductory essay was directed at finding ways to reverse this perspective. He drew on anthropology's own conceptual apparatus to challenge its core tenets and to propose alternative ways of locating Kabyle poetry. For example, he sought to demonstrate how the circulation of Kabyle poems confounded the temporal and spatial boundaries that anthropologists relied on at the time, such as the ethnographic present and the bounded community study. Of more interest to me here, however, are the ways the entextualization strategies he used function to configure the poems as something other than ethnographic objects.

First of all, the way that Mammeri organized the poetry volume suggests that he resisted subordinating the poems to a uniform or elegant classificatory system. Of his five sections, one is organized around the work of the renowned eighteenth-century poet Yusef U Qaci, two around discrete genres (religious legends and proverbs), and two around historical periods ("The Time of the City-States" and "The Resistance to Colonial Conquest"). Second, within each section, Mammeri used authorship as a key organizing device in order to show that the poems were not to be considered as representative of a generalized tradition but rather as positioned products of historically situated individuals. Inverting Hanoteau's layout, Mammeri placed the poet's name, in large type, above each poem at the top of the page; Mammeri also provided a brief historical introduction to most poets (see Goodman 2002b for an example). Mammeri cross-referenced poems in his own collection to the poets or poems mentioned by Hanoteau in order to emphasize the poet's identity and historical trajectory. Instead of showing, as Hanoteau had claimed, that Kabyles had "no sense of history" (Hanoteau 1867: vi), Hanoteau's poems in Mammeri's hands became archives through which Kabyles could lay claim to a history at a time when Berber language and culture were being deliberately erased from Algerian public discourse.

Perhaps the most intriguing way that Mammeri attempted to extract Kabyle poems from the clutches of ethnography was by configuring two separate audiences. This is most apparent in the framing devices that introduce the collection. As noted above, the introductory essay, written in French, is geared to a French-educated readership familiar with anthropological discourse. Directly following this essay, however, a two-page preface addresses a new kind of reader —one capable of engaging with Berber poetry through a medium of print. This preface, written in Kabyle Berber and not translated, takes the form of a personal letter from Mammeri to Muhed Azwaw, a figure meant to symbolically represent "the Kabyle."[30] The letter concludes: "There are no meetings or reunions where you and your generation can learn *tamusni* [wisdom transmitted through poetry] in the way your ancestors learned it. Now, *tamusni* is found in books. I wrote this book for you and your fellow travelers, Azwaw, so that it might serve as a pillar of support, a pillar upon which to build" (Mammeri 1980: 60).

Translation practices also align the poems toward the two audiences. Although the pages are laid out to look like mirror images of each other, closer analysis reveals important differences. First of all, not everything was translated. This is immediately visible in the annotations. In a break with previous practice, both the Kabyle and the French texts are annotated, and these notes are not identical. On the pages with Kabyle poems, the notes are in Kabyle. These notes contain variants of poetic verses, clarification of grammatical points, and explanations of words; unless a long poetic variant is provided, the notes are not usually translated on the facing French page.[31] Footnotes on the French pages rarely contain Kabyle terms; when they do, it is only in order to define them in French. In the French notes, Mammeri, like Hanoteau and Boulifa before him, situated tribes and villages, explained unfamiliar terms, and provided ethnographic details about cultural or religious practices referenced in the poems. The material in these notes never appears in translation on the Kabyle Berber pages.

Mammeri's work further segments French- and Berber-reading audiences through differently configured relationships between the poems and their titles and introductions. This is especially apparent with a poem that appears in both the Hanoteau and the Mammeri collections.[32] Hanoteau had titled the poem "Insurrection of 1856" and made it tell a story of conquest. Mammeri titled the poem in two ways. On the French page, he located it as an example of a more general condition, titling it "An Unequal Struggle" ("Une lutte inégale"). On the Berber page, he extracted a key line from the poem and used it as the title, retaining even its deictics: "If We Stay Like This We Will Not Thrive" ("Ma neqqim akk' ur nerbiḥ") (1980: 416–417). The Kabyle title aligns current readers in relation to the historical community described in the event. Mammeri further anchored the Kabyle poem to an imagined prior utterance through his introduction to the poet. Both Berber and French introductions explain that the poet, Mohand Said, was known as a judge of novice poets, who had to pass a test before him. The French introduction stops there. The Berber one goes on to provide, via direct quotation, the text of what Mammeri imagined that Mohand Said might have said, along with the response of his interlocutors.

French Introduction to the Poem

Mohand Saïd Ou Sidi Ali-ou-Abdallah des Ait Melikech, en son temps prince des poètes, détenait une sorte de maîtrise. Pour être reconnu poète, il fallait composer un poème de cent distiques qu'il jugeait avant de donner une investiture symbolique mais appréciée.

Translation: Mohand Saïd Ou Sidi Ali-ou-Abdallah of the Ait Melikech, in his day the prince of poets, had a certain mastery. To be recognized as a poet, one had to compose a poem of one hundred verses, which [Mohand Saïd] judged, and he then confirmed [the poet]—a symbolic nomination that was nonetheless appreciated. (Mammeri 1980: 417)

Kabyle Introduction to the Poem

Qqaren belli Muḥend Ssaâid Amlikc bbwexxam n Sidi ɛli u ɛbdella di taddart Iɛaggacen d ccix imedyazen l-lweqt-is. Ur iteffeɣ walbaaḍ deg-sen d amedyaz alamma isɛadda kra l-lemṭiḥan zdat-as. Yeqqar-as: "Win a-ṭ-iseffrun ar meyya, ad as sidneɣ." Degmi imedyazen l-lweqt-nni merra mi-d-yeḥḍer ad-d-awin lfaṭiḥa, qbel ad bdun tiyta, qqaren-as: "Lfaṭiḥa akken i-s-yenna Sidi Muḥend Ssaâid. . . . "

Translation: They say that Muḥend Ssaâid Amlikc of the family of Sidi ɛli-u-ɛbdella of the village of Iɛaggacen was the prince of poets in his day. No one could be recognized as a poet unless he passed a few tests in front of him. He [Muḥend Ssaâid Amlikc] said: "He who can [compose poems] to one hundred [lines], I will recognize him as a master poet." It is for that reason that all the poets of that day, when the time arrived, they recited the fatiha [first verse of the Quran, used to mark a religious or special social occasion]; before the contest began, they said: "Here is lfaṭiḥa just as Sidi Muḥend Ssaâid said. . . . " (Mammeri 1980: 416)

The exchange references the reading of the first verse of the Quran, known as *lfaṭiḥa* (from Arabic *al-fatiha*), which would have marked this contest as an important social occasion. This entire encounter is absent on the French page.

The experiential quality conveyed by Mammeri's presentation of the poems in Kabyle may point to the ethnographic occasions (Pels and Salemink 2000) during which he heard some of them. In a discussion with Pierre Bourdieu about oral poetry, Mammeri recalled that when he was a child, his father made sure he was present when "he met with people with whom he knew that a nontrivial exchange would take place" (Mammeri 1991a: 94); his father also brought his son to the markets, another privileged arena for discussion. Mammeri would also spend time in his father's arms-making shop, where people would come by just to converse in the old style, exchanging proverbs and parables (Mammeri 1991a: 95, 97). The live quality of these exchanges may be what Mammeri was seeking to reproduce on the Berber pages. A further example of how Mammeri produced an impression of live performance is found in his Kabyle introduction to another poem (Poem 20), where he reported the poem as speech: "One day Yusef was reciting poems. No sooner had he finished speaking than a widow said to him, 'And my [own] son, why didn't you speak of him [in your poem]?' Yusef replied: [here Mammeri inserted the poem]" (1980: 99). Mammeri did not reproduce this exchange on the French page. Rather, he established an intertextual link with the preceding poem in the collection (and not with an imagined performance situation) via literary terminology; indirect reported speech distances the speakers. The French introduction reads, "The drama is not only a tragedy [a reference to the previous poem], it is also a game. To a woman who complained that the poet hadn't mentioned her son in his verse": [here Mammeri inserted the poem] (1980: 99). Again, instead of using reconstructed dialogue to situate the poem within a prior speech event, Mammeri provided a brief description of the context, using the French *passé antérieur,* a literary tense that by definition is never employed in speech.[33]

If the Berber pages contain sedimented traces of the occasions when Mammeri heard the poems, the French pages are generally silent about them, with one exception. Thus readers learn that Mammeri frequently heard one poem recited by his father, Salem Ait Maammer, who always added the following line from Voltaire at the end: "Ce temps ne se retrouvera plus où un duc de La Rochefoucauld, l'auteur des *Maximes,* au sortir de la conversation d'un Pascal ou d'un Arnaud, allait au théâtre de Corneille" (The time is over when a Duke de La Rochefoucauld, author of the *Maximes,* would leave a conversation with a Pascal or an Arnaud to go to a play by Corneille) (Mammeri 1980: 83). Mammeri adopted the beginning of this line ("Ce temps ne se retrouvera plus") as the French title of the poem; the Kabyle title of the same poem is drawn from a line of the poem itself (as are a majority of the poem titles on the Berber pages). Finally, on the French pages, Mammeri occasionally engaged the French practice of using single poems to make ethnological pronouncements about Berber society. A good example is Poem 21 (Mammeri 1980: 98–99), introduced in French as follows: "The acts of an individual, in a society without organized political power, engage the whole group." This sentence is utterly absent from the Berber side, which delves right into the particulars of the situation in which Mammeri imagined that the poem was recited. Mammeri, in short, configured two separate "contexts" within which the poems could be interpreted.[34]

Mammeri was aware of this double discourse, but his own commentary suggests that he was concerned primarily with the differences that translation effected on the poems themselves, and not with their entextualizing surrounds:

> The two texts, Berber and French, which are on facing pages, are supposed to say the same thing. I tried to translate the original lines into French as faithfully as possible. However, for one who knows both languages, a quick reading is enough to notice that the two versions are actually following two distinct discourses. The differences—or better, the difference—are not in the form: The word-to-word correspondence is essentially respected. It is in the meaning and value that each corpus [i.e., Berber poems and French poems] holds, such that one witnesses the strange result of two texts within which the detail is similar but the overall meaning is different. (Mammeri 1980: 7)

Mammeri viewed entextualization—even his own—as a necessary evil:

> In their original culture, each of these poems is a whole; it has a unique value, a face, a name, a history, and often a destiny. . . . The disorientation of the book removes from them all substance, deprives them of the harmonics of live transmission, which is theirs just as much as the series of words that constitutes them. . . . Many pieces, which I record here like dead documents, came to me magnified, in-

scribed in the dense context of a culture outside of which they are mutilated and extinguished. Some were inscribed in my spirit with the very timbre of the voice of the one who, now deceased, one day revealed them to me. No analysis, with tools elaborated elsewhere and, even if unconsciously, with other designs, can prevail against that, which is not just a lived experience but a reason to exist. (Mammeri 1980: 11, 16)

Through the ways Mammeri entextualized the Berber poems, he did manage to recreate at least a suggestion of the timbre and live quality of his own experience. Yet while seeking to reclaim the poems as "living documents," as "part of the reality that gave meaning to the group that created them and, through the group, to my own existence" (Mammeri 1980: 7–8), Mammeri tacitly acknowledged that they were no longer part of a "reality that gives meaning": "The book is intended not just to preserve [the poems] as 'indifferent documents' but to serve as an instrument in the transmission of Berber culture, *like the poems themselves once were*" (1980: 47, emphasis added).

As Mammeri knew, because the Berber language was not taught in Algeria, only a fraction of the Kabyle population would be able to read his collection in their native tongue.[35] Most Kabyles to whom I showed the text could make out the Berber poems only with some difficulty, making constant recourse to the French translation. If the poems were intended to provide a means through which Kabyles could identify themselves via their oral traditions, such a "return to the source" (Cabral 1973) could occur only from a position that was already estranged.

Stories of cultural difference are told through collections of poetry. Behind the premise that poetry represents an unmediated native spirit lies a dense, highly mediated web of entextualizing devices that worked to orient Kabyle poems to diverse sociopolitical agendas, from pacification and liberalism to nationalism to postcolonial identity. Contrary to views that writing down oral texts fixes them in a so-called original state, from the beginning, Kabyle poetry collection has been a means of configuring Berber culture in relation to metropolitan, nationalist, and postcolonial ideas and ideologies. It was precisely the movement of poetry through these widely circulating discourses that would enable it to be newly appropriated by Kabyles themselves. For it was not the poems as texts but rather the ways they were written about—the metadiscursive paths along which they traveled—that made them available as receptacles of ideology and vehicles for self-constitution.

Processes of refraction and translation are fundamental to identity formation, as the self becomes newly visible through the lenses (and sometimes the language) of the Other. This does not imply a relationship of subordination or derivative imitation; rather, the very conditions of possibility for imagining an "authentic" identity already depend on processes of cultural comparison. As Amselle put it, "It is in thinking oneself [*se pensant*] or in reflecting on oneself [*se réfléchissant*] *in the other* that one confirms [*conforte*] his own identity. . . . Mediation is the shortest route to authenticity" (2001: 9–10, 14, emphasis added).

That an incessant tacking back and forth between self and Other enables ideas about Berber identity to take shape is apparent in the very layout of the poetry collections, where the Berber and French texts seem to mirror each other on facing pages, yet can be made to speak to different cultural universes that derive meaning only from their juxtaposition. Moreover, the mirror points in both directions: As Hanoteau's collection makes abundantly clear, the French also looked to the discourse of the Other to construct themselves in beneficent rather than bellicose terms.

The poetry collections all participate in a regime of textuality that assumes a breach between the author of the poem and its collector. In no case does the collector of the poetic text claim authorship; indeed, locating the text in the Other was largely what allowed these collectors to shape the poems according to their own sociopolitical agendas. The creators of the song *A vava inouva*, Ben Mohamed and Idir, also collected Kabyle village poems and songs. But Ben and Idir would introduce themselves into the text in an entirely new manner, intentionally transforming the older texts even as they continued to view them as sources of an authentic Kabyle culture.

5 Authoring Modernity

I explain the success of *A vava inouva* by the fact that it is both profoundly Berber and at the same time is expressed in a language that is modern, of our times, in a music readable everywhere.

—Ben Mohamed, personal interview with author, August 18, 1994

I try to present the elements of our culture to the greatest degree and in the best way possible, and to lift them to a universal dimension, a dimension that we have not yet known.

—Idir, radio interview, *Inter actualités,* France Inter, June 16, 1976

What is entailed in lifting a village song to a universal dimension? How does a song become simultaneously "profoundly Berber" and "readable everywhere"? How, in short, do village songs need to be reconfigured for a world stage? Ben Mohamed and Idir, creators of *A vava inouva,* reworked several women's texts to imbue them with an aura of universality. When these songs were reconstituted as world music, they refracted back onto their sources, enabling women's village songs to be reinterpreted as objects of tradition and signs of locality.

Like the collectors, Ben and Idir looked to Kabyle village poetry for much of their source material. Yet their songs carve out a different kind of passage from collector to author. Earlier collectors claimed to reproduce poems and songs as they found them, and then surrounded them with their own evaluative essays and annotations. A collector's sociopolitical agenda could be discerned in the relationship between the poem itself and the ways it was framed. In contrast, Ben Mohamed and Idir made no claim to reproduce an "original" poem. Their own relationship to the poetry they gathered is not presented as a separate text but is *folded into* the new text itself. The ways Ben and Idir reworked village songs to enable them to serve as vehicles of a Kabyle cultural modernity is my concern here. I take up in some detail the strategies they developed to make village songs sound simultaneously "profoundly Berber" and "of our times." My focus lies with the minutiae: the specific textual changes, line by line and word by word, that a few songs have undergone in their journeys to a world stage.

In 1992, during one of my first meetings with Ben Mohamed, I asked him how he came up with the texts to some of Idir's early hits.[1] As we sat in Ben's living room in Paris, his newborn daughter's cries punctuating our conversation, he told me about a tape that a friend's grandmother had recorded for him over two decades earlier. It was one of the few things he had brought with him when he immigrated to France the year before. He put it on, and I heard a soft, at times barely audible voice singing in what I would later recognize as "tape-recorder style"—that is, the singing was not in the full, bright voice characteristic of women's public performance in Kabylia but was almost hushed, as if not meant to be heard even in the next room (cf. Ait Ferroukh 1994). I had often worked with similar kinds of tapes during my many years of performing with the women's world music ensemble Libana, but I realized that Ben's process was different. In Libana, we had sought to reproduce as closely as possible what we took to be the originals, listening intently to everything from vocal timbre to word pronunciation. We may have cut out verses here and there to shorten the piece for performance; if the words on occasion seemed to be overly at odds with our own feminist mission, we would simply leave out that particular verse, all the while claiming that we were presenting authentic renditions of the songs of women of other cultures. Even though we were reorienting their songs to our contemporary feminist concerns, it did not occur to us to deliberately change the women's texts—just as it would not have occurred to any of the collectors.

Ben and Idir looked at these texts differently: They viewed them as vehicles for cultural critique. While they drew on the older texts for inspiration, they incorporated what they found valuable in the older texts into entirely new songs, discarding what did not fit their vision. I became fascinated by the spaces that Ben and Idir opened up between the new songs and the older texts on which they are based. Briggs and Bauman (1992) have called such spaces "intertextual gaps," a term that refers to a perceived fit or lack of fit between related texts. In these spaces or gaps—that is, in the discrepancies between the village source texts and Ben and Idir's rewritings—the project of transforming village texts to make them speak to universal concerns emerges with a good deal of specificity. Examining precisely how the older texts were altered reveals particular arenas of Kabyle social life that Ben and Idir (and those with whom they were in dialogue) perceived as incompatible with their modernizing vision. Even those elements of older texts that were retained in the new songs were often embedded in new contexts and invested with novel meanings (cf. Bauman 1993, 1995; Briggs 1993).

Narrow or "minimal" gaps between two texts tend to reproduce the status quo. There is usually little difference, for example, in how a praise song heard at different wedding events is culturally interpreted (although its significance may vary for the particular individuals involved). Wide or "maximal" gaps, on the other hand, are often spaces of exceptional creativity: Setting a praise song text into an alternative frame can allow it to take on an entirely new signification (Briggs and Bauman 1992: 149). The way a text is performed and the circuits through which it travels factor importantly into how a gap is perceived. Indeed, as I show below, gaps can be construed differently even when a text is invoked in dialogue. Intertextual gaps do not determine meaning but rather open a fluid space of interpretation and debate. That Idir's early songs, most of them written by Ben Mohamed, opened this space so compellingly rests in part, however, on the authors' intentional and identifiable manipulations of texts and melodies.

Even as they utterly transformed women's texts, Ben and Idir shared with previous collectors (and Libana) the presumption that "women's song" constitutes a category of cultural discourse. Thus, they collapsed such distinct genres as praise songs, lullabies, saint veneration chants, and funeral dirges under the rubric of female cultural expression.[2] The three songs I consider below are a case in point. The first, *Isefra*, comes from a praise song typically performed by small groups of women at the weddings or circumcision ceremonies of close family members. The second, *Cfiɣ*, is inspired by a lullaby that a woman would sing to a child in the privacy of her own home. The third, *Muhend-nneɣ*, derives from a chant women might sing while visiting a saint's tomb. Moreover, within the Kabyle organization of discourse, religious poetry recited to a melody (as in saint veneration) is not considered "song" (*leɣna*) but is termed "chant" (*adekkeṛ*). Not until they were recorded by Idir did these songs all become "music" in the Western sense.

Ben and Idir also developed a new way of listening to women's songs. John Pemberton makes the provocative proposition that some music is deliberately intended to be *not* listened to (Pemberton 1987). Pemberton likens a form of Javanese gamelan music known as *halus*—a required presence at reception-hall weddings—to the food, attire, and speeches, which are intended to establish a predictable scene of order against which the focus of the wedding can emerge in sharp relief. The gamelan musicians, seated to the side, are invisible to the guests, who "ceremoniously display their detachment by not watching, not listening, and not commenting on anything much" (Pemberton 1987: 28). Were a guest actually to pay attention, turning toward and responding to the musicians as she might in other gamelan performance situations, she could disrupt the ceremony. Kabyle women's songs often play a similar role of background instrumentality, particularly at weddings. I realized this, however, only when I inadvertently stopped listening and noticed that I was not alone. Arriving late to one wedding, I had not brought my tape recorder and did not make my usual effort to sit by the small group of women singers. As they began their ritual songs to accompany the application of henna to the groom's hand, their voices sounded far-off, the words inaudible in the distance. Their songs, I realized, were like the eggs, candles, and other traditional objects arranged around the groom, who sat on a special blanket surrounded by his family, receiving monetary gifts from guests. While their absence would have been noticed, their presence was unremarked. The songs were clearly a backdrop to the ceremony, not its focus.

To transform women's songs into a new kind of cultural product, then, Ben and Idir first had to construct these songs as texts by detaching them from their situations of performance. A few songs came to them from the books of earlier collectors. Some came from their own memories. But many came from tapes they recorded explicitly for this purpose. The songs *Isefra* and *Cfiɣ*, discussed below, are both inspired by the tape of Ben's friend's grandmother, recorded in the village of Ait Hichem in the early 1970s. From there they traveled to Algiers, where Ben began to listen for ways to make them sound both "profoundly Berber" and "readable everywhere."

My trajectory was the reverse. I started from Idir's music and worked backward, trying to find songs in Kabylia that resembled the ones Idir and Ben had drawn on. Back in Paris, Ben and I compared the women's texts (from his tapes and mine) with his own. Why had he erased certain words, altered particular lines, turned a verse on its head? Later discussions with Idir refined, clarified, and sometimes further confused my understanding. I try to convey a sense of these conversations by reproducing portions of them here. Of course, the selection, framing, control, and ultimate responsibility for what I convey here ultimately rest with me. The tape recordings of the women's texts on which we relied were also dialogical products. Those texts that I reproduce in this chapter should not be taken as fixed or static entities but as products of the particular contexts in which they were solicited.

Isefra (Poetry)

The song Isefra,[3] one of Idir's most popular, is also among his most traditional. Both Ben's text and Idir's melody resonate closely with the praise song from which they are inspired. Widely known in the At Yenni, Ain-el-Hammam, and At Ouacif regions of Kabylia, the traditional song also circulated in the missionary literature via a Kabyle Christian woman's account of a typical wedding (Yamina 1960 [1953], 1961 [1953]), to which Ben referred me. I recorded more versions of this song than any other during trips to Ain-el-Hammam and At Yenni, where I stayed in Idir's home village of At Laḥsen (Ait Lahcène). During festivities in the Kabyle region, the village song, which belongs to a genre of praise songs known as tibuɣarin, can be used to laud the qualities of either a newborn male baby or a man about to be married, both celebratory occasions for a patrilineage.

In village celebrations I witnessed in Amkan, tibuɣarin were typically sung by a small group of women (usually postmenopausal) who had both a genealogical connection to and a good relationship with the family hosting the event. The women would sing in two antiphonal choruses, with the second chorus repeating each line verbatim. While the second chorus was singing, the women in the first chorus would sometimes discuss among themselves what the next verse would be, with the de facto leader (the most experienced singer) generally whispering it to the others (unless they sang together frequently). While many women know the melodies and are somewhat conversant with the words, only a handful can recite the texts at any length. Thus, although women's singing may look like a collective enterprise to those watching (including many Kabyles), it relies heavily on a small number of expert singers. These women are referred to as "knowing" the old texts (tessen, "she knows") or as layzbesyalisṭ, a term derived from the French les spécialistes ("the specialists"). In Tamkant, only four or five women were singled out to me as specialists.

A praise song usually starts a village celebration, and Idir often uses Isefra to open his concerts.[4]

Verse 1

A nekker a nebdu cekkṛan
a ncekkeṛ kra da.
Keççini a bab n tmeɣṛa

a mmi-s n tnina.
Yis-ek i nedhent tezzyiwin
di tizi lɣila.

Let us rise and begin to sing praises,
we will praise everyone here.
You, for whom we are gathered in
    celebration,
oh son of Tanina.[5]
It's you to whom your comrades look
in the hour of need.

Verse 2

La leḥḥuɣ luḍa luḍa
yejjujeg umezzir.
Atan ɛadden-d yemnayen
s rrekba d zzhir.
A yuzyin serrej aɛewdiw
ezwir ay itbir.

I am walking in the plain,
the lavender is in bloom.
The horsemen passed by
in a thunderous stampede.
Oh handsome groom, mount your horse,
go to the front of their ranks, oh beauti-
    ful bird.

Verse 3

A timeḥremt n leḥrir
a m' tballiwin.
Yeqqen-ikem-id lbaz ukyis
sennig tɛeyunin.
Ism-is inuda lɛeṛac
yerna timdinin.

Oh silk scarf,
beautifully adorned.
The eagle has attached you
above his brows.
His name is known in every tribe
and even in the cities.

First Reading: Ben Mohamed, June 1993, Paris

My first approach to *Isefra* took place with Ben in Paris. I had already begun my own translation (into French) of the song, but there was much that I did not understand. We began by listening to the tape of the old woman from which he had worked. Ben had a hard time extracting from the tape those verses that he had transformed, repeating several times that he could not separate his words from hers (*"je me confonds avec le traditionnel"*). Finally he found one verse (see below) that he had drawn from to create verse 2 of *Isefra*. As we compared his text against the woman's, I gradually came to understand what he meant by modernizing an older text to imbue it with a sense of universality.

From the tape recorded for Ben Mohamed in Ait Hichem

Yaxi testewḥec luḍa
yejjujeg umezzir.
Atan ɛaddan-d yemnayen
s rrekba d zzhir.
Ay isli serrej i wɛawdiw
ezwir ay itbir.

Oh, how the plain causes fear
The lavender is in bloom.
The horsemen passed by
in a thunderous stampede.
Oh groom, mount your horse,
Go to the front of their ranks, oh beauti-
    ful bird.

Jane: I don't understand the meaning of the song.

Ben: The meaning of the song, first of all it isn't by accident that I titled it "Poetry." The driving idea [*l'idée motrice*], it's the old poems, I tried to look [in them] for the values that we like in our culture, and to emphasize them. What is it that makes us respect this leader, this person who is there when you need him. . . .

Jane: It's a bit of a condensation of the old poems.

Ben: That's it, I took some of them, I extracted the values, then I put them into my text. There is the idea of physical beauty and of the beauty of acts, of conduct, of the ability to be a leader. . . .

Jane: This comes from wedding songs?

Ben: Yes, songs of praise.

Ben attempted, then, to use a praise song celebrating a particular male, a particular family, as the basis for a song of praise for the culture as a whole. To do so, he sought to give his text cohesiveness, whereby one image would flow "logically" into the next, with all subordinated to the message he sought to convey. He changed the first line of the woman's verse, for example, from "Oh, how the plain causes fear" to "I am walking in the plain," because, as he put it,

> I needed to inscribe the line in the overall meaning of the text. And moreover I didn't see the relationship between fear and the blooming lavender [the next line]. . . . It isn't because the lavender is in bloom that one is afraid in the plain. . . . But to say "I am walking in the plain,[6] and the lavender blooms"—there I'm describing the state of a place—and then, before these flowers, the horsemen arrive.

Ben seems to be reading and writing in relation to a notion of narrative structure in which action occurs against a static, natural backdrop. Does the woman's poem link setting and action differently? As Ben and I continued to discuss her text, we realized that perhaps fear was related to the stampede of horsemen (line 4). If so, then the woman's verse had already introduced this impending action within the "setting," via reference to an emotional state. Even had Ben read her verse in that way, though, he still would have changed it, he said, because he did not want an image of fear in his text.

Other references that Ben systematically expunged include what he called religious formulas, which typically open praise songs. Verses 1 and 3, for example, were reproduced directly from the woman's poem—almost. Ben changed the opening words of the song from "*In the name of God* let us begin to sing praises" (*bism'lleh a nebdu cekkran*) to "*Let us rise* and begin to sing praises" (*a nekker a nebdu cekkran*). To him, such framing devices simply took up space, got in the way of addressing "real" problems, and made no sense in relation to the main idea of the text:

> Ben: There were, in the old texts, what I felt the most, it's that most of the time, these religious lines are used as stop-gaps [*bouche-trou*], the essential is said in two lines, then you start with a religious thing [*truc*], you end with another, and it's just to garnish, it sometimes makes no sense in rela-

tion to the main idea [*l'idée maîtresse*] that one wants to transmit. So I said to myself, why not enrich the text, develop its idea, or other ideas, pull together other ideas and transmit them, instead of including these garnishings that have nothing to do with the text.

The rest of our dialogue had less to do with Ben's explicit reading and writing strategies than with his explication of words or images with which I was not familiar. But even this was revealing. To explain *tanina,* for example (a mythical female bird), Ben related the bird's myth to me and then referred me to Mammeri's poetry collection, where the whole myth is recorded (Mammeri 1980: 222–225). To explain the meaning of the phrase *timeḥremt n leḥrir* (a particular kind of silk scarf), he referred me to old women who, he said, would be able to talk to me about the expression because it is from "old Kabyle" (*kabyle ancien*)— a phrase he used frequently.

I better understood Ben's selection of such richly metaphorical, mythological, and "ancient" images when I considered them in relation to those verses that he did not select. While I do not have a full transcription of the tape upon which he drew, I did find numerous poems resembling *Isefra* both textually and melodically.[7] Reading backward from Ben's poem to these, the reasons for the choices he made became clearer still.

Second Reading: Jane, November 1993, Algeria

In the fall of 1993, Karim (a pseudonym), a young man active in Amazigh cultural activities, invited me to visit his village in the Ain-el-Hammam region. Since it was not wedding season, Karim asked his sister and then his older aunt to tape-record songs for me; both sang local versions of the verses that appear in Ben's text. It is possible, of course, that Idir's song inflected what the women sang, but when Karim tried to attribute their song to Idir, his aunt objected vehemently. It was from "the old women of long, long ago" (*temɣarin n zik n zik*), she insisted; she herself had heard it as a young girl. Later that day, I went with Karim's sister to a somewhat larger gathering of women, who collectively produced a more extended version of the song, which I reproduce below. What the text does not capture is the dialogical nature of that performance. Two younger women began the singing but hesitated in the middle of verse 2, and a knowledgeable older woman finished the verse; this is textually visible in the change of rhyme scheme (verse 2, lines 5 and 6). Their voices intermingle throughout the rest of the recording, the younger women taking the lead on some verses and the older woman on others (other women would also chime in or hum along, but their voices do not dominate). Between some verses, they briefly paused for discussion. At one point (after verse 9), one young woman said, "that's all"; the older woman disagreed and went on to sing several more verses. This organization of performance was clearly a function of the recording event; during a wedding or circumcision ceremony, one or several older women would lead the singing, ensuring a smooth flow from verse to verse.

1. Eyyamt a nger aẓeṭṭa
ɣef yiri bb wasif.
Eyyamt a ngezm i uɣanim
bezzaf i_gwezzif.
A aɣa serrej-iw aɛwdiw

tezwireḍ ay ukyis.

1. Come [f.pl.], let's assemble the loom
on the banks of the river.
Come, let's cut the bamboo,
it's too long.
Oh "agha" [Turkish leader] saddle my
  horse
Lead the way, oh handsome groom.

2. Wi-ṭ-ilan lḥara-yinna
yessan s weblaḍ?
Ur ṭ-id-ikeččem yiwen
ḥac' At Sebbaḍ.
[a Sidi Murad Sidi
a lbaz inmewweṛ].

2. To whom does the house belong
that is standing on large, flat stones?
No one can enter it
except those wearing shoes.
Oh Sidi Murad
Luminous eagle.

3. Ay lxir-inu ṛebbi
zewjeɣ-as i mmi.
Bbwiɣ-as-d ḥuṛeṭ lɛin

lehṛuz ɣef timmi.

Ṛebbi ketteṛ-as-d iqcicen
a nehḍeṛ a nili.

3. How great is my joy, oh Lord
I have married off my son.
I brought him one of the beautiful
  women of Paradise
[protected from the evil eye] by amulets
  on her forehead.
God, grant him sons
We will all be witnesses.

4. Ay lxir-inu ṛebbi
zewjeɣ-as i waras.
Bbwiɣ-as-d ḥuṛeṭ lɛin

lehṛuz ɣef ammas.

Ṛebbi ketteṛ-as-d iqcicen
at_tehḍeṛ yemma-s.

4. How great is my joy, oh Lord,
I have married off my brown-skinned boy.
I brought him one of the beautiful
  women of Paradise
[protected from the evil eye] by amulets
  on her hips [i.e., belt].
God, grant him sons
His mother will be present.

5. A timehremt l_lehrir
a m' tballiwin.
Yeqqen-iṭ-id Sidi Sɛid
sennig tɛeyunin.
Ism-is inuda lɛeṛac
yerna timdinin.

5. Oh silk scarf,
beautifully adorned.
Sidi Said has attached it
above his brows.
His name is known in every tribe
and even in the cities.

6. A timehremt l_lehrir
a m' tballucin.
Yeqqen-ikem-id Sidi Murad
sennig tɛeyunin.
Ism-is inuda lɛeṛac
yerna timdinin.

6. Oh silk scarf,
beautifully adorned.
Sidi Murad has attached you
above his brows.
His name is known in every tribe
and even in the cities.

7. Eyyamt at_teddumt a nṛuḥ
s azaɣar a-d-nerr ulli.
A Sidi ɛeziz Murad

7. Come, let's go [f.pl.] together
to bring the sheep to pasture.
Oh, dear Sidi Murad

a taqadumt tecba lemri.
Akk' iqqaren watmaten-is
d amerbuḥ a gma lḥenni.

whose face resembles a mirror.
As his brothers say,
"May the henna bring you prosperity, oh
  brother."

8. Eyyamt at_teddumt a nṛuḥ
ɣer wedrar a-d-nawi lḥecc.
Nniɣ-as keçç ay isli
taqadumt tecba tnefcic.
Kra i nmenna di Ṛebbi.
Ar qabel a nesrebḥ aqcic.

8. Come, let's go [f.pl.] together
to the mountain, to bring back some herbs.
I said to myself, oh bridegroom
whose face is precious.
Everything we desire comes from God.
In the coming year we will gain a son.

9. Ay lxir-inu
tura fukken imeṭṭawen.
A nkkes akw leḥzen
yellan seg wacḥal uɣen.
[unclear] a Murad
amzun yekker-ed wi' yemmuten.

9. How great is my joy
now the tears have ceased.
We are going to remove all the sorrow
that we have known for so long.
[unclear] oh Murad
It's as if the dead have arisen.

10. Eyyamt a nger aẓeṭṭa
ɣef yiri bb wasif.
Eyyamt a ngezm i uɣanim
bezzaf i_gwezzif.
A Sidi Murad
aɛeqq' uẓarif.

10. Come [f.pl.], let's assemble the loom
on the banks of the river.
Come, let's cut the bamboo,
it's too long.
Oh Sidi Murad
seed of wild geranium.

11. Eyyamt a nger aẓeṭṭa
ɣef yiri g_geɣzeṛ.
Eyyamt a ngezm i uɣanim
bezzaf i gɛejeṛ.
A Sidi Murad
aɛeṛjun n ṭṭmeṛ.

11. Come [f.pl.], let's assemble the loom
on the edge of the ravine.
Come, let's cut the bamboo,
it's too stiff.
Oh Sidi Murad
cluster of dates.

12. A tasekkurt yecrurden

ɣef yiri bb wasif.
Tebɛan-ṭ-id iṣeggaden
ḥedd ur-ṭ-id-yeṭṭif.
Wi ṭ-id yeṭṭfen d At Xaled
imawlan n nnif.

12. Oh partridge who walks with tiny
  steps
on the banks of the river.
The hunters followed it
but no one could catch it.
Those who got it are the At Xaled,
a family of honor.

13. Leḥḥuɣ luḍa luḍa
yejjujeg umezzir.
[unclear] amnayen
s rrekba u zzhir.
A Murad serrej i waɛewdiw
tezwireḍ ay itbir.

13. I am walking on the plain,
the lavender is in bloom.
[unclear] the horsemen
in a thunderous stampede.
Oh handsome groom, mount your horse,
go to the front of the ranks, oh beautiful
  bird.

Once I had transcribed the women's verses, I tried to figure out how Ben
Mohamed might have interpreted them, based on our discussion of the previous

summer. Nine of the thirteen verses would not have met Ben's criteria. Verses 1, 10, and 11 would be excluded for their licentious references to sexuality, associated in general with the loom and even more explicitly with manipulating the bamboo wood, described as "too long" or "too stiff."[8] Verses 3, 4, and 8 contain explicit references to the Quran, maraboutic practices, or God. Verses 7, 8, and 12, among others, do not have the "right" number of syllables or rhyme scheme and would be hard to fit to the music. Others contain personal names or other particularities that would not support a generalized cultural message. Read against verses that would be eliminated from consideration, the verses Ben selected take on new meaning. Although they almost exactly match verses in the older song in terms of vocabulary, verse and syllable structure, rhyme, and other formal features, Ben's verses 1 and 3 were explicitly culled from dozens of "rejected" verses. Their selection thus contains within it a series of evaluations that imbue the chosen verses with new expressive value (Bakhtin 1986), making them subtly double-voiced.

The next text further illuminates Ben's writing process. I recorded it with the same group of women, but perhaps because it was later in the session, they sang in greater synchrony, more in the style of a wedding performance, without pausing between verses and with minimal hesitation.

Version 2, Ain-El-Hammam, November 1993, Field Recording

1. A timeḥremt l_leḥrir
a mu tbaliwin.
Yeqqen-ikem weqcic ukyis
sennig tɛeyunin.
Ism-ik inuda lɛeṛac

yerna timdinin.

1. Oh silk scarf,
beautifully adorned.
The handsome groom has attached you
above his brows.
Your [groom's, m.s.] name is known in
    every tribe
and even in the cities.

2. A timeḥremt l_leḥrir
ism-im [Lluja, unclear].
Yeqqen-ikem wecqic ukyis
sennig twenza.
Ism-is inuda lɛeṛac
yerna-d Fransa.

2. Oh silk scarf,
your name is [Lluja, unclear].
The handsome groom has attached you
above his forehead.
His name is known in every tribe
and even in France.

3. A taxuxeṭ yellugg\\u02b7in
ɣef yiri bb wamdun.
(unclear) bab-is di tsulla
at_twennɛe lɛeyun.
A Sidi Murad
acrur uqelmun.

3. Oh ripe peach
on the banks of the pond.
[translation unclear]
[translation unclear]
A Sidi Murad
with tassels on your hood.

4. Axi tsewḥec luḍa
tejjujeg lfakya.
Atan iɛeddan-d yemnayen
s rrekba t-twiɣa (unclear).

4. How the plain causes fear,
the fruits are in bloom.
The horsemen passed by
in a devastating (unclear) stampede.

A Murad serrej i waɛwdiw	Oh Murad, mount your horse,
tezwireḍ a laɣa.	Go to the front of their ranks, oh "agha"
	[a Turkish leader].

5. Axi tsewḥec luḍa	5. How the plain causes fear,
yejjujeg umezzir.	the lavender is in bloom.
Atan iɛeddan-d yemnayen	The horsemen passed by
s rrekba d zzhir.	in a thunderous stampede.
A Lḥamid serrej aɛwdiw	Oh Hamid mount your horse,
tezwireḍ ay itbir.	go to lead them, oh beautiful bird.

Verses 2 and 4 immediately stand out: they laud the young man's qualities via reference to foreign lands or occupiers (France, Turks). Such positive references to foreigners could have no place in Ben's poem, which seeks to "extract cultural values" that are "specifically Kabyle."

Third Reading: Idir, November 1996, Paris

Later discussion of these songs with Idir both supported and complicated earlier readings. As we sat in the basement of the Berber Cultural Association in Paris, I showed him my transcriptions of *Isefra* and related traditional poems. Because the text and melody of *Isefra* retain such a high degree of resonance with women's versions, it is one of the few songs in Idir's repertoire in which he is able to improvise on stage, adding verses as the mood strikes him. He would not add just any verse, however. Most of those that Ben would eliminate, he would eliminate also, for similar reasons.

Jane: Are there images that you would refuse to include?
Idir: The images that we [he and Ben] refuse to include, it's everything that is out of date.
Jane: Which is to say . . . ?
Idir: Everything that is backward-looking, folkloric, static. For example, the marabouts, all those things that don't contribute anything to our society. It was good that we thought of that from the beginning. Sometimes Ben Mohamed goes too far, though. . . .
[. . .]
Jane: A phrase like *hureṭ lɛin* [woman of Paradise, a Quranic reference], you wouldn't use it?
Idir: I don't know, it would depend on the context. *Leḥruz ɣef ammas* [amulets on the hip], I don't think I would use it because it brings up bad associations. Leḥruz it's the thing the marabout writes for you, and I wonder if it isn't time to change speeds now.
Jane: That means?
Idir: If we shouldn't be heading elsewhere, taking the magic we have and then universalizing it a bit, I don't know. . . .
[. . .]

Jane: Talk to me about the history of this song.

Idir: It existed in the things [verses] that you showed me, then Ben picked it up; the militant aspect that he added, it's the [last two lines of Ben's verse 1]: "It's you whom we invoke, whom we call . . . when it's time to go to war or to mobilize." Whereas usually, *bab n tameɣra* is the one who gives the celebration, *mmi-s n tnina* it's the one getting married, who is handsome. . . . In principle, then, lines 5 and 6 should refer to something beautiful as well. But he politicized them. . . . He added a political thing, implying that "we are Berbers." He wanted to replace a religious formula . . . because often those lines say something like, "Muhammad [the Prophet] who chose you." And at the same time [Ben's version] has a political agenda, the hero, that is, the hero of the Berbers who is going to fight against the Arabs. . . . Now Ben's second verse is good, it's complete, it's in the spirit. And the third verse as well. It's just those two lines.

Jane: You still sing them anyways.

Idir: Of course, it's in the text.

All of this suggests that embedding a verse or two of an old song into a newer one involves sophisticated text-making or entextualization processes, beginning with a radical rereading of the older text that already announces a new relationship to it. Here, the older text is interpreted against notions of form and content that center around a guiding master idea. Foregrounded, this idea is set against a supporting ("natural") backdrop and developed "logically" from one line, one word, to the next. Words are seen as detachable from one context and transposable to another because their referents can be double-voiced, or overlaid with new expressive meanings. Not all words can undergo this operation, however. Some are still so tinged by their indexical links to "unacceptable" situations that they require suppression altogether.

The text of *Isefra* appears to minimize intertextual gaps—reducing the distance between Ben's poem and the woman's—in that there are few formal differences. The syllabic, rhythmic, and rhyme structures match. Both employ verses of six lines, divided into three couplets; each couplet has alternating verses of seven and five syllables; the "b" lines of each couplet rhyme at the end. Lexically, the two songs are very close; their differences lie more in the suppression of particular verses or phrases than in the addition of new ones. Melodically, the two resemble each other as well. When I said that I was looking for Idir's songs, the women in Ain-el-Hammam immediately sang for me their version of this one. These matching formal, semantic, and melodic features make the new song sound very close to the older one indeed.

Does this mean that Ben's elaborate rewriting was for naught? Are the intertextual gaps here truly minimal? Addressing these questions involves looking beyond text to music and performance: new instrumentation, a male solo singer, national and international airplay, and circulatory networks that associate the song with the Berber cultural events and the postcolonial currents discussed above. These elements clearly help to support textual interpretations of a certain kind. Because not everyone participates in these contexts to the same degree, different readings of Ben's text may occur. Those highly attuned to Berberist politics or to the potential for censorship by the Algerian state can "misread" Ben's text, as even Idir did, to interpret lines 5 and 6 of verse 1 (and perhaps other lines as well) as a veiled political statement.[9] Such listeners almost certainly would have questioned the song's politics had Ben included references to religion, the Turks, or the French. His suppression of these elements may not have been noticed, but their inclusion would have been, making his textual rewriting essential even though it was probably not explicitly heard.

Cfiɣ (I Remember)

The song *Cfiɣ*[10] ("I remember"), integral to Idir's repertoire, is framed, as its title suggests, through a notion of memory. The melody, composed by Idir, contains no echoes of earlier music. The music, in fact, was written first; Ben then came up with the text.

Verse 1

Cfiɣ amzun d iḍelli	I remember as if it were yesterday
mi d-yebbʷeḍ wejrad tara	when the locusts arrived
ccerq llɣerb yetteggir	from the east and west
adrum ur yezmir ara.	the *adrum* was not able to resist them.
Nekk terriḍ-iyi ɣer dduḥ	Me, you had put me in the cradle
a yemma ur ṭṭiseɣ ara.	but mother, I wasn't sleeping.
Cfiɣ tmutelṭ-iyi	I remember you compared me
ɣer tzurin bbwafrara.	to the green grapes.
Tenniḍ-iyi asmi d-luleɣ	You told me that when I was born
aɛedawen ur-aɣ-bɣin ara.	our enemies did not want us [to have another male].
Yis-i tferḥeḍ mi muqreɣ.	You rejoiced as I grew up.
Tuɣ-am teftilt di lḥara.	The lamp in the courtyard was lit.

Verse 2

Cfiɣ amzun d iḍelli	I remember as if it were yesterday
ɣef usigna mi_gɣumm aggur	the clouds covered the moon,
acekkal yeɣli-d i zznad	the catch of the trigger had let go,
tamurt içça-ṭ unaɣur.	a heat wave consumed the country.
Tmuqleḍ-ed deg-i a yemma	You looked at me, oh mother,
walaɣ ul-im amek yeççur.	I saw how full your heart was.
Tenniḍ-iyi keçç a mmi	You said to me, "you, oh my son,
taḥbult g_girden mi tnur.	glowing beignet of wheat."
Tweṣṣaḍ-iyi ɣef gma.	You put me in charge of my brother.
Ad beddeɣ ɣur-es ad yimɣur.	I will watch over him as he grows.
A-t-afeɣ ɣer tuyat-iw.	I will find him at my side.
W'ur nesɛi tagmaṭ meḥqur	He who is without fraternity is to be pitied.

Like *Isefra,* the text of *Cfiɣ* was written by Ben Mohamed from the cassette recorded by his friend's grandmother in Ait Hichem. Ben transcribed for me only those verses from which his text was inspired.

Version 1, Ben's Tape from Ait Hichem

1. Keççini a mmi	1. You, oh my son,
tiẓuṛin bbwafrara.	bunch of green grapes.
Asmi tluleḍ	When you were born
aɛdawen ur-k bɣin ara.	the enemies did not want you.
Lxir-iw tura muqreḍ	How great is my joy that now you are mature,
tuɣ teftilt deg lḥara.	the lamp in the courtyard is lit.
2. Keççini a mmi	2. You, oh my son,
taḥbult g_girden ma tnuṛ.	beignet of golden wheat.
A mmi f ki-ṭ a gma-k.	Oh son, give it [the beignet] to your brother.
A-ṭ-yeçç, ad yegm, ad yimɣuṛ.	He will eat it, grow strong, and mature.
A-t-in-tafeḍ di tejmɛat.	You will find him in tajmaᶜat.
W'ur nesɛi tagmaṭ meḥquṛ.	He who is without fraternity is to be pitied.

Version 2, At Yenni, November 1993, Field Recording

I heard similar poems in At Yenni, Idir's natal village, as part of a lullaby. I recorded the following text while sitting around a dining room table with three generations of women: Soraya (a pseudonym), a university student active in a regional theater group, who served as my guide; several women of her mother's generation; and her grandmother. The grandmother did much of the singing and was looked to as the expert, but the others also participated, joining in as they could. They had just finished a wedding praise song, and I interjected, "And the one that goes 'keççini a mmi, tiẓuṛin bbwafrara,'" reciting the words but not the tune in the hope that they would sing it. "No, no, that's a different one," they told me, misunderstanding my request. They went on to explain the difference between praise songs and lullabies; the verses I had recited, they said, were sung by women as they rocked their children (*ma ṭhuzzent*). "How does it go?" I asked; after some discussion, one woman recited a verse. "And its melody?" I pursued. Amid more discussion, Soraya's grandmother broke in and sang several verses. Both the recited and the sung verses appear below.

1. Keççini a mmi	1. You, oh my son,
tiẓuṛin bbwafrara.	bunch of green grapes.
Asmi tluleḍ	When you were born
aɛedawen ur-k-bɣin ara.	the enemies did not want you.
A lxiṛ-iw tura muqreḍ	How great is my joy that now you are mature,
tuɣ teftilt di lḥara.	the lamp in the courtyard is lit.

2. Ṭxil-kwent lmalayek
awimt-iyi-d taciṭa.
A mani ansi-ṭ-id awimt
seg wudrar n Jerjeṛa.
A-ṭ-id awimt i mmi
ad yeggan ad yeṛṛeḥa.

2. I beseech you, oh angels,
bring me a branch.
From where will you bring it?
From the Djurdjura mountains.
Bring it to my son
that he may sleep and be blessed.

3. Nniɣ-as keççini a mmi
taḥbult g-irden ma tnuṛ.
Xedm-as lxiṛ i watmaten-ik
i wakken ad-ak-yimɣuṛ.
Lḥif n tejmɛat yewɛeṛ

wu nesɛa tagmaṭ meḥquṛ.

3. You, oh my son,
beignet of golden wheat.
Do good for your brothers
so that they will grow up with you.
Weakness [of number] in tajmaᶜat is
very hard.
He who has no fraternity is to be pitied.

Turning now to the relationship between Ben Mohamed's and the women's texts, Ben's text embeds verses from the woman's lullaby within her son's memory, as the son contrasts his mother's joy at his birth with the destruction of the surrounding land. Like *Isefra*, *Cfiɣ* builds on the earlier texts by imbuing personal, intimate, and locally resonant words with larger meanings. Ben accomplishes this in part by building new textual surrounds for words whose meanings he wants to stretch. One example is the word "adrum" (verse 1, line 4). Whereas its basic referent is the patrilineal Kabyle extended family, Ben used it to represent all of Algeria, attacked from East and West by "grasshoppers"— a reference that refers both to actual locust infestations of previous centuries and to the French colonizer from the West, and earlier, the Arabs from the East. Ben intended for the meaning of "mother" (*yemma*) to expand in a similar fashion, referring to both mother and motherland. Likewise, the word *tagmaṭ* (fraternity) takes on a broader meaning, seen in the next-to-last line of Ben's verse 2:

Woman (version 1, verse 2):   "You will find him [your brother] *in tajmaᶜat* [the village assembly]
He who is without *fraternity* [lots of brothers] is to be pitied."

Ben: "I will find him [my brother] *at my side*
He who is without *fraternity* [brotherhood] is to be pitied."

The shift in the meaning of fraternity that Ben sought to convey required him to eliminate the word "tajmaᶜat"—the men's weekly assembly, usually dominated by stronger, larger, and wealthier patrilineages—and to replace it with the more generalized *at my side*.

Ben: I removed *tajmaᶜat* for two reasons. It bothered me to put in *tajmaᶜat* as a site of conflict. . . . It's true that it is a site of conflict . . . but I prefer to see it as a place where decisions are made for the village, a place of wisdom. . . . Since *tajmaᶜat* is tending to disappear nowadays, I want to preserve an image of *tajma'at* that I like. . . . [In the woman's version,] in *tajma'at* everyone has to have his clan . . . there is conflict, groups that are in confrontation. Whereas for me, when I remove *tajma'at*, I don't involve it in these conflicts. What I say ["I will find him at my side"] holds for any situation. . . . It's broader, and it preserves the image of *tajma'at*.

By removing references to the site where patrilineal rivalry occurs, then, Ben sets up a new frame for the last line, opening the possibility for another reading of *tagmaṭ* (fraternity): from an understanding among relatives (Dallet 1982), it becomes a global feeling of brotherhood.

Most of Ben's remaining changes involved recasting the woman's words from second-person direct address to reported speech and from apposition to explicit comparison. For example, "You, my son, bunch of green grapes, when you were born" becomes "*I remember you compared me* to the green grapes, *you told me that* when I was born. . . .*" In one place, however, Ben altered her words because he felt that they were culturally inauthentic:

Woman: You, oh my son,
        Beignet of golden wheat,
        Oh son, give it [the beignet] to your brother.
        He will eat it, grow strong, and mature.

Ben: You said to me, "You, oh my son,
        Beignet of golden wheat."
        You put me in charge of my brother.
        I will watch over him as he grows.

As Ben explained, "Since I know that among us, it isn't the man who cooks the beignets, who feeds the others, I said to myself, okay, it's better not to cheat." Here, he denies the possibility that the woman might also be using the word "beignet" metaphorically.

In Ben's hands, the woman's lullaby became a wake-up call, pointing to the destruction that the country had undergone from all sides and to its potential resolution via fraternity and solidarity. He recast the older lullaby as memory, suppressed or eliminated words that carried images he did not want to perpetuate, and expanded the semantic reach of other words, turning them into double-voiced terms with both local and universal connotations. These strategies all serve to heighten differences with the older lullaby, creating a maximal intertextual gap: those familiar with it recognize phrases, notice similarities. But they would not be able to sing along. Indeed, the verses of the woman's lullaby are broken up by Idir's music. Six-line stanzas from the lullaby are inserted into separate four-line melodic verses in the new song, such that the traditional poems begin in the middle of Idir's musical verses. (Musical breaks occur after lines 4, 8, and 12, while textual breaks fall after lines 6 and 12, with the "traditional" poem starting on line 7.)

In the song *Muḥend-nneγ*, the use of maximal intertextual gaps to build an interpretive space between old and new texts emerges clearly. The song also reveals significant differences in Ben's and Idir's approaches to the subject of the song: the practice of marabout or saint veneration.

Muḥend-nneɣ ("Our Muḥend")

The song Muḥend-nneɣ[11] ("Our Muḥend") calls both saints and religious leaders to task for their failure to provide for the population in its hour of need. Implicitly, it suggests that the population is deluding itself if it continues to look for otherworldly solutions to its oppression. The text, based on Ben Mohamed's poem Isiditen ("The Saints"), was altered by Idir for the recording (although the text remains copyrighted in Ben Mohamed's name). The song is structured to resemble a typical poem that praises the saints (iɛessasen) (also known as imrabḍen or marabouts in the Kabyle region). Such poems belong to the adekker genre and may be chanted by groups of women or (less frequently) men during pilgrimages to saints' tombs or on other religious holidays. The term adekker derives from the Arabic word dhkir, which refers, in Sufi practice, to the ritual repetition of the name of God in order to call forth his blessing. In Kabyle Berber the meaning of the term has shifted: Adekker includes all religious recitational poetry, from hagiographic legends to funeral laments, from chants about God or the Prophet to poems that laud particular saints (Mahfoufi 1991).

When I asked Yamina, one of the poetry specialists with whom I worked the most closely—who is herself of marabout descent—if she knew of Sidi Yahya Lɛidali, one of the saints mentioned in Ben's poem, she recited this verse:

Sidi Yahya Lɛidali	Sidi Yahya Lɛidali
yezlan azger yessker-it.	slaughtered a cow and then resurrected it.
Sidi Musa t nebder	Sidi Musa, whom we evoke
yerran ṣultan t_tislit.	changed the sultan into a bride.
Sidi Muḥend umalak	Sidi Muḥend, the angel
yerran tigejdit d zzit.	turned a wooden pillar into oil.
Ad ḥelleɣ bab Ṛebbi	I implore my Lord, supreme master
ccedda ttebɛɛ-ṭ talwit.	after suffering comes relief.

"He is my grandfather," Yamina said of Sidi Yahya Lɛidali when she finished. "Where is he from?" I asked. He came, she replied, from the village of Tazmert, beyond the town of Akbu (in the region known as Lesser Kabylia or Petite Kabylie). She then proceeded to list the saint's descendants in a style reminiscent of the biblical "begats," leading down to Sidi Muḥend u Salaḥ, the local saint from her own village from whom her family was descended. "Me, I know history," she said proudly when she had finished, reinforcing her claims to knowledge by using the French term for history, l'histoire: "nekk zriɣ listwar."

Idir gave Ben Mohamed a related adekker text, also from Lesser Kabylia. Ben retained the first four lines of verses 1 and 2 from that text; verse 3 deviates in only one place. He retained formal similarities, making the new text sound like the older one. The metric structure is identical: Both texts follow a pattern of

Yamina, a singing specialist with whom I worked in my host village in 1992 and 1993.

The tomb of Sidi Muḥend u Salaḥ, the local saint from Yamina's village. The tomb had been recently repainted with Amazigh symbols in 1992.

seven-syllable lines found in many genres of Kabyle poetry (Mammeri 1991b). Likewise, the ab-ab rhyme scheme is a frequent pattern in traditional poems. Finally, the opening lines of the new music, while by no means identical to those to which the earlier poem might be sung, nonetheless evoke, according to some interlocutors, the melodic outline of an *adekker* chant.

Isiditen *(The Saints), Ben Mohamed, June 1993, Paris*

Verse 1

Sidi Yaḥya Lɛidali
yemzel wezger yessker-it.
Lemluk sebɣen-t d lwali

win i-t-iɛuṣan ɣurez-it.

Anda yella Lɛidali
mi d-yebbʷeḍ wɛedaw s asqif?
Tendeh tmurt irkʷeli
a sellaḥ sefḍet lḥif.
Waqila lberḥan yeɣli

mi_gebda ṛṣas yeṭṭiẓif.

Sidi Yaḥya Lɛidali
raised from death a slaughtered cow.
The angels consider him our protector saint,
he paralyzes those who would disobey him.

But where was Lɛidali
when the enemy arrived on the doorstep?
The whole countryside cried out,
"Oh saints, make the misery disappear."
Perhaps their magical powers fell to the ground
when the bullets began to fly.

Verse 2

A Sidi Twati Aḥwayli
zdat-ek idurar knan.
Tserrḥeḍ abrid i tmuɣli

lkɛeba a-ṭ-walin lexwan.
Anda yella Weḥwayli
asmi yeṭṭwarez wegdud?
Waqila iɣuc tilelli
ireggwel i rriḥa lbarud.
Yekmen di lxelwa i tili

di leṭṭɛe yeṭṭrebbi afud.

Oh Sidi Twati Aḥwayli
before you the mountains part.
You opened up a path so the eyes of the brothers [i.e., members of a religious brotherhood]
could see Mecca [lit., the Kaaba].
But where was Aḥwayli
when the people were bound in chains?
Perhaps he dislikes freedom,
he flees the smell of gunpowder.
He hides like a hermit, staying in the shadows,
in this refuge he saves his strength.

Verse 3

Si winnat d abbudali.
Yessker taɛekkʷemt igʷelman
kul wa yebded d aḥuli
lḥan ɣef uḍaṛ ar amkan.

Anda yella webbudali
asmi runt tyemmatin
wa yeṛṛez wa d imnejli
wa yenfa wa ddaw tmedlin.
Ula d lemqam-is yeɣli
bbʷint-eṭ themmalin.

"Mr. Joe Saint" is a man of miracles.
He raised a camel-load of animal skins
and changed them into goats,
who then walked to their destination.

But where is the man of miracles
when the mothers cry,
one man broken, another exiled,
one man fleeing, another in the grave.
Even the saints' sanctuary has fallen,
swept away by the flood.

Similarity in lexical organization, formal structure, and, to a degree, melodic structure all act to minimize the intertextual distance between the new song and the *adekkeṛ*, creating a number of resonances between them. But Ben Mohamed breaks sharply with the older text by introducing dramatic shifts in rhetorical structure, forms of address, and referential content. In a typical *adekkeṛ*, after evoking the saint's miraculous feats, participants generally voice their own supplications; Yamina's text provides an example. The evocation of the saint's miracles creates a frame of expectancy, evoking the possibility that miraculous things can happen. After establishing this frame, the supplicant turns toward the divine power to formulate her request, here employing a first-person pronoun marker (-eɣ): *Ad ḥelleɣ bab Ṛebbi* (I implore my Lord, supreme master).

Ben Mohamed builds a different frame. After evoking the saint's miracles, he turns away from the saint to address the population: "Where was Sidi Lɛidali when the bullets began to fly . . . where was Sidi Aḥwayli when the enemy arrived on our doorstep?" In verses 1 and 2, the names of particular saints appear; by verse 3, all particularity is erased, replaced by a universal referent, translated here as "Mr. Joe Saint," which extends the poet's critique to the overall practice of saint veneration.[12] "Mr. Joe Saint" serves as a double-voiced word and as a focal point of the text. Through its placement within an established symmetrical pattern—whereby the listener has been led to expect the name of another saint at the beginning of verse 3—"Mr. Joe Saint" simultaneously evokes the expected referent, highlights its suppression, and serves as a parody of and commentary on the earlier poem.

The initial suppression of the intertextual gap—making the new text "sound like" the old one—is a powerful strategy for setting up maximal contrast between the two texts that is intended to subvert the message of the *adekkeṛ* poem. Ben Mohamed further widens the gap by suppressing referents that are invariably found in *adekkeṛ* chants. In particular, the new text makes no reference to God or the Prophet—intimately connected to saint veneration in the popular imagination (and present in Yamina's text).

Ben's harsh critique of the practice of saint veneration surprised me, for I had found that saints' tombs were one of the few places where women could congregate and literally let their hair down, removing their head scarves and sometimes undoing their braids. I didn't understand why he wanted to take issue with these gatherings. His response:

Ben: You have those [marabouts] who exploit the naiveté of the people, either to extort money from them, or even worse, there are those who abuse women when they're in that state. . . . Otherwise, if it's to let down . . . for a woman who can't speak in her own house because the mother-in-law always has the last word, or the husband . . . she accumulates so much [inside herself that she] . . . becomes completely crazed [in the saint's tomb]. You say to yourself, "all that violence repressed in them." . . . Today, there are women who rebel, but in most of the society the daughter-in-law can never have the last word in front of her mother-in-law, father-in-law, husband, husband's brother, even more distant relatives. And the worst is, when she becomes a mother-in-law, instead of learning from her own life, she reproduces the same system. . . . [Whereas] she should say, this must stop with me.

Jane: So on the one hand, you try to valorize traditional Kabyle culture, and on the other. . . .

Ben: I am very critical. Because we must recover our heritage, but we must not take everything. We should take only the positive side, the dynamic side of this culture, and not the sterile side. . . . The drama of Algeria, it's that we were cut off from our roots. . . . We must come to know all of them, but then be critical, change them, make them evolve.

Muḥend-nneɣ, *Idir, November 1996, Paris*

Idir transformed Ben's poem in small but important ways.[13] First, he shortened the text, combining the first four lines of verse 2 with the last six lines of verse 3. More significantly, seeking to eliminate the local specificities associated with particular saints' names, he replaced the first line of each verse (where the saint's name had appeared) with "*Muḥend-nneɣ d afeḥlī*" ("Our Muḥend is a macho man"). The referent of this line is ambiguous. While "our Muḥend" may represent a generic village saint, it can also stand for any misguided macho leader. Idir standardized the forms of address of the *adekker* lines to make the saint more distant. While in Ben Mohamed's text, the saint is evoked in both the second and third persons, Idir employs exclusively third-person forms of reference. Idir also changed the song's penultimate line: from "even his [the saint's] sanctuary has fallen" to "the village *ccix* [religious leader, from the Arabic term *shaykh*] has fallen."

Verse 1

Muḥend-nneɣ d afeḥli.	Our Muḥend is a macho man.
Yemzel wezger yessker-it.	He raised from death a slaughtered cow.
Lemluk sebɣen-t d lwali.	The angels consider him our protector saint.
Win i-t-iɛuṣan yurez-it.	He paralyzes those who would dis- obey him.
Anda akka yella ufeḥli	But where was this macho
mi d-yebbʷeḍ wɛedaw s asqif?	when the enemy arrived on the doorstep?
Tendeh tmurt irkʷeli	The whole countryside cried out,
a sellaḥ sefḍet lhif.	"Oh saints, make the misery disappear."
Waqila lberḥan yeɣli	Perhaps their magical powers fell to the ground
mi_gebda ṛsas yeṭṭiẓif.	when the bullets began to fly.

Verse 2

Muḥend-nneɣ d afeḥli.	Our Muḥend is a macho man.

S wawal idurar knan.	With only a word from him, the mountains part.
Iserreḥ abrid i tmuɣli	He opened up a path so the eyes of the brothers
lkɛeba a-ṭ-walin lexwan.	could see Mecca [lit., the Kaaba].
Anda akka yella ufeḥli	But where is this macho
asmi runt tyemmatin	when the mothers cry,
wa yerrez wa d imnejli	one man broken, another exiled,
wa yenfa wa ddaw tmedlin.	one man fleeing, another in the grave.
Ccix n taddart yeɣli	Even the village shaykh [religious leader] has fallen,
bbʷint-eṭ ṯemmalin.	swept away by the flood.

Refrain

| Ecc akkin, err akkin | Shoo, go away, |
| s tlufa-k baɛd-iyi akkin! | take your problems far away from me! |

Although Idir loses the parody that makes Ben Mohamed's text so powerful, he makes a strong critique of the living marabout, accusing him of scorning the local population and being ignorant of its hardships. He added a refrain to this effect, voiced in the imperative tense and intended to be spoken by the marabout or shaykh to the population: "Shoo, go away, take your problems far from me. . . . " The loose French translation, printed on the album jacket, is even stronger: "Get away, Go away! Let me meditate in peace. . . . Go far away from me! I'm above your trivial human faults. . . . I'm meditating! Me, I don't do politics."[14]

Idir's text situates the locus of his critique less in the practice of venerating saints who have long been dead and around whom a cultural mythology has developed than with the abuses of power perpetuated by the local village marabout. He explains:

> Idir: I am completely against the ideology [of maraboutism], but completely for the therapy, the illusion, the myth that allows you to go on. When you say that God created someone stronger than you—and yet he is supposed to have created both of us in the same way. He created you, me, with our differences but we are not unequal. Whereas here, God created Sidi Yaḥya but he didn't have more power than you or me. He just knew, via religion, how to create a zawiyya [a religious lodge where people might go into trance], a climate, an atmosphere. That, I'm not against it, the therapy and everything it can bring about. I'm against the beliefs that eclipse the human being, that subject him to the power of these saints. . . . [On the other hand] when someone has been sacralized, I don't think it is by chance. If it's a good man, strong like Ccix Muḥend U Lḥusin,[15] then we have to let the people have their illusions. But as for the petty marabouts who swarm everywhere and who write things on the thighs of women and give potions, they have to be completely attacked.
> Jane: Is that what you meant by "The village shaykh has fallen"?

Idir: The village shaykh, it's the petty marabout . . . who lies in wait for epidemics to see how many deaths there will be this year [so he can collect money from officiating at funerals], or if someone is very old, will he [the shaykh] be able to collect a small commission by praying over him [e.g., at his death], it's that spirit.

Jane: Do you think that people understood your message?

Idir: Not in the way that I'm explaining it here. But I know that I salvaged [the song] because Ben's never would have been accepted. University students might say yes, Sidi Yaḥya, we want nothing to do with him, we can even go and drink wine in his thing [*truc*, i.e., tomb]. But the average man never would have accepted it. . . . If we want to change mentalities, we need to do it slowly.

Beyond Text

In the fall of 1996, I returned to Paris and spent several weeks with my host Lounes and his daughter Sabrina, who had just immigrated to France and was working at a French bank. One night at dinner, I played Idir's *Muḥend-nney* and showed them my typed copies of Ben's and Idir's texts. Lounes's reaction surprised me. He belonged to a marabout lineage, descended from Tamkant's patron saint Sidi Ali. His half-brother, who was also Yamina's husband, had trained in a regional Islamic school (*madrasa*) and served as the shaykh of Amkan for many years. Lounes himself was deeply religious, praying the requisite five times a day, observing the Ramadan fast, and frequently quoting to me from the Quran or the Hadith. Highly respected by Amkan residents in both Algeria and France, Lounes would begin officiating as the shaykh at Amkan weddings in Paris several years later.

Ben Mohamed's text, Lounes insisted, must have been written by a believer: Only someone who had a strong faith could write like that. Taken aback, I asked him how he could interpret the closing lines of each verse as coming from a believer? Didn't the text say, "even the saint's tomb has fallen"? Lounes saw no inconsistency. There was so much misery, he said, that even the saint couldn't defend himself against it. To Lounes, this condition served only to reinforce the intensity of supplication. When I proposed that the text could be read as a parody, with the poet turning away from the saint to suggest to the population that the saints were useless, it was Lounes's turn to be shocked. If that were the intention, he said, the author would have to be an atheist—but to Lounes it was inconceivable that an atheist could have written the text, which strongly resonated with his own experience, down to the miracle performed by his own ancestor, Sidi Ali, which was similar to that allegedly performed by "Mr. Joe Saint" (Sidi Abuddali). For Lounes, the apparently minimal intertextual gap generated in the initial four lines of each verse overdetermined the rest. That is, the "traditional" frame was so strong that it not only overwhelmed Ben's intended critique but also worked to intensify the supplicatory properties of the *adekker* itself. But Lounes then turned Ben's text face down, and he looked at Idir's text

(Ben Mohamed's text *Isiditen* was never recorded or published; Idir used it as the basis for his song *Muḥend-nneɣ*). "Profoundly atheistic" were his first words. The term *afehli*, a man who gained power by force rather than wisdom, had no place in such a text, Lounes said: The angels (*lemluk*, see verse 1) would never have given him respect. He was equally outraged by the penultimate line, "the village shaykh has fallen." To him, the shaykh was a figure to be respected, but here he was being ridiculed. Paradoxically, if Idir had tried to soften Ben's critique, here the song had the opposite effect.

Lounes's reaction surprised his daughter Sabrina, who was more familiar with Idir's song. Sabrina had always thought of Idir's Muḥend as a virile man who could accomplish a lot, but she did not interpret the song as undermining the saints. Yet she did see the intended parody in Ben's text. It triggered her memories of the many conversations she had with her girlfriends and her brother during her high school and university years, when they would question why saints were venerated as if they were God, whether saints had any real power, and why rituals that seemed illogical to them—such as the practice of kissing the saint's tomb—were still being observed. She went to the saint's tomb in her village, she said, out of respect for her ancestry, but for Sabrina, the saints had little to do with divinity.

By embedding older texts into newer ones, the songs of Idir refract back onto their sources, turning the initial texts—whether praise songs, lullabies, or religious chants—into objects of culture that can invite critical reflection (cf. Kirshenblatt-Gimblett 1998). They do so by generating spaces between old and new texts in which interpretive possibilities are especially fluid. These spaces or intertextual gaps can perhaps be likened to what Homi Bhabha has called the "Third Space of enunciation"—"a contradictory and ambivalent" space that ensures "that the meanings and symbols of culture have no primordial unity or fixity . . . that even the same signs can be appropriated, translated, rehistoricized, and read anew" (Bhabha 1994: 37). Through their layered intertextuality, Idir's early songs kaleidoscopically generate this space of indeterminacy. In part through the use of intertextual relationships, Ben and Idir produced songs that could be understood as "profoundly Berber" and "readable everywhere," but they did not achieve this by joining two fields that had separate, a priori existences. Rather, through the strategies discussed in these pages, the songs simultaneously resonate as both "local" and "universal," "traditional" and "of our times," creating a single field from apparent polarities. The sites of tension pointed to in these pages both lie between and help to constitute such polarized fields: relationships to saints and to God; patrilineal forms of social organization; elaborations of new cultural values; and the generation of collective memories from a fragmented past.

Yet as my talk with Lounes shows, not everyone interprets these texts along a tradition/modernity axis, and those who do may construe the relationship differently from what the author intended. Thus even Idir "misread" Ben's *Isefra*, taking a couplet that came straight from the grandmother's tape as a veiled and somewhat awkward political statement that Ben had added to the text. If interpretation can go so far afield from authorial intention—if intertextual gaps can be construed in ways that actually contradict what the author meant—why look to the author at all? Why not simply begin with the song in circulation?

Paradoxically, one response lies in circulation itself. Looking to a song text for an underlying authorial intention (as even Lounes did) has come to seem natural precisely because songs like Idir's can circulate only with an author's name attached. A song's institutional mooring, in other words, fosters its interpretation in relation to notions of authorship. This becomes clear when comparing the new songs against their village sources, not only in terms of text but also in relation to the contrasting regimes of textuality through which they move. The regime of copyright helps to produce a notion of authorship, in turn inflecting Kabyles' relationship to what is now seen as women's song.

6 Copyright Matters

> Textualizing the author's proper name necessarily projects "the signature" into unanticipated sites for signification.
>
> —Rosemary J. Coombe, *The Cultural Life of Intellectual Properties*

Recall what may have seemed a minor point in the last chapter: Idir's politicized "misreading" of the first verse of Ben Mohamed's text *Isefra*. Imagine such a reading by a radio censor charged with eliminating political references to Berber culture—a daily occurrence in Algeria throughout the 1970s and 1980s. Picture Ben playing him the tape of the old woman singer from Ait Hichem, where those very lines appear. Now envision a related dispute in the copyright agency, this time over whether Ben should be credited as the author of a song like *Isefra*. If most of the song text can be readily located in village repertoires, shouldn't it instead be attributed to the public domain? What makes Ben the author?

Such a scenario is not merely hypothetical. Disputes about which songs have "folk" origins and whether they were properly registered extend beyond the agency, animating both living room gossip and courtroom proceedings. The more I discussed the resonances between new songs and village repertoires with singers and producers, old women and activists, the more I realized that talk about origins was frequently accompanied by a disgruntled subtext: Had the song been accurately registered (*déclaré*) at the copyright agency? That is, was it listed as a folksong or otherwise attributed to the public domain? Or was the song circulating in the singer's name? It gradually became apparent to me that the moral and creative character of songwriters was being constructed in relation to the institutional inscriptions of their songs. Moreover, the question of whether or not a song had "folk" roots turned out to be less than straightforward. For a long time, I sought to come up with a definitive response, backed up by some sort of proof—locating traces of a song in a village performance or in an older anthology, or establishing its genealogy through the singer's admission or the testimony of older women (the legal terminology here is telling). Disjunctures between these evidential realms (which carried different weights in my mind) would leave me in a quandary. What if a singer's claim did not match what I thought I had found? What if neither correlated with how the song was registered at the copyright agency? What if the singer contradicted himself or herself at different points in time? Gradually, I came to realize that the tensions surrounding the question of origins were more revealing than the responses. For whom was this a charged issue? Why?

Of the many conversations I had about origins,[1] one of the more difficult occurred with Idir in Paris.[2] I had just returned from Kabylia, and I thought he would share my enthusiasm about the songs I had found in his home village and the connections I had begun to draw with his work. I also hoped he would shed light on his own highly creative processes of transformation, explaining which changes he had made and why. But our conversation quickly soured, as he insisted not on the resonances between his repertoire and the village one, but on their differences. He would hum for me the village melodies and then his own, challenging me to explain where I thought they were similar. "There are too many levels [in my music]" he kept repeating, "*trop d'étages.*" His tone was defensive, bordering on angry, leading me to believe that this was not the first time he had had such a conversation. It was as if his own creativity was under attack.

Conversations with editors and producers revolved less around creativity than honesty. Each singer, it appeared, had acquired a reputation. Those known as "honest" accurately and consistently declared songs with village origins as belonging to the public domain. The others were seen as self-serving. (I feel compelled to mention here that Idir and Ben are considered among the "honest" ones.) Producers and editors would evaluate each other in similar terms. Dishonest editors, I was told, exploit the singers by declaring the singers' works under their own names. "There are some singers," a music video producer explained, "who have never touched a single royalty. That isn't how it should be." The opposite case can also occur: "You find the same work declared two or three times, under different names."[3]

Others cast the declaration of origins as a cultural mission. To Boualem Rabia, a former singer-songwriter with the 1970s new Kabyle song group Yugurten who has long been active in the Berber cultural movement, failure to correctly attribute the origins of a song is tantamount to erasing the Berber cultural heritage from the Algerian landscape—thus carrying out just what the government wants. If anything, listeners like Boualem may overemphasize connections between contemporary and village songs. Zahra (a pseudonym), a young immigrant friend from Amkan involved in Berber cultural activities in the diaspora, had a similar reaction. She decided to transcribe her mother's songs so she could sing them with a Berber chorus she was helping to form in Paris. She found many of the melodies almost identical to those recorded by a singing group under its own name. Furious, she sought to reclaim the songs, using her chorus to restore their connection to the villages.

What of the old women who sing the songs from which the new repertoire is drawn? "He dresses them up" (*Igerrez-itent*), one woman replied when I asked her how one singer had changed songs she knew. Some failed to comment on the transformations, or else would become confused while listening, unable to sing along with the new songs but not sure exactly why. Others would say, "It's not like that" (*maçç' akka*) and then sing their version, covering the singer's voice. Often absent were the character judgments or moral evaluations made by other listeners, but this was not always the case. Saliha (a pseudonym), an older, literate woman who spent some twenty-five years in France after a childhood in At Yenni, knew women's repertoires well. As we listened together to one singer's recording at her apartment in Paris, she was disgusted: "He added some zig-zags . . . he twisted it . . . he stole things lived by the people before there were professional singers. Had he taken it from the professionals, *they* would have received royalties." Yamina, the elderly singing specialist from the village where I worked, always made sure to tell me "on her honor" which songs belonged to the women and which to the professionals: "*I* do not lie" regularly punctuated her comments—clearly implying that others did. One older woman, who composed texts for her children's Paris-based band, went further, casting me as a potential thief. When I told her that I was interested in her poems, she thought for a minute: "There's one I can give you," she replied, "because it has already been registered with the copyright agency."

Such talk is not confined to private settings. The Kabyle singer Cherifa had recorded dozens of her own songs—many drawn almost unaltered from older female repertoires—beginning in the 1940s. Like most singers of that era, she had never registered her songs, thus leaving them open for subsequent appropriation. In a music video made for public release that Saliha made a point of showing me,[4] Cherifa lamented this and accused new singers of stealing songs she had written. I learned of a similar situation from a representative of the French copyright agency SACEM (Société des Auteurs, Compositeurs et Editeurs de Musique). The female Algerian rai singer Cheikha Remitti, who redefined the genre in the 1950s, reportedly accused a contemporary rai star of plagiarizing some of her songs.[5] According to a SACEM representative, dozens of such cases exist.[6]

In stark contrast to this running commentary, which extends from courtyards and kitchens in Algeria and France to the courtrooms of both countries, when I inquired at the copyright agency, I was met with disquieting silence. One employee initially agreed to look up, in his vast database, a few songs of whose village roots I was relatively certain. Many had been registered as original authored compositions. The next time I interviewed him, he was chagrined: He did not have the authority to provide me with this information, and begged me not to use it. I felt like a spy.

Why is the matter of how some new Kabyle songs are linked to their origins fraught with secrecy, accusation, anger, or moral evaluation? How are scholars to understand this clamor of voices, alternately raising issues of creativity and heritage, profit and property, honesty and theft? Why does how a song is legally registered seem to matter—not only to the professionals but also to a growing number of ordinary listeners? And why is it that old women are the ones who are cast—and are increasingly casting themselves—as the plaintiffs against whom singers must defend their copyright declarations, whether in kitchens or courts? While I never set out to work on copyright matters, the contentiousness surrounding these questions drew my attention. What does copyright—and in particular, the notion of public domain—mean to differently positioned Algerians? Is copyright law mediating new relationships to local women's repertoires? If so, for whom and in what ways?

Such issues are not specific to new Kabyle song, of course, but point to some of the tensions inherent in the enterprise of world music. Scholarly accounts of world music alternate between what Steven Feld (2000) calls "celebratory narratives," which valorize ethnic differences and applaud the production of hybrid identities through creative musical fusions, and "anxiety narratives," which foreground, among other things, world music's potential for exploitation and commodification. The latter are pervaded by an almost tortured moral and, in some cases, fiscal accounting (see, for example, Feld 1988, 1996; Meintjes 1990; Seeger 1996; Zemp 1996). Were particular Third World musicians ripped off by Western recording artists? What financial arrangements were made for these musicians' services? Are their royalties commensurate with their contributions? Were song credits appropriately distributed? If direct remuneration was not feasible, was a philanthropic contribution made to an appropriate institution in the native country? Ethnomusicologists making commercial recordings of local musical traditions articulate similar kinds of anxieties. In some cases, entire articles have been devoted to prescriptive advice about how to address such concerns within ethnographic practice so as to mitigate what all seem to recognize as an inherently inequitable relationship (e.g., Seeger 1996).

Like the conversations I had (or, better, the disgruntled comments in the margins of our discussions), these anxieties point beyond the morality of particular musicians to some of the fault lines that underlie intellectual property law (more popularly referred to as copyright law), illuminating some of the "intellectual quicksand" (Rose 1993: 142) on which it rests. Yet here, too, critique focuses on the perceived injustices stemming from incompatibilities between the categories of copyright law and local organizations of musical performance (see McCann 2001; Seeger 1992). This literature is similarly pervaded by a confessional tone, as scholars call for changes in the law or detail how they have attempted to overcome an inherently unjust legal system by developing creative remuneration arrangements with local musicians, often at considerable personal expense (for example, Feld 2000).

As important as this work is, it perpetuates the presumption that indigenous peoples are necessarily and exclusively disadvantaged by copyright law. As such, it fails to recognize the ways they may also be refashioning the law's categories in relation to their own organizations of discourse and performance. The ways in which the notions of authorship and the public domain are being locally engaged in relation to new Kabyle song appears to challenge one of the foundational conceits of copyright law: that authorship and the public domain constitute mutually exclusive categories. Considering copyright law in relation to Kabyle organizations of performance suggests that Kabyles are appropriating the notion of public domain to generate novel conceptions of authorship with regards to village repertoires.

The Public Domain in the Western Imagination

Much of the scholarship on intellectual property law emphasizes the constraints, prohibitions, and limits that the law places on the circulation of cultural texts (see, for example, Burke LeFevre 1992 and Gordon 1989, among others). In this view, the interests of creators and consumers stand opposed, with private, authorial control and public access in constant tension. As the creative subject, the author is thought to generate—in almost "magical" (Litman 1990: 1008) or "religious" (Rose 1993: 142) terms—original works that spring up from the depth of his (*sic*) being and constitute expressions of his spirit (see also Jaszi 1991; Woodmansee 1984). In Foucaultian language, the author-function (the way a work is institutionally inscribed in relation to a notion of authorship) operates to reward such individuals—who typically occupy a particular gendered and class position (Coombe 1998: 250–257; Spender 1982)—for reproducing dominant ideologies about the self as the point of articulation between notions of individuated autonomy, labor, and rights to property.

The public domain, in contrast, is characterized by the absence of authorship: It contains no creative subjects recognizable as such under the terms of the law, and holds nothing that can be legally constituted as individual property. This absence seems to have afforded scholars a certain license to view the public domain in romanticized or nostalgic terms.[7] Organic metaphors abound, with the public domain said to constitute a source of "raw material" (Litman 1990: 967) that authors may "harvest" or "mine" (Litman 1990: 987, 1010), a place "from which all may freely draw sustenance" (Carman 1954, cited in Lange 1992: 151 n. 20), or "the territory of the creative subconscious" (Lange 1982: 176). More prosaically, the public domain has been characterized as a "hodge-podge of unprotectible material" (Litman 1990: 993) or "the space that is left over after all else has been parsed out" (McCann 2001: 99 n. 4). It is often imbued with a celebratory or even subversive character in that its contents—unencumbered by authorship rights—belong to all and can be freely accessed by anyone (see, e.g., Burke Lefevre 1992; Gordon 1989). Further, the public domain lends itself to being "Othered." It is like the "fragile tundra of the Alaskan North: wild, vast, inaccessible, beautiful, but singularly unsuited to colonization" (Lange 1982: 176). Like other sites of modernist nostalgia, the public domain is viewed as at risk: "encroach[ed] upon" by copyright law (Lange 1992: 147) and even in need of its own legal police (Lange 1982: 176; cf. Collins 1993).

Indigenous forms of knowledge, including oral texts and music, are almost always "relegat[ed] to" (Mills 1996: 60) the public domain because they lack the criteria—nameable author, tangible medium, original product (Mills 1996: 63; cf. Jaszi 1991: 501)—that would enable them to circulate as authored compositions under the terms of intellectual property law. Indeed, as Steven Feld notes, the term "oral tradition" itself slips readily from a way of describing "that which is vocally communal" and circulates without an accompanying written text to come to mean "that which belongs to no one in particular" and thus is open to appropriation (Feld 2000: 161).[8] Anthony McCann, in an otherwise engaging discussion of Irish music, goes so far to claim that " 'public domain' is synonymous with uninhibited exploitation of the music or song" (McCann 2001: 99 n. 4). The absence of legal "protection" for so-called oral traditions seems to have called forth a compensatory response. Scholars, activists, and government officials alike frame these "public domain" materials in protectionist terms and propose prescriptive solutions to prevent their exploitation or appropriation (see, e.g., Collins 1993; Jabbour 1982; Mills 1996; Ndoye 1989). From this perspective, intellectual property law and indigenous regimes of knowledge appear to present a "fundamental clash" (Mills 1996: 60).[9] Western scholars may also gravitate toward cases in which indigenous populations are indeed disadvantaged by the law. Thus, even Rosemary Coombe, who makes it clear elsewhere in her work that intellectual property law is not only prohibitive but also productive of new forms of public expression (see, e.g., Coombe 1998, chaps. 2–4), demonstrates how Western intellectual and cultural property laws[10] force indigenous groups (in her case, First Nations peoples) to "make their claims using categories that are antithetical to their needs and foreign to their aspirations" (Coombe 1998: 241). Here, the West and the Rest are opposed, with Western law viewed as destructive and limiting as it "rips asunder what First Nations people view as integrally related" (Coombe 1998: 229).

While Western regimes of intellectual property have no doubt negatively impacted many indigenous groups, the disputes I witnessed about the origins of some new Kabyle songs suggest an alternative possibility. As Kabyles encounter the Western legal discourses through which new songs must circulate, they are reshaping these discourses to produce a markedly different understanding of the relationship between authorship and the public domain. Instead of being conceptualized as an arena where unauthored and unowned materials float freely, available to all, the notion of the public domain in Algerian discourse is being evoked to constitute entirely new conceptions of authorship—conceptions that are not opposed to the public domain but emerge from it. As copyright law introduces new ways of ordering the women's songs from which new songs are inspired, the ways women situate themselves and are being situated in relation to their songs are undergoing subtle but significant shifts. This occurs as songs that typically circulated among specific locales and events, and were indexed to particular gender and age groups, are being legally reconstituted as authored compositions.

The Public Domain in French and Algerian Copyright Law

Artistic works and, in particular, musical compositions have long posed both metaphysical and moral challenges to property law, for they transect fundamental categories on which the law depends. Indeed, ownership itself—the very premise on which the law pivots—is not straightforward: Is an artistic product the sole property of its creator, or does a broader public have rights in the work? How can a "work of the spirit," as French law terms artistic creations, be subject to individual ownership without foreclosing public access? Intellectual property law has attempted to resolve this conundrum by splitting a work, in Cartesian fashion, into intangible (immaterial) and tangible (material) components. While the former, the province of the mind or soul, are thought to be eternal, the latter, like the body, will eventually expire. In Anglo-American law, this split is understood in terms of the "ideas" that a work carries, seen as free and available to all, versus its material "expression," which is the target of the law and the source of the author's profits. French law—largely adopted throughout Continental Europe as well as in some former French colonies including Algeria—instead divides an authored composition into "moral" and "patrimonial" bundles of rights.[11]

Moral rights protect the author's sovereign spirit in the work. During the author's lifetime, they give the author certain privileges in the work (such as, for example, the right to control aspects of its circulation).[12] Ultimately, however, moral rights separate a work from the physical body of the author, for they continue to reside in the work after the author's death. In seeking to protect a work's moral attributes, the law is concerned with preventing the work from being altered in a way that violates the spirit within which it was conceived. Patrimonial rights, in contrast, link the work to the author's material presence on earth. During the author's lifetime, he or she has exclusive rights to the work and may use it to gain monetary profit.[13] Upon the author's death, patrimonial rights are transferred to his or her descendants for a set period of time whose length has continually increased, along with the expected lifespan (it is now seventy years in France, fifty in Algeria, mirroring the average time period in which the author as a material presence would linger in descendants' memories).[14] Those who inherit patrimonial rights in a work are seen as continuing the author's physical presence, and they receive all royalties until patrimonial rights expire. In Foucaultian language, the author-function shifts when all traces of an author's body—whether in actuality or as an image in memory—have disappeared.

With the expiration of patrimonial rights, a national community takes precedence over the author. Indeed, as Michel Gautreau notes, "before having patrimonial value in a commercial sense, a work of the spirit belongs to the *cultural heritage of the national community* that permitted it to be hatched" (1970: 67, emphasis added). A "work of the spirit" appears to be imagined, then, not only as the product of its creator but also in relation to the nation as a unique cultural heritage. Authors may borrow from this stock during their lifetimes, but must eventually relinquish their patrimonial rights—their material claims on the work—and deposit the work in the public domain when they vanish from the nation.

On January 1 of each year, the public domain opens up to receive the songs of all authors or composers whose material traces have disappeared. All village or "folk" songs are attributed to the public domain under this law, because the law presumes that since they have passed from generation to generation, they are beyond the seventy- or fifty-year limits.[15] This makes it clear that French copyright law has no way to categorize songs as authorless, since songs in the public domain are all assumed to have authors—now long dead—at their origin.

As already noted, in the West, the public domain is popularly conceived as a realm "free" from intervention by the law, where certain kinds of texts can circulate without regulation and are available for use by anyone. However, a recorded song may also be legally attributed to the public domain. A singer may "arrange" a public domain song (popularly referred to as a folk song) and declare it to the copyright agency as "public domain."[16] Here, the author-function undergoes a slight shift. Someone who uses a public domain melody is considered not a composer but an arranger under the law; one who borrows a public domain text is not an author but an adapter.[17] The key point here is that no song may enter the copyright register as "public domain" unless it is attached to the names of these individuals. The public domain recording circulates, in other words, only through an author-function.

Money Matters

French copyright law as concerns music is administered through SACEM. The French copyright agency also administered copyright law in Algeria until April 1973,[18] when the Algerian agency ONDA (Office Nationale des Droits d'Auteur), modeled after SACEM, was formed.[19] Even after ONDA opened, however, Algerian singers with legal residency in France would generally register their works with SACEM because they perceived it to be more "honest." All of the professional singers with whom I work operate through SACEM, not ONDA.

Contrary to popular belief, royalty payments for songs declared to SACEM as public domain do not differ significantly from those earned by "original" compositions. Royalties are determined through temporal and spatial relationships between a song's performance and its audience that the law terms *reproduction* and *representation*.[20] Reproduction describes a temporally deferred encounter between performer and audience, as when a recording is purchased for later consumption. In contexts of reproduction, royalty payments are the same for recordings of public domain songs and original compositions: When recordings are sold, the arranger and the adapter receive full royalties. Representation refers to a Kantian realm of immediate sensory perception within which spectators are in direct physical contact with the performance of a work. It includes both concert performances and radio or television broadcasts, where the spectator's immediate presence is imagined. In contexts of representation, the public domain fees are lower, following a two-tiered schedule. Fees for live concerts consist of one-twelfth of the full royalty for an original song (if arranger and adapter are the same individual, he or she receives two-twelfths of the full fee). For radio/television broadcasts, fees of one-sixteenth of the full royalty are disbursed to the arranger and the adapter each time the song is played. In both cases, the rest of the monies go into a special public domain fund established and run by SACEM.[21]

The situation in Algeria is somewhat different. Although I could not locate an official royalty schedule, the Algerian weekly *Algérie actualité* ran a series of articles on copyright in Algeria in the early 1980s. In a February 1984 piece, reporter A.D. (presumably Abdelkrim Djilali) stated that the sale of recorded works attributed to the public domain generated 6 percent of royalties for the author, as opposed to 10 percent for original compositions. This would make it far more profitable for producers to attribute a work to the public domain, and it may explain why, of the 29,000 cassette titles that A.D. claimed were registered with ONDA in 1983, more than 16,000 were so situated (A.D. 1984).[22] The public domain in Algeria is linked even more explicitly to nationalist considerations than it is in France. The use of works considered part of Algeria's national heritage requires prior authorization from the Ministry of Information and Culture (Moussaoui 1980b; cf. for Ghana, Collins 1993; for Senegal, Mills 1996 and Ndoye 1989).[23]

In both France and Algeria, any number of artists can declare themselves arrangers or adapters of the same public domain piece, and each will be paid according to the schedules described above. However, another scenario sometimes transpires. If a work that originates in the public domain (that is, a folk song) has never been declared by anyone, the first to use it may register it under his or her name as author/composer and receive full royalties, including payments from others who may use the song later. This can lead to a kind of steeplechase: "We hear tales of stolen music or scenarios . . . [based on the knowledge] that 'he who declares [registers it] first is supposed to be the author of the work'" (N.S. 1984). Here, the copyright agency has no jurisdiction to intervene unless someone contests the first singer's declaration. The agency then investigates, and if the singer is found guilty, it may "return" the song to the public domain. In that case, however, the song will still be attached to the names of all those who record it, and each will receive royalties keyed to the public domain schedule.

Finally, the public domain also includes composed songs that have never been copyrighted by an author, even if they have been recorded. This means, for example, that the recordings of earlier Maghrebi singers such as Cherifa or Cheikha Remitti that were never registered with the copyright agency may now be appropriated by a contemporary singer, who can lawfully put them in his or her name and receive full royalties.[24] One exception: An author-composer may borrow up to eight measures of another work with impunity, whether or not the work is in the public domain. (The extensive and generally undeclared use of village refrains in contemporary song may fall under this provision.)

The Public Domain in Algerian Discourse

It is with the songs that are (or "should be") declared to the copyright agency as "public domain" that Algerians seem to be most concerned. For them, the term public domain does not appear to evoke an undifferentiated mass of unauthored and freely circulating material. Rather, a public domain designation marks local repertoires in an altogether novel manner. It designates songs as cultural heritage, it associates them with a notion of origin, it imbues them with an aura of belonging to a national (or, in the Kabyle case, subnational) community, and it creates the possibility of imagining original authors. These new associations are then indexed to the executors of the local repertoires; in Kabylia, this usually means older women.

That women tend to be associated with cultural heritage under nationalist regimes is well attested, but less attention has been paid to how such an association may be transforming relationships to women's knowledge. Old Kabyle women were frequently described to me as archives or libraries containing vast amounts of valuable material waiting to be tapped. This depiction is resonant with Western definitions of the public domain, but with a key difference: It locates what the West considers public domain material not in a neutral zone of free circulation but within female bodies. Such statements are made not only by politically active youth interested in reclaiming Berber heritage but also, increasingly, by the women themselves, who are coming to see their knowledge as worthy of recording. When I expressed interest in learning women's songs during one weekly female gathering at a local saint's tomb in Amkan, several older women urged me to bring my cassette and they would "fill it up" (*a neççur takkasseṭ*). On another occasion, a woman informed me that I needed not just a cassette but a *fawṭay* (armchair, from French *fauteuil*) so I could sit back, listen, and get it right. A few women seasoned by the taping practices of an ethnomusicologist native to the village[25] even asked me for a *purbbwar* (tip, from French *pourboire*) in exchange for their songs. In short, as women's songs start to circulate as heritage, the ways women—as the producers of these songs—are perceived also begin to shift. Women are increasingly being seen and seeing themselves as containers for and generators of cultural value.

A particularly vivid illustration of the way women's knowledge is being revalued as cultural capital via new Kabyle songs took place at a wedding in Amkan in the summer of 1993. Hend, founder of a new village children's chorus and a drummer in Tamkant's wedding band (*iḍbellan*), had the chorus perform Idir's song *Tamacahuṭ n tsekkurt* (The Tale of the Partridge), which originates in a well-known folktale (the tale was published in Mammeri 1980: 222–225, and was initially released in 1973 on the flip side of the 45 containing *A vava inouva*). As the children sang, Hend invited the old women to rise together and dance. The "dance of the old women" caught on and was repeated at the next wedding, keyed again by Idir's song. "It's for our 'class of people,'" one woman said to me as she rose, smiling, to dance with her peers.

Viewing women as holders of heritage is not the same, however, as seeing them as authors. Processes of preservation alone need not necessarily generate an authorial relationship to the village material. How is it that many Kabyle listeners—including some older women—are beginning to identify women as the "original" authors of the older songs from which the new ones are sourced? The possibility of imagining women as authors is enabled in part through the particular modes of textual circulation entailed within copyright law. When a song is registered in the public domain, it must circulate in the name of the singer who so situated it (cf. Bigenho 2002: 220–221). The singer's name and a public domain attribution, placed up against a work that is already familiar from local performance contexts, seem to open a new, shadowy space where the figure of an earlier author can then emerge. In the contrary case, if the singer "dishonestly" declares the song in his or her own name, the work is nevertheless known to many listeners. Here, although the singer's name appears to erase the possibility of an earlier author, it may make that possibility loom larger still. By trying to write over the new "public domain" space where an earlier author can now be envisioned, that space of erasure may become even more prominent and thus all the more contentious. In short, as songs are lifted out of the villages, registered in the copyright agency, and recirculated in a singer's name, the women who know the songs from which the new songs are sourced are beginning to be imagined, and to imagine themselves, through a lens of authorship. The form of authorship through which women are coming to be seen is not, however, identical with the romantic view of the single creative individual, but rather assumes a collective character, inflected by local conventions of production and performance.

The Performance Economy in Kabylia

Contrast the modes of authorship and circulation made available through copyright law with the organization of women's songs within village performance settings.[26] Songs in village contexts are indexically linked to discrete performance events and are governed by particular participation frameworks. One song might be sung at a specific moment in every wedding, and only then; another might be pulled out once a year, in a particular saint's tomb, to commemorate only that saint. Furthermore, not just anyone can sing. The women who participate in wedding songs, for instance, must have both a genealogical connection to and a good relationship with the family hosting the event. Women's wedding songs also participate in an economy of matrimonial exchange, marking key moments in which food, money, and, of course, the bride herself, move from one patrilineage to another.

Women's singing awakened me at seven o'clock in the morning on a hot July Thursday—the start of the Algerian weekend—in Amkan in 1993. Said, a twenty-six-year-old member of my host family, was getting married, and around a dozen women of his extended family had gathered to begin preparing food for the several hundred people who would be arriving for meals over the next two days. As they tackled the eighteen crates of fruits and vegetables that would be served to the guests, the women sang songs of celebration and praise for the groom (*isli*) and his family in two antiphonal choruses, marking the opening of the wedding event. The singing felt fairly informal to me. While older singing specialists like Yamina tended to start the verses, women of any age could join in. Songs were interspersed with talking and laughing, and a woman could move into and out of the songs, alternately singing and chatting with her neighbors.

I continued cleaning vegetables with the women until just past noon, when I donned my wedding finery and went with a group of some thirty guests specially invited to a traditional luncheon at the home of the bride (*tislit*). Called *ṭṭeeyen*, this event also entails a substantial gift of food from the groom's family to the bride's (in this case, sixty kilograms of semolina flour, fifty kilograms of beef, and fifteen liters of olive oil). As we waked down to Tamkant's public square and piled into two hired vans for the seven-mile (twelve-kilometer) trip to the bride's house, we were dispatched by the songs of women, who accompanied us to the square in two groups, arms joined as they sang. At one point, a younger woman grabbed a jerry can and began drumming as others clapped, layering a rhythmic texture into the women's songs.

Singing stopped at the dinner hour, when the women served the meal they had prepared earlier that day. As dusk fell, I walked with Said's sister Samira and her female cousins to the public square I call Xamsa Iberdan ("Five Paths"), a broad, sloping intersection where five paths come together. Each of us carried a *takwersiṭ*, a small, low stool that we would sit on for the next five or six hours. There we joined a crowd of close to five hundred people—virtually the entire summer population of Tamkant plus a few families related by marriage from other village sections. I sat with the women on one side of the square, our stools pressed so closely together that we would have to clamber over each other as we got up to dance. The men stood together on the other side, surrounding a troupe of four *iḍbellan* musicians—two zurna players and two drummers. As the musicians began to play, most women of the groom's family got up to dance, transforming the dusty patch of earth into a dance floor aglow with their shiny white dresses and red and yellow outer-skirts (*fuḍa*-s), adorned with imaginative designs crafted from brilliant rickrack and glittering sequins. Dancing continued, with most wedding guests participating at one point or another, until midway through the evening, when Said's mother, sister, and aunts walked back to his home to gather objects for the henna ceremony: colorful woven blankets; cushions; a candelabra; a basket containing eggs, wheat, and a *tabzimt* (a piece of his mother's jewelry indicating that she had borne a son); another basket with cookies, candies, and cubes of sugar; and, of course, a box of henna dye and a vase of water. Processing back to the square amid loud ululations and *iḍbellan* music, they set up the objects on the blanket and began applying henna to Said's right hand, a ritual that takes place on the first night of every wedding. As they did so, a small group of older women led by Yamina sang in two antiphonal choruses, alternately praising Said and his family and evoking the courage, prosperity, and long life that the henna would bring to them. Perhaps in recognition of the groom's new potential as a progenitor, the women singing for the henna ceremony had to be well past their childbearing years. Moreover, they all were closely related to Said. Although women from more distant patrilineages knew the songs and would sing them at weddings in their own families, it would not have done for them to join in. For a younger woman to sing would have consti-

The groom and his mother before the henna ceremony in Amkan, July 1993.

The groom's father and grandmother at the henna ceremony. The jewel (called *tabzimt*) on the grandmother's forehead indicates that she has borne a son.

tuted an even more serious breach of propriety (*d lɛib*); it is hard for me to imagine that the idea to sing along would even have crossed the minds of the young women I knew.

If the henna songs (*leɣna l_lḥenni*) symbolically marked Said's passage from youth to man, they also accompanied monetary gifts. As the older women continued to sing, a representative from each invited family got up to place several bills on the blanket in front of Said. Yet although the songs served to sonically carve out the ritual space of the henna ceremony, they were barely listened to; while the women sang, most other guests were talking at full voice. Like the eggs, candles, and other ritual objects placed around the groom, the henna songs appeared to serve an instrumental function, marking this moment as transitional rather than constituting a focal point in their own right. This may be changing: At Said's wedding, the women were seated in close proximity to one another, but did not stand out; at another, they had to scramble over others to be near enough to each other to sing together. At a third, however, which was hosted by Zahra's family, the old women—some of them vacationing immigrants from Paris—brought their stools to the center of the circle, positioning themselves somewhat apart from the crowd, and sang while Zahra, sister of the groom and an immigrant for most of the year, recorded them.

On the second day of Said's wedding (Friday), old women's songs punctuated three events, all similarly set off as times of heightened transition: when the groom's family went to get the bride, displaying their pride in numbers with a procession of fifty-one cars plus a large rented bus, horns honking all the way; when the bride left her home;[27] and when the bride arrived in Amkan and crossed the threshold of the groom's house. Here, too, the women's singing was not a focal point; indeed, sometimes it was almost covered by the loud zurnas and drums of the *iḍbellan* troupe. On the third day of the wedding (Saturday), songs would usually mark two further moments, both meant to encourage fertility: a small, private ceremony at the groom's house where the new bride is outfitted with a special belt (*aggus*), which is fastened around her waist by the groom's father or brother (or, in the case of one wedding I attended, by the groom himself); and a procession to the village fountain, where the bride gives a young boy from the groom's family a sip of water drawn from the well (which he would promptly spit out, the well in Tamkant being polluted). (The events of the third day did not take place at Said's wedding, as he and his wife left immediately for a honeymoon in France, but I participated in them at another wedding.) At the end of the wedding, the women singers were acknowledged by the host family; although they were not paid for their songs (as were the male musicians), each woman received a stack of beignets or a box of store-bought French-style pastries.

Weddings are the sites where women's performance is the most public, but women also sing in other places outside their own homes. For the birth or circumcision of a boy, they gather in the home of the male child and sing songs of celebration and praise, customizing the texts—as with wedding songs—to the particular family (see Mahfoufi 1991, chap. 1). During religious festivities at saints' tombs, women engage in melodic chanting of religious poetry called *adekkeṛ*. In addition to a shared corpus of *adekkeṛ* texts and melodies, older women know particular *adekkeṛ* poems for each saint, which may be chanted as infrequently as once a year.

Kabyle women's songs circulate in relation to events, not individuals. Indeed, the songs are referred to by the action they help to produce: songs of applying henna (*leɣna l_lḥenni*); songs for picking up the bride, taking her to the well, or attaching the *aggus* around the bride's hips (*leɣna t_tislit*). Notions of authorship are rarely invoked. As the Kabyle novelist and poetry collector Malek Ouary put it, "In Kabylia . . . we are not at all interested in the personality of the creator [of a poem or song]; we don't even remember their names. Only the most famous [poets] are able to transcend this indifference and leave their mark. . . . Even then, it does not even enter their heads to exercise ownership rights in their work" (Ouary 1974: 21–22). Particular stanzas are occasionally attributed to specific women. For instance, one of my interlocutors shared with me several henna verses she had created; another recited for me her own poem about a ne'er-do-well bride from the perspective of the mother-in-law. The women are not considered proprietors of their texts, however; the texts enter the shared village repertoire, their authors are gradually forgotten. Moreover, songs travel in village performance contexts not as unique and inalterable cultural products but as part of a fluid, improvisatory musical economy. Within related genres, text and music are frequently detachable. The same text can be sung to a variety of melodies; conversely, the same melody can accompany any number of texts (Berkani 1972; Boulifa 1990 [1904]; Mecheri-Saada 1979). During my first working session with Yamina, I told her that I could sing the melody of a wedding song but didn't know the words: Could she tape them for me? I hummed a few bars and she sang what I thought was a full rendition of the song. Later, her niece Samira, helping me to transcribe, told me that Yamina had given me pieces of many different poems that would be sung to that tune during different phases of the wedding ceremony; the same tune, Samira said, could be used for many different sets of words.

While women's songs travel and are shared by one or more publics, they are not understood as belonging to a nationalized public domain. They are not subject to copyright regulation, do not generate royalties, and are not yet tokens of heritage. These songs do not freely circulate, equally available to all—as a public domain designation would suggest—but are indexically linked to specific events and participation frameworks. Only when the songs are extracted from local circulation, inscribed in a national register, and recirculated through an individual singer's name are they labeled "public domain," becoming available for national and international consumption. But as women's songs enter world music circuits via a public domain designation, they carry with them the histories of their use, which inflect the ways the public domain is conceived by those familiar with the songs' local lives. As songs previously indexed to distinct events and participation frameworks are drawn together as tokens of cultural heritage and are connected to the emergent figure of an "original" author, that author almost always is imagined as female. By extension, the "public domain" in Kabyle discourse appears to be not neutral but gendered, acquiring a primarily female aura. At the same time, the figure of the author imagined by some Kabyles does not appear to be that of the romantic individual with vested property rights in his or her work, but rather is a collective female entity (cf. Bigenho 2002: 217–225).

This collective figure may also work, however, to obscure a division of musical labor that goes officially unacknowledged. Younger Kabyles seem to think that in the past everyone knew the traditional songs, but that this knowledge had been gradually lost, surviving in the memories of a small group of older women whom they call specialists. It seems at least as likely, however, that the role of female poetry specialist has long been important to the organization of village performances. This may explain why specialists like Yamina or Saliha are particularly concerned with the appropriation of women's songs by the new Kabyle singers. Kabyle conventions of female morality make it unlikely that a woman would publicly claim and display her specialized knowledge; instead, she whispers it to the other women in her group and they sing collectively. If this is the case, disputes around copyright may also point to some of the unarticulated tensions between individual expertise and collective knowledge in Kabyle women's performance.

To return now to the clamor of voices with which I began: Evaluating the singers in terms of their character, motives, honesty, and so forth may be understood less as a critique of any one singer than as a way of participating in and commenting on a broader reclassification of local repertoires to nationalist ends. Intellectual property law, rather than "protecting" an existing national public, is helping to produce that public, and this occurs in part through the contested category "public domain." Older women, in turn, are increasingly viewed—and sometimes view themselves—as authors of what is now becoming known as "their" repertoire.

As Mark Rose notes, copyright law operates through a "chain of deferrals" that moves from property rights to a transcendent individual spirit. The legal concept of intellectual property is rooted in the particularity of the text, which in turn is underwritten by the notion of originality, itself guaranteed by the concept of personality, behind which stands original genius (Rose 1993: 128). Only such a "transcendent signifier" could provide copyright law with "a category beyond the economic to warrant and ground the circulation of literary commodities" (Rose 1993: 128). With new Kabyle song, this chain of deferrals is constituted in new ways. The form of authorship attached to the recorded song text recursively provokes a notion of an earlier author. It is this second author—the Kabyle woman—who is viewed as transcendent, for it is she who serves as a vehicle for the "culture" latent in the work. Ultimately it is culture, thought to be beyond material interest, that serves as the guarantor of a work's "spirit." Small wonder, then, that the economic value that accrues to the new songs provokes such heated debate.

The intertextual relations between new and old songs extend far beyond the simple embedding of one text in another, entailing the interpenetration of Western and indigenous regimes of textuality. In locally specific ways, copyright law, understood as a particular mode of circulating texts through their attachment to authors, is being used to generate new relationships to women's repertoires in Algeria and to produce new notions of who can be imagined as an author and how authorship itself can be conceived. New songs also move beyond the author, however, circulating as signs of an indigenous modernity in novel performance spaces.

Part Three.   *Performances*

7   Staging Gender

July 21, 1993, Tamkant. Said, the oldest son of my host family, was getting married, and his friends in Amkan's four-year-old village cultural association had been preparing a surprise. For several months, they had been working with village boys and girls to create a chorus that would animate the evening urar at Said's wedding. Although I feigned interest, I failed to share their anticipation, privately picturing the off-key, uninspired, and, well, boring children's concerts that I had both sung in and sat through in the Boston suburbs where I grew up. When the night of the urar arrived, I settled in to wait until the chorus finished and the "real culture" returned. But during the performance, my boredom gradually gave way to profound interest. Through the chorus, I realized, village youth were attempting to reconfigure the way relations of generation, lineage, and especially gender were imagined and experienced. As they put it, the chorus was a way to begin to change people's "mentalities."

Struggles for Berber/Amazigh identity seek not only to recover heritage but also to build the foundation for a new "project of society" (*projet de société*). In Algerian parlance, the term refers simultaneously to the premises and principles on which a national government should be founded and to the social practices that could help bring this vision into being. Since the 1980s, two competing "projects of society"—broadly conceived as secular-democratic and Islamist—have framed ideological debates in the Algerian public sphere. Kabyle writer Tahar Djaout, in the last column he published before he was assassinated by the Armed Islamic Group in June 1993, characterized these positions in evolutionary terms, casting the democrats as "the family that moves forward" and their opponents as "the family that moves backward" (Djaout 1993: 15). For Djaout, to "move forward" meant to work toward transparent, democratically run institutions and away from factional or clan-based politics; to cultivate an "open-minded" rather than a "fatalistic" world view; and to advocate for gender parity in mode of dress, access to education, the work force, and even political office. To "move backward" was to return to a past social order perceived as autocratic and obscurantist.[1]

Gender is perhaps the most contentious and problematic field on which these polarized visions of Algeria's future are being played out. At issue is the very nature of the Algerian public sphere: Should it be gender-segregated, following what some consider Islamic principles—the most visible of which is the practice of using the veil to mark women's bodies? Or should it be secular (*laïque*), organized through what Algerians call *"la mixité"*—awkwardly translated as mixed-gender interaction—in which men and women occupy the same public space on apparently equal footing? The dispute took an especially bloody turn in the mid-1990s, when women's bodies literally were caught in the crossfire. The Armed Islamic Group (GIA) announced that it would start shooting at unveiled women; in return, Berber militias threatened to target women who chose to veil. In such a climate, a man's position—or as Algerians would say, his "mentality"—with regards to *la mixité* became the most telling index of his political leanings.

Kabyle youth use the same evolutionary language to characterize divisions that they perceive in their own villages. Traditionally, Kabyles have used a language of shame or modesty to explain why young women are hesitant to walk alone outside their village section, why some girls stop schooling when they reach adolescence, why young men defer to their fathers and uncles in village assemblies, or why immigrant women refrain from smoking in front of their families (cf. Abu-Lughod 1986). The commonly used verb *iseṭḥi* describes the feeling of modesty (sometimes expressed as shyness or reserve) and its accompanying behaviors, called "relationships of respect," expected in front of one's social superiors. Relationships of respect prevail between individuals in particular social categories. From a male perspective, these include a man and his parents (father, mother, grandparents); a man and all of his siblings; a son-in-law and his parents-in-law; and, more generally, any relationship between a man and all women with the exception of his wife when they are in an intimate and private setting (Mahfoufi 1991: 53–54). From a female perspective, relations of respect should prevail between a woman and her father, brothers, uncles, and grandparents as well as her parents-in-law, and between a woman and all men outside her household. Relations of respect are relaxed when women are among themselves (unless an elderly woman is also present), when men are among themselves (unless one of the categories above is present, such as an older male relative), or between Kabyle men and women who are perceived as outsiders (such as European or American women), unless these women are associated in some way with the lineage-based organization of the village (for example, guests of a family, as was my situation).

Increasingly, however, relations of respect are being reframed as reflections of the "old mentalities" that need to be swept aside in order for the village to enter modernity. Activist youth are taking it upon themselves to reform their own villages by introducing new mentalities, or "evolved" ways of thinking, regarding questions of generation, lineage, and, especially, gender. Key sites where these projects of reform are being formulated are Amazigh cultural associations, which "sprouted like potatoes" (in one man's words) after the violent youth demonstrations that took place throughout Algerian cities in October of 1988 brought to an end the twenty-five-year rule of the FLN (National Liberation Front) and led to a multiparty system.[2] Change was already in the air—in 1987, the Algerian government had recognized the right of citizens to form local, non-political associations without governmental authorization[3]—but it was not until after the October riots that cultural associations began to flourish.[4] At the end of the summer of 1989, 154 youth-dominated associations had been officially established in Kabylia; by 1995, there were reportedly more than 1,000 (Chaker 1995).[5] While a handful are located in urban areas, most are found in the region's 1,500 mountain villages. And the phenomenon has also taken hold in the diaspora.[6] A basic goal of the associations is to promote the Tamazight language and Amazigh culture. Some associations offer language classes; the most enterprising produce mimeographed newsletters or linguistic manuals. Members also gather what they consider endangered cultural capital, such as proverbs, folklore, traditional medicinal remedies, the "original" names for plant and animal life, or artifacts that have fallen into disuse.

Many associations have another project that is less tangible but far more ambitious. Young Kabyle activists are creating new kinds of performances—both staged events and seemingly more mundane interactions such as meetings—to develop and display novel forms of social relationships. During the early 1990s, cultural associations on both Algerian and Parisian sides of the village of Amkan were using performances to bring what they saw as modern ways of thinking to bear on local practices. For them, performances operated as sites of heightened reflexivity (Bauman 1977; Turner 1986) through which they could critique prevailing forms of social organization and experiment with new identities. At the same time, the cultural association performances constituted nodal points where discourses and practices that tend to be cast as local, national, and global were being brought into a new configuration—one in which gender was profoundly implicated. In using the terms local, national, and global, I do not imply that they represent inherently distinct orders of reality that come into contact in performance. Rather, I use them to invoke different "acts of positioning" (Tsing 1993: 31) through which actors orient themselves to particular contexts and concerns. These acts address—singly or together—village-based morality, national ideology, or performance forms associated with a world stage. The village here is not a target of "global" forces presumed to lie beyond it, but a site where representations and experiences of locality and globality are being co-produced.

In the Algerian case, a new performance form—the children's chorus—was being introduced into an already familiar performance landscape, the wedding. This produced a break with expected practices, interrupting the repetitive performance of gender (Butler 1999 [1990]) and opening a reflexive space that both enabled novel possibilities for gender interaction and produced new grounds for critique of existing practices (much like the "intertextual gaps" that, as we have seen, allowed for critical reinterpretation of older songs by embedding them in newer ones). In the Parisian case, the very creation of the cultural association itself was a performance through which its founders—including a young woman who would be elected president—intentionally sought to model for the larger village what new forms of gender relationships might look like. Talk coming from villagers in both Paris and Algeria converged around the public presentations of the young female university student who served as the as-

Kabyle artifacts that have fallen into disuse are being reappropriated as signs of cultural heritage by young activists. These objects were on display in Tizi Ouzou on April 20, 1993.

Old Kabyle pottery is laid out and labeled. Although this exhibit took place in Tizi Ouzou, village cultural associations also mount their own displays.

sociation's first president. In some quarters, she was evaluated as someone who was not constrained by "old mentalities," while in others, she was described as the "village donkey." Caught between these competing evaluations, the young woman ultimately found herself in a situation where her own performance was closed down, her words ventriloquized by one of the association's (male) founders. In her case, experimenting with alternative social roles and practices led not to "new mentalities" but to communicative breakdown. The debates surrounding the creation of the cultural association also speak to the ways in which the Algerian and Parisian populations of the village have each other constantly in view, each imagining how their actions and initiatives might appear to those across the sea.

Both the Algerian and Parisian cases give rise to a vexed paradox: As men seek to construct themselves as proponents of *la mixité*, they are dependent on recruiting women who will enact their vision (and on excluding those who will not). To what degree, then, do these initiatives simply reinscribe gender hierarchy under the guise of a project that is characterized as forward-looking? At the same time, although men may be helping to create new subject positions for women, their control does not necessarily extend to the performances of the embodied women—their sisters, cousins, daughters—who take up these positions. Those disjunctive moments when women's performances deviate from the "evolved" roles into which activist men seek—albeit ambivalently—to place them make apparent some of the competing pressures women face as they attempt to balance modernist gender ideology with village-based social morality.[7]

Dancing toward *La Mixité*

August 11, 1993, Tamkant. It was another hot summer night, and the third of four late-night weddings in a row. I watched with jaded interest as first women, then men, occupied the dancing space—a circle carved into a dusty village square, around which women spectators sat on one side and men stood on the other. The party seemed to be winding down. Many were readying to walk the mountain paths back to their homes. Suddenly, our attention was galvanized as three young boys, ages nine to thirteen, came out onto the patch of earth that served as a dance floor. The boys danced with all they had, one tying a scarf around his hips for added effect. Excitement crescendoed when after several minutes, three young girls went out to join the dance. At first, the girls danced in their own circle, as is customary among Kabyle women, but it was not long before the six children had formed three male-female couples. Amid intense rhythmic clapping, ululations, and shouts of encouragement from the wedding guests, the children continued their dance for nearly an hour—three to four times longer than most dances last. What mesmerized the crowd was the suggestion that a deeply rooted behavioral code was beginning to shift. The young boys and girls, most in early puberty, were unrelated. A brother and sister were indeed dancing—but not with each other. That the couples were not considered "just children" is evidenced by the fact that as the dancing heated up, each girl discarded her *fuḍa*—an outer skirt that Kabyle women don whenever they go out of the house—and was outfitted with an *aggus*—a thick woven belt wound tightly around the hips that signals a woman's eligibility and emphasizes her sensual beauty.[8] It was as if the three dancing couples had begun to open a new social imaginary: The unthinkable, in Bourdieu's terms, was becoming thinkable (1977: 21). A shift in "mentalities" was taking place.

The dancing of the children was not an innocent event. It was the direct result of a conscious effort to change ideas about gender that members of Amkan's cultural association (created in 1989) had been preparing for several years. They had initially formed a theater troupe as one way to provide humorous critique of such subjects as the lifestyles of immigrants or the corruption of local politicians. But after four years, the young men were frustrated. For one thing, they had difficulty finding women who would agree to appear onstage. This was not as clear-cut as it may sound, for several women had reportedly volunteered to join them (particularly during the later seasons) but were found wanting: One, an immigrant, was rejected because she apparently did not know the language well enough; others were rebuffed for having what the men saw as "ulterior motives." The upshot was that men ended up playing the women's roles. Moreover, the men felt that their message was not getting through—people laughed at the plays, but nothing changed. So in early 1993, one enterprising twenty-six-year-old, Hend (a pseudonym), decided to try another performance medium. Seeking to instill a new relationship to *la mixité* in the young while setting an example for the audience, Hend mounted a children's chorus under the cultural association's auspices. It was no accident that the young adolescents who got up to dance all came from this newly created group.

Hend viewed the chorus as a means of redressing internalized beliefs and behaviors surrounding gender. At the same time, he hoped to break down intra-village alliances by recruiting children from all four of Amkan's village sections. Getting the chorus started had been no simple matter. He first had to fight for permission from the tajmaᶜat to use a public building (also the site of tajmaᶜat meetings) for rehearsals. Permission was initially accorded only to children who lived in the Tamkant section of the village—others were considered outsiders. To recruit members, Hend went to see each child's father, explaining the project and asking for cooperation. He had wanted older teenagers, but each time he would request the elder daughter, the father would propose the younger one. Sometimes, permission granted would later be withdrawn with no explanation.

Hend described to me how he felt when he entered the first rehearsal.[9] "I was shocked," he recounted. "I saw a group of girls in one corner, and a group of boys in another. That blew me away, it just killed me [Ça, ça m'a énormément choqué, ça m'a tué]. These kids are innocent. . . . If I created this [chorus], it was in order to change, to revolutionize, if you will, people's mentalities, to give an example." But Hend said nothing to the children and simply began to teach them songs, interspersed with informal skits to foster a climate of play and trust. As weeks passed, his strategy began to bear fruit. As he told it, the children became so engrossed in the work of the chorus that they began to forget about whom they were standing next to: A boy would find himself between two girls, or vice versa. By the end of the summer, things had become completely "normal," said Hend: "The children play together . . . without complexes, without anything." So much so that on a hot summer's evening, they were able to galvanize an entire village.

The children's chorus appears to have carved out a new space in which modernist gender ideologies were being brought into relation with village-based performance practices. What was being performed onstage was *la mixité* itself. The particular pieces the chorus sang were perhaps less important than the fact that boys and girls were performing together and interacting in new ways. The children's bodies became conduits for Hend's vision. He had specifically arranged them onstage to promote mixed-gender interaction. At their first show, the children stood in a semicircle on the makeshift plywood platform, with several boys on the left, the five girls in the center, and the rest of the boys on the right. Several concerts later, Hend deliberately rearranged them in a boy-girl-boy-girl order. For one number, the children executed a simple dance step while they clapped and sang. For another, Hend brought one boy and one girl to the front of the stage, where they performed a short dance as a couple—in effect modeling the kind of dance that would come later.

The stage itself helped to constitute the performances as sites where new gender relations could be tried out. Stages had no place in the traditional *urar* (wedding dance); in 1993, they were hastily erected only for certain kinds of performances on the morning of the event itself. In Amkan, the traditional *iḍbellan* (wedding band) performs while standing in the men's section of the audience. Older women who sing as henna is applied to the groom's hand sit among the other women guests and sometimes are not even in immediate proximity to each other. Only recently, with the hiring of outside dance bands who use electric instruments that require amplification, have stages begun to be built and microphones rented. Even then, however, the dance bands are not themselves the focus of the event but are engaged to energize the dance. The chorus, in contrast, was not performing to accompany another activity but was configured as a focal point. This produced a new "organization of attention" (Berger and Del Negro 2002) in which performer and spectator positions were constituted around the consumption of a spectacle rather than collective participation in a shared event.

If, as Judith Butler has suggested, gender is produced through performative repetition, and if changes in gender identities involve a break, even partial, with that structure of repetition, the chorus performance appears to have constituted such a disjunctive moment. Two aspects of their performance merit particular attention because they were taken up almost immediately within new contexts, opening up the possibility that they would become sedimented into new social practices. One day after the chorus performance, a group of boys and girls who lived across from me (but who were not in the chorus) began singing one of the chorus songs, even reenacting the dance steps and clapping that had accompanied it. Here, the new modes of gender interaction staged in performance inflected local forms of play. The couple dance on stage had an even more public impact, as three chorus couples subsequently danced at the urar itself for nearly an hour, commanding the attention of the entire audience. In Amkan, men and women would typically dance in gender-segregated circles or lines; sometimes men and women of the wedding family would dance together in a group, but never as couples. That the children formed male-female couples broke entirely, then, with ways that gender segregation was conventionally reproduced in dance.

The forward-looking vision of *la mixité* that Hend sought to create through the chorus drew its authority from the fact that it was framed not as a merely local initiative but in relation to broader struggles for Amazigh identity. This was achieved through his selection of repertoire. Much of the chorus's music was drawn from the recordings of the most acclaimed new Kabyle singers—especially Idir, Ideflawen, Aït Menguellet, and Ferhat. This clearly brought Amazigh subnational interests to a local stage, where they were enacted and instantiated in the very bodies of the children performers. At the same time, new Kabyle song lent authority to other numbers in the repertoire. This was especially apparent in one piece—a poem that Hend wrote about the death of Kabyle cultural leader Mouloud Mammeri, which his sister Dehbia recited. Behind her, the chorus hummed the melody of one of the most well known new songs, Ferhat's *Tizi bb wass-a* (Ferhat 1979), which has become a Kabyle political anthem of sorts, sung at rallies and even intoned by a group of political prisoners as they made their way from the courthouse to the jail. Hend thus contextualized his sister's performance in relation to the authoritative protest song made popular by Ferhat, and by extension, to the broader struggle for Amazigh identity that both Ferhat and Mammeri embodied. Finally, of course, the new performer and spectator subject positions enacted by the chorus drew on an organization of performance associated with concerts of new Kabyle song and related popular music genres.

The repertoire alone does not necessarily determine its reception. At a wedding I attended in another village, culturally active young men decided to perform some new Kabyle songs during a part of the wedding usually reserved for antiphonal male and female singing (an unusual arrangement that is apparently specific to that village). They rented microphones, brought out their guitars, and launched into the new songs, effectively silencing the women. Here, the appropriation of new song worked to produce a gendered segregation of a usually "mixed" performance space. Constrained by the force of the performance by their brothers and cousins, the women were cast in the unfamiliar role of passive listeners, where their sole recourse was to complain of boredom. In the case of the Tamkant children's chorus, in contrast, the choice of repertoire was aligned with the organization of performance in such as way as to enable discourses of Amazigh ideology and practices of *la mixité* to be mapped onto each other and experienced together.

"It Was a War in the House"

The challenges posed by the chorus proved substantial. Recruitment was initially difficult. During the first year, not only were all the children from Tamkant, but they came from within Hend's *adrum* (patrilineage), and most were from two of the *adrum*'s four subpatrilineages—Hend's own and a closely related one. To recruit members, Hend relied on established communicative conventions. He made no public announcement but drew on personal ties to young men of his own age throughout the village and used his own family ties within Tamkant. Getting boys to join was relatively easy, so he focused on finding girls. Hend described to me his initial efforts: "I didn't have a relationship with the families [of the other three villages], so I would ask the brother [of a girl I wanted] . . . he would give his okay, but then would never do anything. . . . I got sick of waiting for them, so I decided to create [the chorus] just in Tamkant. There, I could go about it directly. One weekend I got home from work, I contacted all the parents, I saw them all, almost all of them gave me permission, but then some people seemed to regret it, pulled back, refused to let their sisters or daughters go, so the beginning was really difficult."

The oldest girl in the chorus was Hend's own seventeen-year-old sister Dehbia (a pseudonym). Her presence was to prove controversial. By the time of the third wedding performance of the season, the chorus was gaining approval from many villagers and grudging acceptance from even the most recalcitrant. But this night was different. It was the wedding of Hend's brother, and Hend's father would be present. Hend had with much difficulty persuaded his sister to perform a solo. Stepping to the front of the stage, Dehbia spoke clearly and dramatically into her handheld microphone in front of hundreds of wedding guests. She recited a text written by Hend that betrayed some of Hend's own ambivalence about gender relations. The text simultaneously evoked a perceived gulf between men and women, a belief that men had to liberate women in order to gain their own freedom, and the apparent enmeshment of women in the domain of love. Hend built it around traditional proverbs that locate woman as the foundation (*asalas*) of the house and man as the roof. In the text, the man complains that the foundation is falling apart; he has done everything in his power, he says, to liberate his wife, including quitting his job to attend to the crumbling foundation. From the woman's perspective, no man has ever come to liberate her; if her husband quit his job, it was because he was seeking any excuse not to work. The man laments his loss of freedom, which has evaporated on a "sea of hope." The woman regrets her lost love; even if she goes elsewhere, her heart will remain behind on the roof (that is, with her husband).

The day after Dehbia's performance, as Hend told it, "it was a war in the house." For a young woman to appear on a public stage, speaking of love and freedom, in front of the entire village and in her father's presence, was—according to the old "mentality"—to compromise her modesty and to call into question not only her own reputation but also that of her father and brothers. Predictably, Hend's father exploded; for weeks afterward, stony silence alternated with outraged outbursts. Hend also became a target of village gossip. Suddenly, his every movement became suspect. Greeted time and again with his mother's tears, he was continually plied with her questions about his whereabouts.

Attacked from all sides, Hend felt more clearly than ever the weight of the "traditions" he was up against. "*La mixité*, it's something that all Westerners have," he said to me. "You were born into it. But it's because your ancestors, long ago, lived through changes that allowed you to be who you are today. . . . So now it's up to us to sacrifice ourselves. It's not for me that I'm working for '*la mixité*,' it's for my son, for the future."

Voice and Footing

If the chorus represented an early attempt of the Amkan cultural asso-ciation to address the question of gender, this enterprise was complicated by the fact that the initiative was controlled by men—from the initial vision to the or-ganization of the performance to the details of staging, voice, and footing. Al-though Dehbia performed a solo piece, the text was written by her brother Hend. In Erving Goffman's terms, she was the animator (the one performing the text), while Hend was both principal and author—he composed the words and was responsible for the opinions behind them (Goffman 1981; Hanks 1996: 208–209). That Dehbia was essentially ventriloquizing his text became especially ap-parent when she stumbled over a line, and Hend—who had been standing on the sidelines—walked over and prompted her; he remained by her side for the rest of the performance, mouthing the words. And although Hend encouraged his sister to take the stage, he had virtually substituted himself for her father. "I'm the one who brought her up," he told me. "[When our father started] mak-ing her account for her every move, for every last penny she spent, I told her, 'Look, don't take his money any more, I'll take care of you.' . . . But I also set conditions . . . because giving a woman total freedom, in our country, is impos-sible. It can't be done. She has to be prepared for that freedom and that's what I did with her. . . . Now she's responsible, and I can let her do what she wants. . . . '*La mixité*,' it must be prepared for."

Hend, buoyed by the relative success of his efforts, seemed unaware of his conflicted relationship to *la mixité*. Other young men were at once more self-conscious than Hend and more tormented. Farid (a pseudonym), a founding member of Kabylia's first mixed theater group and strongly committed to "sweep-ing away old ideas," sadly recognized that his upbringing left him with "marks" (*taches*) from which he couldn't seem to recover. Makhlouf (a pseudonym), liv-ing in Paris where he is active in the Kabyle artistic community, encouraged his niece not to hide the fact that she smokes and drinks, but then acknowledged that he would be lying if he said it didn't bother him on some level. In his words, "It's as if there's a war in my head."

Unfortunately, the war was not just in Makhlouf's head, since the regulation of women's activities in public space is among Algeria's most heavily charged ideological sites (Carlier 1995; Lazreg 1994; Messaoudi and Schemla 1995; Slyomovics 1995). It is a site where men not only construct their sense of honor and self-respect but also forge their cultural and political identities. In the ideological frame in which the Algerian civil conflict was then occurring, Hend's action took on added significance. By placing his sister on the village stage—one of the most controversial public settings of all—Hend implicitly positioned himself on a national stage, proclaiming his adhesion, however partial, to the contested principle of *la mixité*. By choosing to make his sister's body publicly visible, Hend displayed his own political allegiances, demarcating himself from certain groups and identifying with others. Control over *la mixité* remained in male hands.

Or did it? The boys and girls on that hot August night drew on their experience in the chorus to transform the dance space. Their experience on stage with a new performance form refracted into and helped to reshape, for all to see, one of the primary performance events in the Kabyle village—the dance. Nor was this a onetime occurrence. Subsequent chorus performances that summer spontaneously concluded with a "mixed" dance by the chorus members. The children's dance, from this perspective, can be understood as a site where modernizing notions about gender equality were inflected and transformed in unexpected ways within local organizations of communication and performance. While Dehbia's appearance in the unfamiliar role of a female soloist—deliberately planned to counter prevailing gender ideologies—provoked overt controversy, the boys and girls took dance, a popular and acclaimed performance genre within the village, and began to shape it into something new.

"An Association for the Twenty-first Century"

March 1994, Paris. The phone rang in my host family's apartment in the suburbs of Paris, where I had been staying since escalating civil conflict had forced me to leave Algeria the previous December. On the line was Kamal (a pseudonym), a forty-three-year-old man from Tamkant who had been living in France since 1980, working as a carpenter. We had met a few weeks earlier, while helping out with a family move. Although Kamal was from a different adrum than my host family, they were related through maternal kin. As the representative of his sub-adrum in Paris, Kamal was frequently on the phone to collect money for repatriation costs or other village projects, which he would turn over to his adrum representative. But this time he had a different request. He had been thinking, he told me, that younger immigrants from Amkan—many born and raised in France—needed a way to get to know each other. Although the Paris village committee (tajmaᶜat) worked well for repatriation, it was not a forum for organizing community activities in France. Further, the committee, made up of five older men, had been in the hands of the same families for decades. Kamal's vision was of another kind of organization—in his words, "an association for the twenty-first century" (*une association caractère l'an 2000*)— that would bring together Amkan residents in Paris across gendered, generational, and lineage-based lines while forging new connections with the Algerian village. He recognized, however, that to succeed, this enterprise would require the active participation of the young, and especially the young women. Could I possibly call Zahra (a pseudonym), one of my immigrant friends from the village, and see if she would be willing to help out?

Zahra, age twenty-three, had lived in France since she was two years old, and came from a highly respected family. Her parents and all but one of her siblings were in France, where they owned a comfortable home in the suburbs of Paris. Her oldest brother had remained in the family's large, contemporary house in Amkan, to which the whole family returned every summer; in 1994, he was serving as the head of the Algeria-based village committee. Passionate about her heritage, Zahra was active within the large Berber Cultural Association (Association Culturelle Berbère, ACB) in Paris, where she taught Kabyle language classes for children. She and I had met two years earlier in a different Kabyle language class, which she was taking so she could learn to write her native tongue; she would later complete an advanced degree in Berber studies. She was also studying English at the university, so each week we traded language lessons over coffee and soon became fast friends.

When I called Zahra to pass along Kamal's request, she was interested but did not immediately acquiesce. After sounding out her network and learning that he was respected in the village, she agreed to come to a meeting, bringing her sister and several female cousins along. So it was that a few weeks after Kamal's phone call, thirteen of us—twelve Amkan residents (seven men and five women) plus myself—met in a café owned by one of the men. Myself excluded, all but two of those present were from Tamkant. One of the two (I'll call him Djamal) was from the large village section bordering Tamkant, and he had been specially invited by Kamal as the youngest and the most "forward-looking" of the five-member village committee in Paris. The other, a young woman, had strong maternal ties to Tamkant and was related to Kamal's family.

Figure and Ground

Amkan's cultural association in Algeria generated new performance opportunities that were framed and staged to stand out from the surrounding context. Duranti and Goodwin (1992) have called such focal events "figures" within a broader figure-ground relationship. With the wedding—a major and well-respected social institution—as its ground or setting, the choral performances stood out as something new that nevertheless did not challenge the legitimacy of the wedding itself. In contrast, in Paris the ground for creating the kind of association Kamal had in mind was not established but had to be produced. There was no precedent for distantly related men and women to come together in a Parisian café. Over the course of numerous meetings in the spring of 1994, this association did organize two staged performances. But by far the greatest amount of our meeting time—for they generously invited me to be present whenever I could—was spent talking about how to frame and organize the association itself: What was its mission, how would it take shape, and especially, how would it gain legitimacy in the eyes of the Amkan communities in both Paris and Algeria? Under debate were the very terms of how the ground would be set: for example, where to meet and how to recruit members; what background music to play at the first event; what would be the spatial layout of tables and chairs in the meeting room; what language (French or Berber) would be used to communicate; what would be the legal structure of the association vis-à-vis the French state; and what would be the association's relationship with the existing village committee in Paris. The difficulty of the enterprise was succinctly voiced by Kamal: "If we succeed in getting people to acknowledge that this kind of meeting exists, it's already a step forward."

In Kamal's view, the success of the association pivoted on establishing a new subject position for women—one in which they could take an active role in the association without being encumbered by "old mentalities." If women stayed away from the association, he thought, nothing would have changed. At the same time, Kamal acknowledged that the association needed to establish a new basis for credibility, legitimacy, and appeal without entirely breaking with existing structures like the village committee. For if the association were marginalized, villagers would not participate. It was important to Kamal, then, that a respected group of young women involve themselves in the creation of the association. Zahra, he hoped, would help to get such women on board.

Setting the Stage

Again, the phone rang, this time in the café where the thirteen of us had gathered.[10] It was for Kamal. He left the table to take the call and returned a moment later, shaken. An anonymous caller, he told us, had shouted "Kamal, you are a fool," and then slammed down the receiver. Clearly, establishing credibility—winning the respect and support of the village—would be of utmost importance.

After greeting us, Kamal opened the floor for discussion. The discursive conditions that would frame the next several meetings, and ultimately determine the shape of the association, were established quickly. Two competing bodies of knowledge about how the association could work emerged to frame the debate (see Lindstrom 1992). Zahra was the first to voice them as alternatives: "Will we register [the association] with the police [i.e., under the French law of 1901[11]], or continue in the old way?" Zahra's question launched a debate about the relationship between the village committee and the new association that drew on participants' understandings of how each operated. These understandings were highly uneven, structured by both gender and age. Of the seven men present, three were directly involved with the village committee: Djamal was a village section representative; Kamal and one other man were sublineage representatives, responsible for collecting money from their "branches" of the adrum.

The women and several younger men felt completely separate from the committee and barely knew how it operated: "My father pays for me, that's all I know," said one.

Some argued that with the assistance of the village committee, the association could gain members and financial support quickly. Djamal presented himself as someone who could marshal committee backing, offering to discuss the association with the other members and to "tell them to support it." He emphasized the force behind a "unanimous, five-out-of-five decision," contending that when the village committee threw itself behind a project, it was sure to gain credibility. Kamal and others, including several of the women, countered Djamal's claims by recasting the village committee in relation to "outmoded" and "cumbersome" structures; it operated, Kamal argued, through cronyism, factional pressures, and collective obligations rather than voluntary decisions. While Djamal thought the advantages of a village committee mandate for the association outweighed these concerns, most of the other men, and all of the women, disagreed. In contrast, they argued, structuring the association in relation to French law would provide it with autonomy and enable it to organize events and activities as it saw fit. And participation would be voluntary—no one would be "forced" to attend or contribute, the way they were under village committee mandates. Despite the desire to move away from a lineage-based organization, however, it proved difficult for even Kamal to discuss questions of recruitment without recourse to lineage considerations. At times, Kamal spoke about recruitment targets in relation to a notion that entire lineages or village sections could be "swayed" through the presence of a few key individuals. If the village committee were not the vehicle through which such connections could be activated, another would have to be found.

April 3, 1994.[12] The café, which its Tamkant owner had closed to the public for the afternoon, gradually began to fill with men and women from Amkan. Men stood at the bar, which was not serving alcohol at the association's request (Zahra's initiative). Women occupied the café's restaurant, separated from the bar by a movable divider that felt like a moral threshold. Crossing it, one was clearly in the other's territory. From time to time, Kamal ventured across to bear a message to Zahra or his niece Sabrina (a pseudonym). At first, Sabrina had been at the bar, but as the spaces became more clearly gendered she moved to the women's side, saying she felt too awkward. More than an hour after the announced meeting time, Kamal clapped his hands to begin. Men crossed into the restaurant side and most took seats, along with the women, around café tables that Sabrina and I had arranged in a long rectangle. Behind the tables, we had set up several dozen chairs. Seated on one chair was Kamal's wife; the two on either side of her were left empty. The remaining chairs were all occupied by men. Overall, some forty people were present, and while most were from Tamkant, the other three village sections were all represented by one or two individuals. Djamal, however, was noticeably absent.

Kamal opened by voicing his hope that a meeting place for the Amkan community in Paris could be created. He then gave the floor to Zahra, positioning her from the outset as someone with knowledge and authority. She spoke about the goals of the association, evoking such possibilities as organizing cultural days or collecting medications for the Algerian village; she framed these initiatives in relation to globalizing cultural or humanitarian missions such as *Médecins sans frontières* (Doctors without Borders), whose legitimacy was already well established in France. Kamal then set these proposals in relation not to the village committee but to the larger Berber Cultural Association (ACB) in Paris by passing out ACB brochures and explaining that association's mission. He linked Zahra to the ACB, explaining that she taught Kabyle language classes there. From the beginning, then, Kamal presented Zahra as experienced with association projects and Berber cultural activities, framed her as someone with specialized knowledge of how associations operate, and created specific opportunities for her to speak, which she accepted. Yet from early on, their voices were becoming commingled in ways that would soon prove problematic.

During the course of the ensuing discussion, one participant, not present at the previous meeting, asked if the plan was to create an "association 1901"—that is, an association based on a French law that governs the rights of associations organized by foreigners. Zahra and Kamal answered together in the affirmative, citing the material benefits: It would give them access to a meeting space and a legal way to raise money and perhaps even receive state funds. Zahra then provided a succinct overview of how associations are typically structured under this law: "Four or five people are at the head, another forty are actively involved, the rest are ordinary members. Usually, a president represents the association, a secretary keeps minutes and takes care of paperwork, and a treasurer handles finances. Active members join committees and organize events or projects, the others just come to the events." She then turned from these descriptive statements to ask a performative question that effectively brought the structure into being: "Who wants to be part of what?" Debate ensued about whether representatives should be drawn from each village section, but most countered this suggestion as reinforcing "old ideas" and "feudal divisions." Discussion also centered on how the association would finance its activities—would it be through dues, individual contributions, or fundraising events such as a dance? Once again, Zahra took the amorphous discussion and reshaped it into a summary statement of what she thought had been proposed: first, to make the association official; second, to hold a conference on village history; and third, to attempt to raise money through a special event. She then asked another question with performative effect: "How do we decide on the candidates [for office]?" Within two minutes, a slate of six officers had been proposed by different individuals, and it was no surprise that she was nominated as president. Without further discussion or vote, this slate was accepted. It was evenly split by gender, with a female president, a male vice-president, and joint male-female appointments for secretary and treasurer. Kamal had not been nominated.

In sum, over the course of the first few meetings, discursive conditions were put in place that enabled a young woman with Zahra's credentials to assume a

position of high visibility and at least limited authority. This involved both establishing the bodies of knowledge that would be taken as authoritative and
identifying discourse strategies through which credible claims to knowledge
and authority could be made. Two explicit bodies of knowledge were evoked,
one pointing to lineage politics and the village committee, the other, to the autonomy and independence enabled (at least in theory) by French law, and modeled by the larger ACB. Djamal attempted to peddle his influence with the village committee to gain support for the association. Zahra, in contrast, established
credibility through her experience with institutions of French society—most
directly, the Berber Cultural Association, but also the school system, which had
presumably helped to foster her ability to make summary presentations before
an audience. She also aligned the association with broader cultural and humanitarian missions whose legitimacy was uncontested. Whereas Djamal would have
gone outside the association, meeting separately with the village committee to
seek a mandate, Zahra issued well-timed performative questions that helped to
bring the association structure into being during the meeting itself. Finally, she
benefited from Kamal's help as, on several occasions, he deliberately directed the
flow of conversation to point to her qualifications and expertise or to give her
the floor. It was not long, however, before tensions surrounding Zahra's role
would come to the fore.

May 15, 1994.[13] For the past week, a few of us had been busy preparing for the
next meeting, a discussion of the history of Amkan and the surrounding region.
Most of the Amkan immigrants had been invited by a letter, which also announced the creation of the association. Zahra had signed on to research the
region's early history. Kamal would speak about the history of emigration, and
I had volunteered to prepare something on a sixteenth-century Berber kingdom
in the Amkan region.[14] When the day of the event arrived, we met not in a café—
judged too controversial a setting to encourage female and family attendance—
but in a large room at the Berber Cultural Association.

Meanwhile, pressure on Zahra had been building. Her father had warned her
that she risked being viewed as the "village donkey" (*l'âne du village*) were she
to associate herself with the new initiative. A phone call from her oldest brother
in Algeria, who had heard about the association, echoed this concern. While
some of the other young women had also been pressured by their families, Zahra
was in the most visible position. Perhaps, she worried, she was acting too fast.
Zahra had enjoyed working on her short presentation, and shared with me her
excitement about discovering references to Amkan in early colonial works. The
day before the conference, however, she informed Kamal that if she were to read
her own talk, she would provoke a family controversy, which she was unwilling
to do. She would be responsible for the writing, but he would have to find a
replacement presenter. So it transpired that on the conference day, Kamal got
up to read Zahra's work.

Kamal was clearly uncomfortable. He rose to welcome people, then announced
the day's agenda. "The first part," he told the assembled audience of some fifty

people, "will be on the origins of the village." Despite Zahra's absence as a speaker (she was in attendance), he insistently invoked her presence in several ways. First, he linked her work to my own presentation, making it sound like we had worked on a joint text that I would read: "Jane and Zahra have worked on Kabylia. . . . This part will be presented by Jane." He then added that he himself had "two or three lines to read to you" on the early history of the village. "I must tell you," he confessed, "that these three lines are the result of a labor of many hours spent in the library, and I will say that this was the work of Zahra." Kamal went on to read Zahra's statement, framing it as reported speech:

Kamal: "Zahra tells us that around the sixth and seventh centuries, the Zouaoua were located in the province of Bejaia, more precisely, between Bejaia and Dellys. They lived on the mountain peaks, inaccessible to outsiders. . . . "

Here, Zahra interrupted: "You could perhaps explain who the Zouaoua were."

Kamal: "Go ahead, explain!"
Zahra: "The [Ait *Tribal Name*] are our tribe, the Zouaoua is the race to which our tribe belonged."

Kamal's presentation of Zahra's text continued in a similar fashion. At one point, he could not make out her handwriting, and she had to explain what she meant. She went on to sum up her main points, speaking rapidly and with occasional nervous laughter, while remaining seated in the audience.

Voice and Footing, Again

To recall the discussion of voice and footing above, Kamal was clearly only the animator—the presenter of the text—while Zahra was both author and principal, responsible for its organization and content. Unlike Dehbia, who in a similar performance situation had layered her own expression into the text her brother wrote, Kamal's reading was flat, uncreative, and distanced. Through his use of reported speech, his failure to contextualize the text, his inability even to make out parts of it, and through continuous references to Zahra as the author, he clearly displayed his discomfort with Zahra's stance. Kamal's commentary, in which he framed the text as Zahra's and distanced himself from it, called attention less to the text she had prepared than to her refusal to present it. Simply put, she had stepped away from the subject position he sought to create, and he was furious. Later, he complained to me at length: If people like Zahra would not take responsibility for changing things, he lamented, they would never change. As disagreements between the two of them continued to emerge in subsequent small-group discussions, he reiterated to me his concerns, fearing that she would not stand up to her parents. Perhaps, he wondered, it would not work after all to have her as president. Perhaps their visions were simply too different.

For Zahra, it was important that things not move too quickly, and that her involvement in the association be viewed as respectable by her father and broth-ers. While this certainly related in part to her own internalization of behaviors of modesty as a basis for gaining the village's esteem, she was also persuaded that change had to happen slowly. Zahra was committed to the creation of the association, but she felt that taking an onstage, focal role would detract from her own credibility in her relatives' eyes and serve to delegitimize the undertak-ing altogether.

Kamal wanted Zahra to be a spokesperson for the association and strongly supported her performance in that role. When she sought a less visible presence, he felt that his own vision was threatened. To him, only strong female leadership within the association would enable the emergence of new forms of relation-ship not based solely on the "old" divisions. For Kamal, the performance events themselves should model and display the new "mentalities" he sought to instill. For Zahra, in contrast, creating credibility for the association—simply getting people like her parents to positively acknowledge its existence—required an ap-proach that took into account their concerns about appropriate female behav-iors. Zahra gradually removed herself from positions of visibility. She deliber-ately signed her name illegibly on a letter that "la Présidente" (the [female] president) sent to the village, and she refused appear on a panel at a subsequent association event. Ultimately, Zahra would resign as president, but that is an-other story.

During the remainder of my stay in Paris, the association moved increasingly toward a focus on humanitarian intervention in the Algerian community. Its primary project centered on how to get an adequate supply of prescription drugs to the Algerian village. While this project ultimately failed, it was the only place where the cultural association in Paris sought to forge ties to the Algerian vil-lage. Yet it did so in a way that clearly positioned the two places as separate and unequal. Unlike the tajmaᶜat organizations, the cultural associations were not places where movement between Algeria and Paris was managed. Although the two cultural associations shared the related goal of instilling "new mentalities," their trajectories and projects were almost entirely distinct.

The cultural association performances on both Algerian and Parisian sides of Amkan constitute nodal points where discourses, ideologies, and practices associated with a secular modernity are brought into relation with local per-formance practices, furnishing another example of branching interconnections. The village is not, however, the endpoint or target of the "global," its last place of penetration. Rather, the village is precisely the site where globality and lo-cality are made to co-articulate. Gender is a privileged site where this articula-tion occurs. As the performances illustrate, a globalizing discourse of women's rights has taken on a particular valence in the Algerian political context, where a woman's appearance on a public stage is already a political statement. When this discourse is pushed up against village-based forms of social organization, both are reconfigured into something new, such that to demonstrate a "forward-looking mentality" with regards to women in an Algerian village setting entails not so much advocating for workplace benefits (as it might in the West) as confronting lineage-based forms of social morality.

I am left with two scenes of ventriloquism: Hend mouthing the words of his own text as his sister recites it; Kamal flatly reading Zahra's text as she punctuates it from the sidelines. Both speak to men's abiding ambivalence about women's performance in public space, despite their professed political leanings. In Hend's view, Dehbia required constant coaching; in Kamal's assessment, Zahra had caved in to the "old mentalities." Both women were critiqued for failing to embody—literally—the men's vision. In short, these men seem to be endorsing a subject position without a subject. Yet if their halting dance toward *la mixité* was conflicted, it also produced unexpected openings. With the children's dance, it was precisely in an unscripted moment that new forms of gendered interaction began to take shape. In another performance—this time, a video production in Paris—women's bodies would be literally erased.

8   Village to Video

May 1994, Paris. The curtain of the Olympia Theater rose to reveal a traditional Kabyle Berber village. Before a painted backdrop of mountains, five chorus women—myself and four Kabyles—sat surrounding a water fountain. We were cloaked in the region's brilliant red and yellow colors. Eight chorus men, all Kabyle, occupied an outdoor square where the public assembly (*tajma^at*) would be held, and four children engaged in play with antique Kabyle toys. A female dance troupe further enlivened the event, helping the chorus to enact a traditional wedding ritual and other village scenes. We were the supporting cast for the star of the show—Lounis Aït Menguellet, one of Algeria's leading Berber political singers. With more than three dozen commercial cassettes and CDs selling from Algerian kiosks to Tower Records, Aït Menguellet has been singing to packed houses on both sides of the Mediterranean for three decades. He is seen as a contemporary bard, a crafter of words who produces penetrating commentary about Algerian politics and history in a richly metaphorical language packed with proverbs, legends, and popular wisdom. A staunch advocate for Amazigh language, culture, and identity, Aït Menguellet has seen his songs censored on Algerian national radio, served time in prison,[1] and been threatened by the Islamist opposition.[2]

Behind the scenes, another scenario was unfolding. A commercial video of this performance was being made, to be marketed to Berber communities across France, Belgium, and North Africa (Aït Menguellet 1994). After the video had been shot and edited, the choruses staged a heated dispute about whether they would sign releases. Ultimately, the men signed release forms, accepting to appear without remuneration; most also accepted a 1,000-franc (about $200) token of appreciation for their participation in the five concerts. The four Kabyle chorus women, in contrast, refused to sign without payment ranging from 2,500 to 5,000 francs ($500 to $1,000) each. Aït Menguellet, rather than pay the women, instead paid more than twice what they were asking to delete them from the video. The video was subsequently reworked: Signs of this dispute include five permanently empty microphones, women's voices on the soundtrack but no women singers on the stage, and a new female soloist, recorded after the fact and then spliced into the video, who is both out of tune and out of relation to the rest of the cast.

Why did the women singers have to become invisible before the video could go on the market, with disembodied voices as the only trace of their performance? As I discussed this scenario with a range of interlocutors, two narratives emerged. The first sought to locate the women's invisibility in relation to conventional views about the problematic public display of women's bodies in

North African and Middle Eastern societies. Here, the story goes, women gain self-respect and the respect of others by behaving with modesty in public spaces. This entails not a fixed set of behaviors but a perceived "continuum of public-ness" (Seizer 2000: 250 n. 8). In a village context, it might mean donning a *fuḍa* (outer skirt) before leaving the house; avoiding the public square where the men gather; or making sure no men are in the vicinity before breaking into dance or song on a lazy afternoon. In urban or diaspora settings, modest behavior might entail avoiding makeup (or at least removing it in front of one's family), dressing conservatively, or refraining from drinking or smoking in the presence of one's brothers, fathers, or uncles. In either location, women on a public stage risked compromising their modesty, for they were potentially making themselves avail-able as sexual objects for public consumption (see Jansen 1987; Kapchan 1996; Van Nieuwkerk 1995). The video intensified this effect, for unlike the perform-ances, which were onetime, fleeting events, it would fix a woman's image on tape, where it could travel far and wide and be seen for years to come. Not only would it be available for consumption by new publics, but it might also come full circle, falling into the hands of the very family members whom a woman had chosen not to inform about her participation in the concerts. This narra-tive, then, locates the crux of the matter in the women's refusal to allow their images to circulate via a mediated product. Their request for money is ex-plained, in this scenario, as a ruse: The women "had to know" in advance that their request would be denied, so their stance was simply a way of saving face by not appearing to be bound by "old mentalities."

The second narrative, in contrast, foregrounds the women's erasure. This story—which plays especially well among feminist audiences—seeks to demon-ize the singer for his unwillingness to pay the women. Its larger subtext is the familiar tale of female oppression at the hands of exploitive men, as the dispute becomes yet another example of how politically liberal men draw on women's labor to achieve nationalist or subnationalist goals, only then to deny women political visibility and economic parity (see Parker et al. 1992). Here, patriarchy itself is cast as the culprit, and the women are lauded for standing up for their "rights." Erasure, not refusal, is emphasized; the women are seen as having been removed from the video despite their efforts to negotiate a fair place for them-selves.

While each of these narratives touches on issues that no doubt were partially implicated in the videotape dispute, neither satisfies me. In their own ways, both are deeply conventional. The first relies on traditional images of North African women whose relevance to this particular situation may be questionable at best. For the chorus women were living in Paris—one had come as a child, one as an adolescent, and one had never set foot in Algeria. Only the soloist, whom I will call Delila, had recently arrived in France. Evoking exclusively "traditional" norms of gendered behavior to explain their choice is insufficient. The second narrative is underwritten by western feminist ideology that often cannot see past its own culturally based assumptions. Both take it for granted that the dis-pute pivots on the "women's question," although they approach it from competing perspectives. At the same time, the diasporic arena in which the dispute took place tends to recede. I argue, in contrast, that the diasporic location of the performances was crucial. Over the course of the concerts, a gap began to emerge between the production of a collective cultural identity mediated through images of the homeland and the lives of the Paris-based Kabyle performers who were engaged for the show (see Brah 1996: 124). Whereas the staged concerts were oriented to a diaspora nostalgic for images of traditional village life, the ways in which diaspora and home were linked behind the scenes spoke to an entirely different set of allegiances and concerns. This split became particularly acute for the women in somewhat paradoxical ways. The disjunctive spaces in the video offer a compelling image of this gap.

On- and offstage ways of conjoining diaspora and home were increasingly set against each other during the course of the performances. Aït Menguellet's vision for the concerts and video drew on images of the homeland to support a vision of a collective political identity. In contrast, representations of diaspora and home were constituted by the men and women of the chorus in relation to the material conditions of their engagement. They put into play an opposition between a dynamic, relational form of financial negotiation linked to "Algeria" and a "transparent," contract-driven negotiation style linked to "France." At the same time, the women's chorus authoritatively invoked memories and images of home to position themselves in relation to the hired troupe of Arab and French dancers. In the way that they did so, they reconstituted traditional ideas about authentic female performance in relation to the adjacent discussions about money matters. It was this move that ultimately produced a breakdown.

Lest my own voice become the most disembodied of all, I briefly locate myself. I was engaged differently from other chorus members. Whereas the other women and men were recruited to help out Aït Menguellet, I asked him if I could participate. As a result, I did not feel justified in requesting remuneration, so I did not join the chorus women in their financial negotiations, although I was present for most of them. My goals, too, were dissimilar. As an anthropologist, I saw the experience as an opportunity to deepen my understanding of Kabyle musical and performance practices. As an amateur singer of nonwestern music, I hoped to further develop my own vocal abilities. I also love performing and was delighted to have the opportunity to be on stage. Finally, my material situation was entirely different. I was not giving up work time or income but was engaged in grant-funded research. I mark my own split perspective deictically, using the pronoun "we" to talk about our collective role as singers in the performance, and "they" to talk about the Kabyle Berber women as they positioned themselves through payment issues.

Setting the Stage

The Olympia concerts represented a departure for Lounis Aït Menguellet. Known as shy, unassuming, and somewhat reclusive, he chooses to spend much of his time in his natal village of Ighil Bouamas (although he holds a

French residency permit to facilitate recording and performing abroad). Unlike most other Algerian artists of his stature, he remained in his village even at considerable risk to his own life when, during the mid-1990s, artists and intellectuals were among those under siege by Islamist insurgents.[3] For Aït Menguellet, the village is not simply a locus of nostalgia and loss, it is where he lives, has raised his family, and does most of his work. Yet he is widely seen through a nostalgic lens—for the Kabyle public, he embodies the values and behavioral codes of an older Kabylia in which one's word had value, in which forthrightness and respect governed social relations. As video producer Ammar Arab put it, "Aït Menguellet is the very personification of the village . . . he conducts himself in the same way whether he is in the village or the Place de la Concorde." Aït Menguellet's image is one of simplicity, sincerity, and generosity, and these qualities were borne out in all of my interactions with him.

As an artist, Aït Menguellet is strongly associated with the Kabyle region's bardic tradition, in which a poet served as the political and ethical voice of his people (Mammeri 1980; Nacib 1993; Rabia 1993). The language of his poetry is deceptively simple: It draws on metaphors, images, and allusions sourced in daily life to formulate incisive commentary that both critiques the neocolonial and anti-Berber politics of the Algerian state and chastises the Kabyle population for acquiescing in its own disenfranchisement. Although his poetry is informed by Kabyle poetic traditions, Aït Menguellet's project differs considerably from that of Idir and Ben Mohamed. Aït Menguellet does not share what he calls Idir's "archaeological" vision; he is not interested in recovering village songs or in reconstituting them through a lens of universality. To the contrary—he considers village texts and melodies to be rather limited, offering inadequate frameworks for the kind of messages he seeks to convey. Of 104 songs reproduced in a 1989 collection of his works (Yacine 1989), he identified only five as having any links to village repertoires. When he does work with a traditional song, he told me, it is "because something in it struck me and I wanted to make something else of it."[4] In short, Aït Menguellet seeks less to represent traditions through a modernizing lens than to work from within traditional poetic genres and speech styles to create texts that address contemporary concerns. Furthermore, his music is not particularly innovative; as was the case with earlier bards, he places far more importance on text than music. He has traditionally accompanied himself simply by strumming the melody line on a guitar adapted for quarter-tone scales;[5] folk-rock instrumentation or harmonies have never entered into his songs (although his son Jaffar recently added a synthesizer to the mix). Yet Aït Menguellet is considered very much a new Kabyle singer because his songs speak strongly to Berber identity issues (see Cherbi and Khouas 1999).

Nor is Aït Menguellet in the habit of creating multimedia productions. While he has performed at venues like the Olympia dozens of times, he typically sings alone, with just a percussionist on the bendir (frame) drum and perhaps another string player to accompany him. Being on stage does not come easily to him. He was visibly trembling at the beginning of our first show, and has on more than one occasion described the discomfort he feels on stage: "As for being on stage, I have a terrible fear [*une peur bleue*] of it. If I could avoid doing live concerts, I would do so with joy" (Ourad 1984: 30; see also Aït Menguellet 1993; Ouazani 1988). Not until he had been performing for several decades did he start organizing larger "gala" productions. This effort began in his own village, where he worked with the nascent cultural association in the early 1990s to develop a program that included, among other things, a children's chorus; he performed a version of this show in Paris.[6] The May 1994 production went considerably further, involving extensive stage sets, casting, and scripting. The stage itself was turned into a village, and several scenes—the wedding and the grand finale—entailed coordinating a cast of several dozen performers. A village jester periodically enlivened events on stage. Aït Menguellet's son Jaffar, just coming into his own as a musician, was featured not only on synthesizer but also in a dance number in which he waltzed with a young girl, accompanied on the keyboard by a child. Indeed, children were a significant part of the act, participating in the staged wedding ritual and other village scenes. A number of prominent Kabyle singers and cultural figures made guest appearances.[7] During one performance, Aït Menguellet himself—usually an austere and somewhat distant figure on stage—was shown in a fatherly role: His manager made a "surprise" phone call to Aït Menguellet's family in Kabylia, and Lounis spoke via telephone on stage with his young toddler, creating a familial touch that at the same time viscerally recalled the immigrant situation, with the telephone often the only point of contact between family members "here" and "there."

The Olympia show was created not only for the live audience of 10,000 spectators but also in anticipation of a video public that would be drawn largely from the diaspora. The video intensifies the representation of Berber identity via idealized images of home even as it reinforces a dramatic split between the diaspora and the homeland. The diaspora presence is configured almost exclusively in terms of spectatorship. In the opening frames, concertgoers are seen entering the Olympia; vivid audience shots of Kabyle men and women dancing in the aisles and clapping punctuate the entire video. The only other representation of diaspora is through an arrival scene, filmed when Aït Menguellet and his son were met at Paris's Orly Airport. The remaining video footage moves between the stage of the Olympia and Kabylia itself. As Aït Menguellet sings, the painted backdrop of mountains gradually fades into a shot of the snow-capped mountains of Kabylia. The viewer is transported from the tajmaᶜat set recreated on the stage to a tajmaᶜat meeting (also apparently staged) held on outdoor stone benches in a Kabyle village. Footage of old-style Berber houses, their interiors intricately painted with indigenous geometric patterns, alternates with shots of gnarled old women engaged in traditional tasks, their foreheads tattooed with traditional designs. Juxtaposed against these shots of village life are powerful scenes of Amazigh political demonstrations in which Aït Menguellet's image floats against a sea of impassioned Kabyle men marching in city streets, chanting, pumping their fists, and holding signs demanding linguistic rights and political representation.

The staged representation of Berber identity produced for consumption in the diaspora clearly pivots on a dramatic divide in which the homeland was constituted as a locus of nostalgia while representations of the diaspora were virtually excised. Backstage, however, a different kind of split between home and diaspora began to emerge in ways that would make such an idealized portrayal problematic. Remuneration became a central symbolic locus around which competing ways of conjoining home and diaspora took shape.

Money Matters

Explicit agreements about remuneration were reached prior to the concerts with all performers except the chorus. One of the female chorus members, Delila, who also sang three solo numbers, retroactively claimed that an agreement had been made. During the intermission of the last performance, she told the other women that over an informal couscous dinner with Aït Menguellet, his manager, and other friends, which took place before the other chorus members were recruited, a figure of 500 francs ($100) per concert had been tossed around (another participant at this dinner told me that this sum had been mentioned but not agreed upon). The rest of the women and all of the men were engaged after this dinner, without discussion of financial terms.[8] It wasn't until a week after the final show that the manager telephoned each of us to offer a token "reimbursement" (*défraiement*) of 1,000 francs ($200) for the five concerts. Only at that point did he ask us to sign video releases. To present the transaction in this summary fashion, however, is to obscure the ways in which it was discursively constituted as the performances unfolded.

Over the three-week period during which the concerts took place, chorus members gradually began to frame their experience in terms of two forms of contractual relationships, which they linked to "France" or "Algeria" even as they recognized that transactions of each kind could occur in both places. Their "French" model, described as direct, impersonal, transparent, and professional, is based around a prenegotiated wage in exchange for an agreed-upon service. It may involve written contracts or be based on standardized pay scales that explicitly connect time and labor with wages. Beyond this fee-for-service transaction, no relationship need bind the parties. In their "Algerian" model, while service is performed and money may change hands, the exchange transpires differently in both discursive and temporal terms. First of all, financial negotiations are indirect, especially among acquaintances. For example, a request for service may be formulated as a favor. However, if the scope of work exceeds what could easily be returned in kind, both parties usually harbor expectations about future remuneration, but these remain unspoken, and both act as if payment were not at issue. The one performing the service, if asked, may well claim that he or she has no thought of accepting money. Second, while payment is usually necessary, it is not sufficient. As one chorus man explained to me, the person doing the work must also feel "well received" by the host. For example, the host might provide a meal accompanied by stimulating discussion. When I talked about the concert situation with a member of my own host family, he invoked a common proverb to explain that the sharing of a meal is thought to establish a trust between both parties: "*neçça tagʷla d lemleḥ*" ("we ate wheat and salt"—the proverb implies the creation of a bond). Theoretically, this sharing of food seals the relationship and makes betrayal unthinkable.[9] The temporal dimension in which a transaction unfolds also helps to constitute the exchange. Not only is it unseemly to negotiate up-front, but once payment is offered, the matter is far from settled. The "worker" may make an initial show of refusing the money, claiming that payment was the last thing on his mind. The "employer" then presents it as a gift, implying that a refusal would be insulting. The amount of money is crucial. The worker has generally made a mental calculation of what he thinks the job is worth. If the amount offered is too little, the worker may refuse the amount altogether out of a sense of pride, may defer collecting for months or even years, or may up the ante and demand a much larger sum. Breakdowns in this system are described in a relational or familial idiom, with the phrase "*txedmeḍ i xalti-m*" ("you are working for your aunt"). In other words, because the worker is "family," the aunt doesn't think she needs to pay him much, while the worker is convinced that because he is family, he will be paid more.[10]

Pierre Bourdieu situated these kinds of exchanges in what he called a "good faith economy," within which economic transactions are disguised by the discourse in which they are formulated (see esp. Bourdieu 1977: 171–183). Economic relations among individuals bound through kinship or other personal interests, he argued, are not subject to the objective structures (such as minimum wage or union rates) that could otherwise regulate exchanges among disinterested parties. Rather, transactions among kin are negotiated through the communicative norms—the manners of speaking—in which the exchanges are carried out. The tenor of the interaction—the choice of words, smiles or frowns, gestures or tones of voice—is as important as the "material" exchange. In short, it is only through intricate communicative maneuvering that economic relationships can unfold even as they are officially denied.

In the Olympia performance situation, a good faith economy had little structural necessity. That is, most participants did not depend on each other for future services, so had no economic need to maintain good relationships. It did, however, have discursive authority. Over the course of the weeks leading up to the concerts, a "good faith" language was clearly used to constitute the chorus. Chorus members were treated as "part of the family"; indeed, wanting to create a family atmosphere rather than a formal, professional environment may have been one of the reasons nonprofessional singers were used. The audition process was informal. No official announcement was made; instead, singers were recruited on the basis of personal connections. All of the women were contacted either by Aït Menguellet directly or by his friends and supporters and asked to help out. Delila, the soloist, knew him already and had sung with him in Algeria. Another woman was related to a close friend of his. During rehearsals, a congenial atmosphere prevailed. Aït Menguellet would go out with some of us afterward, and on at least one occasion he took the entire chorus out for a meal. Payment seemed to be the last thing on anyone's mind. Indeed, to be working with a contract would have taken away the "charm," as one chorus man later told me. In fact, some chorus members may even have refused contracts had they been offered at that point.

As a discursive or a narrative frame, the good faith economy may have held together, functioning through chorus members' nostalgic desire for more "human" forms of relationship that they associated with their distant Algerian homeland, had the atmosphere created in the rehearsals extended to the concerts. This was not always the case. Aït Menguellet, preoccupied with the demands of his own performance, delegated responsibility for the chorus to his manager. We were required to arrive between 7:00 and 9:00 A.M. for a 3:00 P.M. show; we generally could not leave until 9:00 P.M., and we spent well over half of this time sitting idly backstage. It was sometimes difficult to obtain complementary passes for family members, and many of us ended up paying for at least several tickets, at 125 francs ($25) each. Meanwhile, some were losing money. Two women gave up weekend jobs, several men lost work time. Some chorus members felt improperly spoken to by the manager, whose style tended to be authoritarian. A woman was told to "shut up" when she repeatedly questioned a managerial decision; a man was dressed down in front of everyone for his "overly enthusiastic" stage presence; another was sharply criticized for not having made prior arrangements to obtain a complementary pass for his sister. The familial idiom through which the choruses were constituted seemed to prevent chorus members from raising concerns as they arose. For example, one man had a brother-in-law who worked for the manager; he chose not to voice his grievances so as not to disrupt his brother-in-law's relationship with his employer. In short, the discursive conventions through which a good faith economy was supposed to operate—and through which the choruses were positioned—were being gradually undermined. Meanwhile, chorus members learned that the dance troupe had been engaged differently: They were being paid through the "French" contract model. Rumors put their salaries as high as $500 per day.

Only as these perceived injustices gradually built up did chorus members begin to grumble about payment.[11] In fleeting comments shared in the dressing room between numbers, the chorus women began to berate themselves for having been taken in by the "Algerian" way of doing business. For although each had believed that she would be fairly remunerated, not one had discussed payment when she was engaged. "I told myself, 'he'll surely give us something,'" said one woman. Another, who had grown up in France and worked in a legal environment, said that she was usually scrupulous about getting everything in writing; she did not do so in this case, she said, because her aunt was a friend of Aït Menguellet. During a negotiating meeting between the chorus women and the video producer, held two weeks after the final show, the women reconstituted themselves through the terms of the "French" model. They framed their grievances in contractual terms, calculating the time they had spent at rehearsals as well as the money they had lost by giving up jobs or paying for childcare. They also sought to invoke the law, arguing that the use of their image entailed legal rights to compensation (here, however, they had no legal grounds to stand on).[12]

From Aït Menguellet's perspective, the women's request appears to have widened the gap he already perceived between diaspora and home. As they moved toward the "French" model, he aligned himself even more closely with what he described as an "older Kabylia" where one's word "replaces documents, replaces writing." When he and I spoke after the performances, he characterized his way of seeing things as not "rational," "modern," or "logical"; nevertheless, he said,

> I take responsibility for it [*je l'assume*] because I have the memory of that era that was disappearing. I lived it a little bit. And it's that era that really marked me. I can be modern, but in reality, all my foundations, all my roots, are deep into this ancestral, older time, really antiquated [*desuet*], outside of time . . . I don't refuse modernity, but maybe I refuse it only in certain areas. Where, for example, a paper can replace a man, a paper can testify [*faire foi*] more than the word of a man, I refuse modernity. Do you understand? But I don't refuse, for example, recording equipment that allows me to work, a computer that lets me have all my information. Not at all. But I refuse modernity when it crosses a threshold and puts man himself in question [*remet l'homme en doute*].

Aït Menguellet has never worked with written contracts, he emphasized, even with his own editors and producers; from the start, he was against asking chorus members to sign releases. To him, the matter was straightforward: "If someone doesn't want to be in the video, I'll take them out." His discomfort with financial negotiations had led him to delegate all such matters to his manager:

> I refused [to get involved] right from the beginning, and moreover I was careful to discuss this with [the manager]; I told him, in the shows we're going to give, all the people that we contact, I'll talk to them only about technical and artistic things. Everything having to do with money, you work it out with them . . . work it out with the Olympia to define salaries, such that we will have achieved our goal of putting on a really strong show, even if I don't make a cent . . . I would not know how to receive someone [i.e., to discuss payment] because [laughs], I don't know, because, to receive someone who says to me "I want to be paid," I'll say, "How much do you want?" He says a million, I'll go get him a million, I'll give it to him. I am incapable of negotiating [this] . . . of telling someone, "no, you're asking for too much because there's a law that says [such and such]," I don't know these laws, I don't want to know them. . . . If I hadn't found someone [to handle the money], I would have . . . performed alone, as I usually do, so as not to have problems.

Money matters took shape, then, around opposing representations of diaspora and home, differences that sharpened dramatically over the course of the performances. Unlike the video images, however, in backstage conversations it was the homeland that was increasingly disparaged. As the discursive gap between diaspora and home widened, the players, too, became polarized. For the chorus women, representations of the homeland as an idealized site of nostalgia receded, replaced by images of a Kabylia mired in unwieldy and often corrupt traditions or "mentalities" that were simply not workable in the world in which they lived. Their move pushed Aït Menguellet, in contrast, to embrace even more strongly his vision of Kabylia as a place of human values, where one's word had pride of place. To include the women in the video, under their terms, was to allow the Kabylia that he stood for to be undermined.

Performing Authenticity

The situation of the women's chorus was further complicated by their relationship to the dance troupe. Here, the women configured the homeland in yet another way, situating themselves as representatives of Berber cultural traditions in relation to the dancers—two Algerian Arabs, one Moroccan Arab, and a French woman.[13] It was especially galling for the chorus women that three of the dancers, including the director of the troupe, were Arabs who had been engaged to represent Kabyle dance practices. Although only two chorus women had spent more than a few years in Kabylia, they collectively constituted themselves against what they perceived as the dancers' inauthentic portrayals of Kabyle dance styles. Matters came to a head at the dress rehearsal, when the lead dancer was positioning the chorus for the wedding scene. The dancer planned to have the bride enter the stage seated on the crossed arms of two men, and this outraged the chorus women. "It can't be done that way, that's not how it's done, the public will never accept it," said Delila. "A woman would never enter on the arms of men." When a dancer told Delila to loosen up and "play" with her more during one song, Delila refused. "I'm not there to play with her, I'm there to sing. I'm not going to lower myself to their level. . . . That's just how Arabs are," she told me later. "They have no shame [ulac leḥya]. . . . We have a word for these kinds of women in Kabylia—they're called ticeṭṭaḥin."

Historically, the term ticeṭṭaḥin describes the women belly dancers who were paid to perform provocatively with itinerant dance musicians in front of the men of each village they passed through. Delila was using the term, however, not in a referential but in an evaluative and performative fashion, attributing to the dancers essentialized qualities against which she could define herself. This is a good example of what Crapanzano (1992) calls an "arrest" in the ongoing dialectical movement between self and other, through which an illusion of a fixed self is produced when the other is assigned, for example, character traits, a "personality," a particular psychological makeup, or a societal role. Through her scorn-laden "ticeṭṭaḥin," Delila constituted the dancers as provocative and promiscuous while positioning herself at the opposite end of an intricate scale, mapped onto the body, that measures a woman's moral character through her mastery of modes of moving in space.[14] Here, fine gradations of posture, eye position, gesture, or dress are all used to project an image of respectability and self-control. Mastery of context-appropriate performance modalities is part of this embodied knowledge. Conventionally, women singing by themselves would fall at the high or more acceptable end of the scale, and public belly dance would occupy the low end, with a range of intermediate positions. Receiving payment for any kind of performance automatically moves it down on the scale; in other words, an inverse relationship obtains between respectability and remuneration.[15] Delila reconstituted this moral discourse, casting a condemnatory judgment of female performers (of which she herself was one) onto the dancers while crafting herself as a different kind of performer, one who practiced only "respectable" song, one who would never perform a belly dance on stage. "Kabyle women perform a belly dance," she told me, "but we do so only among ourselves, never in front of men."

The role of the women's chorus on stage facilitated Delila's move. We embodied a representation of traditional Berber women. Our positioning on stage mirrored the ways women would have sung by themselves in an ideal-typical village setting. First of all, we were physically separated from the men. Whereas they stood before stone benches designed to evoke memories of the village assembly, we were in front of a replica of a water fountain, historically a key symbol of women's social space in a Kabyle village. We joined with the men on many refrains, but were not involved in the most political songs. We did one number by ourselves—a lighthearted lament about marriage that was written by Aït Menguellet in a style intended to imitate the kinds of songs that village women improvise.[16] We also participated, with the men, in a song whose refrain was inspired by the women of Aït Menguellet's village. Aït Menguellet inserted their tune into a larger composition in which he, joined by the men's chorus, sang verses about the trials of immigration to France.[17] We women, left back at the village fountain, punctuated the verses with a refrain about the glittering world to which the men had been lost. Lighting also helped to create the illusion that we women were singing by ourselves. During our refrains, the men were plunged into darkness while we were under the spotlights. In short, the role of the women's chorus on stage was to represent the ways Kabyle women would traditionally sing together in village settings.

Had the chorus women been defining themselves solely in relation to traditional performance behaviors, however, they should not have asked for money. Refusing payment could, in some ideal cultural sense, have constituted a further way of distancing themselves from the dancers and reaffirming their own moral superiority. Yet the dancers were doubly resented because they were paid more for their work. Furthermore, it seemed to the singers that the dancers received better treatment from the manager. They received complimentary passes; were given a spacious dressing room; and in general were well spoken to. Payment for performance in this situation appeared to be accompanied by public acknowledgment and professional respect. As the discrepancy between the treatment of singers and dancers widened, Delila informed the other chorus women of the initial dinner meeting, in which a figure of $100 per concert had been tossed around. During the intermission of the final performance, the women decided that they were entitled to this payment. "I would feel like I was betraying myself if I just smile and say nothing," Delila said. "How long are they going to get away with treating people like this?"

The chorus women, by explicitly requesting remuneration, attempted to open up a new space in which they felt recognized for their embodied knowledge of Berber traditions. To do so, they removed economic negotiations from a relationally oriented and indirect "good faith" frame. Instead, they used a contractual discourse to seek acknowledgment of their roles as performers. The chorus men were unwilling to take this step.[18] Furthermore, they judged the women harshly. Delila, in particular, was seen by one man as being "worse than a French woman: Because she didn't say anything about money at the beginning, she acted as if she were in Algeria, and then afterwards, she acts like a French woman in demanding it. She wanted to give an image of herself as being something that she isn't; she wanted to see herself as 'evolved' [évoluée]." For this man, Delila was "acting like" another kind of woman, be it a "traditional" Algerian or an "evolved" French one. Her own situation as an Algerian woman living in a complex diasporic situation was utterly invisible.

Over the course of the Olympia performances, the chorus women constituted themselves as performers by playing representations of diaspora and homeland against each other in a flexible and shifting fashion. They drew on their diasporic location to distance themselves from "Algerian" styles of negotiation and to demand remuneration. At the same time, they constituted themselves in terms of cultural authenticity with regards to the dance troupe of mostly Arabs. This ambivalent relationship to tradition, in which some aspects are valorized while others are disparaged, was utterly absent from the performances themselves. On the concert stage, Aït Menguellet had tried to create a representation of an authentic Kabyle culture positioned far away from the modern world. It was this image—one that nearly all spectators could embrace—that furnished the backdrop against which the specific messages of his songs were articulated.

The concert video is more equivocal. In some ways, it reinforces the traditional roles that the women were asked to play onstage, for as the video was reworked, frames of the chorus women were replaced for the most part by footage of old women in Kabylia engaged in traditional tasks. In other ways, however, the disjunctive aspects of the video—the occasional shots of five empty mikes in front of the fountain; the disembodied women's voices on the soundtrack; the new, out-of-tune soloist—suggest a more compelling image of the multiple currents traversing Kabyle diasporic society. The women on the stage were visible to the audience within the performance frame, as representations of women in traditional Kabyle culture. Outside the frame, the real-life women, those who had given up jobs and time with their families, who had faced the disapproval of some members of their community, those who sought respect for and understanding of their situations, those who made demands, were in turn made invisible. Aït Menguellet's wish to create a video image of an older world was ultimately subverted not by anything so simple as greed, but by the need of Algerian women living in France to invent new ways to locate themselves in a world whose contours are constantly shifting.

The Olympia concerts provide a vivid illustration of the ways in which the production of Berber identity as a collective project intended for public consumption and political mobilization may work to erase adjacent "axes of differentiation" (Brah 1996: 124). Within the diaspora, such axes of differentiation may be especially acute, as family relationships constituted in terms of morality are crosscut by new economic and social pressures. Women's positioning is particularly contentious, for it is largely through women's bodies that novel ways of configuring home, work, and leisure are being organized and experienced. Ultimately, however, differentiation recedes in cultural products destined for widespread circulation. The concert video, despite several awkward scenes, in the end does not reveal its own history. As the video travels from France to Belgium, Montreal, and beyond, its idealized images of the homeland generate a unifying vision of collective identity that obscures its own location in a profoundly heterogeneous trans-Mediterranean space.

Epilogue

As I write in Bloomington, Indiana, in the summer of 2004, Berber cultural movements have become a force to be reckoned with by states across North Africa and the diaspora. In 1995, following a regionwide boycott of public schools in Kabylia, Tamazight began to be taught on a limited basis in some Algerian public schools. On November 28, 1996, the Algerian Constitution was amended to acknowledge "Amazighité" (Amazigh-ness) as one of the three "fundamental components" of Algerian identity, alongside Islam and "Arabité" (Arab-ness) (Algerian Constitutional Council 1996). In 2003, following a yearlong insurgency in Kabylia, Algeria amended its constitution to recognize Tamazight as a national (although not official) language. The Moroccan government, long hostile to Berberist concerns, established the Royal Institute of Amazigh Culture in 2001, and in 2003 introduced the language into a group of pilot schools. In 1995, France included Berber (*Taqbaylit* and *Tacelhit* varieties, from the Algerian Kabyle and Moroccan Chleuh regions, respectively) as one of the foreign language options on the nationwide baccalaureate exam.[1] In March 2002, the parliament of the Spanish region of Catalonia adopted a resolution in support of Amazigh language, culture, and identity. Even Washington's attention was momentarily captured. On July 12, 2001, on the occasion of a meeting between Algerian President Abdelaziz Bouteflika and President George W. Bush in the U.S. capital, Berbers demonstrated outside the White House to protest the Algerian government's assassinations of over one hundred activist youth in the Kabyle region. The World Amazigh Congress brought Amazigh issues to the attention of the United Nations at the twenty-seventh meeting of the U.N. Committee for Economic, Social and Cultural Rights (Geneva, Switzerland, November 2001) and the World Conference against Racism (Durban, South Africa, September 2001).

If Berbers have succeeded in garnering global attention, it is because they have been profoundly attuned to how discourse travels. This study has been concerned with the skill of Berbers in fashioning relationships between representation and circulation. Starting from the tensions between the seeming naturalness of identity discourses and the conjunctural nature of their constitutive networks, I have been interested in the multiple processes through which a sense of Berber or Amazigh identity has taken hold among Kabyles. I have argued that it is through linkages and interconnections to a range of products, events, and ideologies that such an identity has come to seem natural, and I have attended to a number of specific locations where such interconnections have been forged. The reflexive and refractive nature of these linking processes—encapsulated by the image with which this book opened of two video cameras taping each other filming a cultural performance—is of paramount importance. For seeing one-self through distancing lenses is precisely what enables a sense of unique cultural identity to crystallize.

Cultural products (such as the song *A vava inouva*) and events (the Berber Spring) that are discursively described in terms of an originary Berber identity turn out to be configured through circuits that extend far and wide. By obscuring their own historicity and hybridity, such products can circulate far more easily than they otherwise might. The search for stable signs through which groups can be represented is of course hardly limited to Berbers but has long been central to a range of political and scholarly projects. Attending to the circulatory flows that constitute the Berber village both elucidates and unsettles the ways in which colonial, anthropological, and activist interests have converged around the village as an originary entity where culture is thought to be at its most authentic.

Texts and performances offer especially productive locations to tease out the specificities of the branching encounters through which a unitary Berber identity has been fashioned. This may at first seem paradoxical: What could be more bounded in time and space than a printed text, a recorded song, or a staged production? Yet attending closely to such microsites—whether poetry collection, songwriting, children's concerts, copyright disputes, or the making of a music video—has enabled me to track the precise locations where Kabyles are coming to see themselves in cultural terms in a world where to lack a culture is also to lack a political voice. Such practices as creating village archives, engaging in protest marches, forming independent associations, mounting cultural exhibits, or developing new performance initiatives geared to "democratic" reform speak to the development of a new collective agency that must formulate itself in terms readily recognizable to a wider world community to have any hope of political survival.

A number of scholars concerned with the emergence of a modern social order all emphasize, as do I, the centrality of texts and their circulation to the creation of new publics (see especially Anderson 1991; Taylor 1999; Warner 2002). Yet what these accounts tend to take for granted is the textual product itself—a newspaper or pamphlet simply appears on the scene, leaving a new community in its circulatory wake. What I tried to detail in chapters 4, 5, and 6 are the specific ways in which texts have been constructed so as to invite particular kinds of allegiances. On the one hand, this entailed close attention to the regimes of textuality in which new notions of authorship, creativity, and individuality have been brought to bear on indigenous texts. At the same time, it meant looking into the concrete practices of text-making in which situated individuals—from a nineteenth-century French military man to a postcolonial Berber scholar-activist—have made choices about how to present and represent Kabyle songs and poems.

Yet texts alone do not tell the whole story. Following new Kabyle songs and related products as they are taken up within new performance spaces, whether weddings, kitchen conversations, or multimedia productions, reveals some of the tensions and fissures that have emerged in the collective project of creating Berber identity. Yet these "axes of differentiation" (Brah 1996: 124)—of which gender is among the most salient—are understandably not represented in collective cultural products destined for widespread circulation.

Initially, this work was conceived differently. Imagined under the title *Village to Vinyl*, the book was to follow the trajectories of women's songs as they left the villages and moved to a world stage. I hoped to identify the processes involved in transforming a "local" repertoire for a "global" market. The problem, of course, is that this presumed an origin that proved to be a mirage. The village songs that Ben Mohamed took as originals came to him already on tape or in print. In a process of creating "originals" for Ben, his elderly female informant, seated before a tape recorder in the early 1970s, was already reconceptualizing the songs in relation to Ben's request. Nor is it sufficient to go one step beyond—to arrive in a village, as both Idir and I did, tape recorder in hand, and try to capture the songs live. For the process of collecting introduces into the collected object new mediating structures, as the object is reimagined in relation to assumptions about tradition that already deeply implicate modernity itself. Although the new Kabyle songs claim rootedness in earlier village traditions, their trajectories begin not in the past but in the present. There is no linear move from village to vinyl; rather, the two locations are linked through a series of branching interconnections that extend in multiple directions.

As it turned out, I did follow songs, but not those of the old women. I followed a few of the first new songs—primarily those of Idir—and they led me to most of the sites I have explored in this work. I pursued their orientations to nationalist and postcolonial discourses, world music markets, and local repertoires. I looked into intertwined colonial and anthropological convictions about poetry as a form of unmediated cultural expression. I considered the assumptions about authorship, ownership, and cultural property on which the new songs rested. I explored the ways these various orientations and associations refracted into situated performances, where they were sometimes taken as authoritative but at other times utterly reshaped. In so doing, I sought to move across and between contemporary ideologies, historically shaped metadiscourses, and situated practices.

If cultural identity is formulated in discourse as stable and unitary, as soon as one begins to follow culture in circulation, this apparent stability vanishes. We find in its place a series of branching interconnections that I have elucidated only partially in this work. Ben Mohamed perhaps best captured the difficulty of trying to track culture in a remark he made to me during one of our last interviews. Although he was referring to the failure of the Algerian government to halt the Berber Cultural Movement, his comment applies equally well to anthropological projects. "Culture," he said, "is something that one can never fully master. There is always something that escapes."

Notes

Introduction

1. This brief history of Berber populations in North Africa is necessarily over-simplified. For a fuller account, see Brett and Fentress 1996; Camps 1987; Chaker 2004; Julien 1994 [1951]; Lorcin 1995.

2. Brett and Fentress (1996) locate Berber in the Afro-Asiatic language family, also linking it to both Semitic languages and old Egyptian (1996: 4). I believe that their difference with Chaker is merely one of terminology.

3. For locations and sizes as well as maps of Berber-speaking populations, see Chaker 1989; Brett and Fentress 1996.

4. North African Jews were treated by the French as a case apart, and in 1870, with the Crémieux Decree, were granted French civil status.

5. The first use of the term "Amazigh" in Kabylia may have been in M. Idir Ait Amrane's memoir, privately published in the 1940s, titled "Rise, oh son of Amazigh" (*Ekkr a mmis oumazigh*) (Ait Amrane n.d.).

6. For charts of election results that compare Kabylia with the rest of Algeria, see Mahé 2001: 498, 503.

7. Eventually, armed resistance was carried out by many different groups and subgroups. See Martinez 2000, esp. chap. 9; and Mahé 2001: 506–507.

8. During that period, I spent from October 1992 to mid-February 1993 in Paris. I subsequently worked in Paris from December 1993 to August 1994.

9. The total number of people with Algerian origins living in France in 1989 was approximately 1.5 million; of those, about one-third were Berber, primarily Kabyles (Chaker 1989: 49). Figures for Algerian immigration as a whole have not changed significantly since the 1982 census (www.INED.fr, accessed November 20, 2004), so I presume that this percentage remains accurate. Chaker's figures include both Algerian nationals and Algerians of French nationality.

1. The Berber Spring

1. I am grateful to the Association Culturelle Tafrara, Commune Maatras, Wilaya Tizi Ouzou, for allowing me to reproduce their account. They appear to have drawn it in part from Imedyazen 1981b: 10.

2. The potential crowd had been estimated at 10,000, but the demonstration was officially cancelled by French authorities (Chaker 1982: 421).

3. For comprehensive press coverage of the events of 1980, see Imedyazen 1981b.

4. Yugurtha was a Berber political leader in ancient Numidia (now Algeria) during the second century B.C. Because he fought the invading Roman forces, he is reclaimed as a hero by contemporary activists.

5.   Two exceptions to this view are Colonna 1996 and Roberts 1983.

6.   Accounts conflict about whether there were fatalities at the Cherry Festival. Ouerdane reports three deaths (Ouerdane 1990: 185), as does Imedyazen (1981b: 7), but Rachid Chaker does not note any (Chaker 1982: 389).

7.   The events of 1980 were so dramatic that many people, both activists and scholars, remain convinced that there were fatalities. Rumors of fatalities circulated in the French press in the days immediately following the events (see Imedyazen 1981b). However, these were not confirmed in subsequent reports, and an account in the Algerian newspaper *Algérie actualité* that appeared a week after the events confirmed that no fatalities occurred (Blidi 1980). Moreover, the accounts by Berber scholars and activists that I take as the most authoritative (and that would have a strong political interest in reporting fatalities) make no mention of any deaths. See Chaker 1982; Chaker 1989; and Ouerdane 1990. Finally, I interviewed eyewitnesses who confirmed for me that no fatalities occurred.

8.   Chaker 1989 and Mahé 2001 briefly note the importance of the university to the events but do not pursue this line of analysis.

9.   See Grandguillaume 1983 for a detailed account of Algeria's Arabization program. See also Taleb-Ibrahimi 1995.

10.   Personal interview, Ammar Lakehal, Montreal, Canada, March 10, 2002. Ammar wishes his full name to be used.

11.   I am indebted in this section to the history of associations developed by Karima Slimani-Direche (1997, esp. chaps. 4–5).

12.   According to Slimani-Direche, ABERC produced one issue of the journal *Amazigh: Revue du monde berbère et des entités ethniques* (Slimani-Direche 1997: 92 n.2). Ouerdane reproduces some of the statutes of this organization (Ouerdane 1990, Appendix 4).

13.   Salem Chaker has described the differences between the two associations in terms of "activist" versus "culturalist" orientations (Chaker 1987a), with ABERC on the culturalist and the Agraw on the activist end.

14.   Bessaoud was a controversial figure. He had served as an officer in the Algerian army (Armée de Libération Nationale, ALN) during the war, but found himself marginalized afterward, as an opposing faction took control of the state. For two years (1963–65), he participated in an insurrection seeking to topple the government. When it failed, Bessaoud went to Paris. See Bessaoud 1963 and Ouerdane 1990.

15.   According to Slimani-Direche, the Agraw produced the journal *Imazighene* monthly beginning in 1970. I have not located publication information about *Iṭij*, which translates as "Sun."

16.   The alphabet may have been easier to circulate than the journals, but being caught with the alphabet could be cause for arrest. The regular column "Faire le point" (Taking Stock) in the journal *Tafsut* tells of a group of young people who were brought to court in 1982 for having been caught with the alphabet in 1976 (Tafsut 1981a: 42).

17.   Goodman 2002a provides a graphic representation of this character.

18. The French law of July 1, 1901 governed the rights of associations organized by foreigners in France until 1981, when it was replaced by the law 81–909. See Benamrane 1983: 358.

19. On the creation and mandate of the Groupe d'Etudes Berbères, see the *Bulletin d'études berbères* 1972–73: 4–14.

20. Redjala was the first instructor (*Bulletin d'études berbères* 1972–73: 1–14); Slimani-Direche claims that he also founded the Groupe d'Etudes Berbères (Slimani-Direche 1997: 114 n. 3).

21. A list of members of the board can be found on the inside cover of each issue.

22. Colonna 1996 makes a related point in an essay considering the various uses of the street in postcolonial Algeria.

23. I am indebted to Rachid Chaker for his detailed daily journal of the events. His account opens as follows: "The notes that follow . . . are those of an observer who followed closely the events that shook Kabylia and, secondarily, Algiers. Completed and rearranged, the information and the observations contained in the lines that follow will perhaps serve as the basis for a broader analysis, which remains to be accomplished" (1982: 383). I hope that my discussion suggests the contours of such an analysis.

24. The UNJA was previously named the UNEA (Union Nationale des Etudiants Algériens, National Union of Algerian Students). By 1971, the UNEA had become dominated primarily by communist party (Parti de l'Avant-Garde Socialiste, Avant-Garde Socialist Party, PAGS) affiliates. The FLN shut it down and opened a new organization that it called the UNJA (Union Nationale de la Jeunesse Algérienne, National Union of Algerian Youth); this, too, soon came to be dominated by the PAGS. See Redjala 1988: 111.

25. The communist PAGS party (formerly the Parti Communiste Algérien) was tolerated by the Algerian government because of the supposedly critical vantage point it provided on the socialist state.

26. Most of the information in this section about dates and events is drawn from R. Chaker's comprehensive account (R. Chaker 1982). I have not provided the detailed daily account offered by Chaker but have tried to sketch the overall movement of the events.

27. Salem Chaker notes the hesitancy and indecisiveness of the state security as well as the fact that a new president (Chadli Bendjedid) had just taken office as factors contributing to the duration of the occupation (Chaker 1989: 48).

28. This missive from the Ministry of Higher Education is reproduced in Imedyazen 1981b: 108.

29. The international press stories are reproduced in Imedyazen 1981b: 240–266.

30. Most of the material in this paragraph comes from Chaker 1982.

31. Officially, classes resumed, but in practice, only 20 or 25 percent of students were attending (Chaker 1982: 435).

32. On the Seminar of Yakouren and its aftermath, see Mahé 2001: 513–515.

33. Mahé provides a brief history of the journal *Tafsut* and lists its founders (2001: 515 n. 1).

34. "Pour l'amazighité la lutte continue," *Liberté* 250, April 21, 1993. Photograph by Hamid Kouba.

2. Refracting Berber Identities

1. *A vava inouva* was released in Algeria on a 45 by Oasis-Disques (no. 11.001) in 1973, and in France and Algeria on an LP of the same name by EMI/Pathe Marconi (C 066–14334) in 1976 (Idir 1973; Idir 1976a). I have retained the orthography found on the record jacket. Using contemporary Tamazight orthography, the title would be written as follows: *A baba-inu ba*.

2. Informal discussion, December 2, 1992, Paris.

3. The documentary was later turned into a commercial video, *Ramparts of Clay* (*Remparts d'argile*) (Bertucelli 1970). This was filmed in Algeria but not shown there (Etienne and Leca 1975: 65).

4. Unless otherwise indicated, Ben Mohamed's remarks are drawn from interviews I conducted in Paris on December 1, 1992; December 23, 1992; June 21, 1993; August 18, 1994; and October 30, 1996; as well as several follow-up email exchanges.

5. Interview, December 1, 1992, Paris.

6. This strike was ultimately unsuccessful. See Duvignaud 1970 [1968] and Bertucelli 1970.

7. This statement comes from the speech made by a member of the Guinean delegation to the festival (Société Nationale d'Edition et de Distribution 1969: 94–104).

8. See, for example, the speech of Guinean President Ahmed Sékou Touré (Révolution Démocratique Africaine 1970: 11).

9. Festival publications are liberally peppered with quotations from the anthropological literature, but they also critique anthropology's links to colonialism and its use of an "an unscientific cultural pluralism" to "dilute" issues of historical materialism, class struggle, and cultural imperialism. See Révolution Démocratique Africaine 1970: 23ff.

10. The idea for the festival was initially proposed at the Conference on Education and Culture in Kinshasa in 1965 and consolidated in 1967; in September 1968, Algiers was selected as the site. See Organisation de l'Unité Africaine 1969b (Bulletin 2): 38–39.

11. See Organisation de l'Unité Africaine 1969c (Bulletin 5): 43–46.

12. China, despite a related effort to revive traditional culture (see Litzinger 2000; Schein 1999) was not in attendance—no doubt because of its ideological rift with the Soviet Union, with which Algeria had close ties. Also notable for its absence was most of the Arab Middle East; only Lebanon and the Palestine movement El-Fath were present.

13. A list of festival participants, guests, and observers can be found in Société Nationale d'Edition et de Distribution 1969: 193–208.

14. Ben told me that he went to all of the theatrical productions and two-thirds of the films, where such emerging luminaries as Egypt's Youcef Chahine and Senegal's Sembene Ousmane were screening early works.

15. At the Symposium of Algiers, which accompanied the festival, speeches were given by a high-level representative (in eight cases, the president) of every African nation in attendance and by officials from the Soviet Union, North Vietnam, and the Palestinian liberation movement "El Fath." An additional forty talks were given by various intellectuals and writers from around the world. See Société Nationale d'Edition et de Distribution 1969.

16. Ben initially wrote these remarks as part of a course paper. His instructor wanted to give him an A+ (in the Algerian system, a 19 or 20 out of 20), but did not dare to because he feared that the paper would be reviewed by the school administration. Later, Ben used this paper as part of a text responding to the 1976 referendum on the creation of a new Algerian constitution. The text was published anonymously in France (N.A. 1976); Ben's section was subtitled "Constitutive Cultural Elements of the New Algerian Man" and drew explicitly on the works of Fanon, Cabral, and Ki-Zerbo.

17. Unless otherwise indicated, remarks by Idir are from interviews I conducted with him in Paris on February 10, 1994 and November 4, 1996.

18. A version of the tale can be found in Amrouche 1979 [1966]: 111–113. In some versions, including the one used by Idir, the ogre is replaced by a more generic monster (lwaḥc).

19. Scott defines "problem spaces" as "conceptual-ideological ensembles, discursive formations, or language games that are generative of objects, and therefore of questions" (Scott 1999: 8).

20. At the time, Messadia was responsible for "orientation and information" for the FLN.

21. Personal interview, Ferhat Mehenni, Tizi Ouzou, May 9, 1993.

22. See, e.g., the dictionary of neologisms Amawal (1990). The journal Tafsut ("Spring") regularly printed a chart of the Berber alphabet as well as some grammar lessons. Tafsut also published a special "Scientific and Pedagogical" series that developed terminology in Tamazight in subjects like mathematics.

23. Taleb-Ibrahimi, speaking at this seminar on the role of the INM (Institut National de Musique), summarized the nation's musical politics as follows: "Adapting music to our national realities, enriching it by modernizing it and establishing its scientific basis, teaching it to the next generation—these are the imperatives of our Cultural Revolution" (Taleb-Ibrahimi 1973).

24. Early festivals included the National Folklore Festival (est. 1966), the National Festival of Classical (i.e., Andalusian) Music (est. 1967), the National Festival of Popular Music and Song (est. 1969), and the National Festival of Algerian Song (est. 1973). Later on, there would be festivals centered around political song (est. 1979), unity (est. 1979), protest song (est. 1982), and youth (est. 1985), to cite only the most prominent. On music festivals, see also Déjeux 1975.

25. It is unclear whether the figure of 20,000 participants refers to the festival in Algiers, or to the multitiered festival structure that preceded it.

26. Houses of Culture began to be built throughout Algeria in the mid-1970s; their role was defined by a decree of December 6, 1974 and is further elaborated in the 1976 Constitution (Front de Libération Nationale 1976: 85). The House of Culture in Tizi Ouzou opened in 1975; see A.M. (presumably Achour, Mouloud) 1975.

27. I was unable to secure copyright permission to reproduce the full text of *A vava inouva*. The refrain comes from a traditional text in the public domain.

28. Oasis Disques no. 11,001; the flip side of the recording contains the song *Tamacahuṯ n tsekkurt*.

29. In exchange for promoting the album, Chappell took 25 percent of the royalties earned by Idir and Ben. This kind of arrangement, exploitive from the perspective of the artists, was apparently common, especially with singers coming from the third world. See Wallis and Malm 1984: 79.

30. The "Big Five" recording companies included EMI, RCA, CBS, WEA, and Decca. According to a Decca producer, for a recording to break even, it needed to sell at least 30,000 to 40,000 copies (Wallis and Malm 1984: 89).

31. *Nueva canción* ("new song"), for example, had emerged in the 1950s and 1960s with Chile's Violeta Parra and Victor Jara. It enjoyed a resurgence in the 1970s, when it also began spreading to other Latin American and Caribbean nations as well as to Europe. See Wallis and Malm 1984 (esp. 41, 132–134, 219, 336–343). See also Fairley and Horn 1987; Manuel 1987; Tumas-Serna 1992.

32. One such group was the French duo Dominique et David. I was unable to locate other groups, but heard about the multiple translations on a number of occasions and from different sources, both print and personal. An article in the French paper *Libération,* for instance, refers to the song's translation into "numerous Mediterranean languages" (B.D. 1992).

33. Personal interview, Paris, June 27, 1994.

34. The phrase "moved through the world" is inspired by the title of Greg Urban's book: *Metaculture: How Culture Moves through the World* (Urban 2001).

3. The Mythical Village

1. Other colonial accounts that draw on related images of the village or the house include Genevois 1962; Masqueray 1983 [1886]; Maunier 1925, 1926. Bourdieu's concentric circles model was later reproduced in both Basagana and Sayad 1974 and Mahfoufi 1991. On Bourdieu's possible political motivations for portraying the Kabyle village in ahistorical terms, see Goodman 2003.

2. See esp. Mitchell 1988.

3. In using a pseudonym for the village, I am respecting my host family's wishes. They did not wish to draw attention to their village, given the continued possibility for political instability in Algeria.

4. Michael Herzfeld defines "structural nostalgia" as the "collective representa-

tion of an Edenic order—a time before time—in which the balanced perfection of social relations has not yet suffered the decay that affects everything human" (1997: 109).

5. I established a census of Tamkant based on a ledger of names kept in the Algerian village, and with the further assistance of two men actively involved in village affairs, one in Tamkant, the other in Paris.

6. Montagne 1954 provides a fascinating series of maps that illustrate where in Paris immigrants from particular Algerian regions settled. See also Massignon and Gérolami 1930 and Slimani-Direche 1997.

7. The agreement reached between Algeria and France in March 1962 that officially ended the Algerian revolution and laid out a thirty-year framework governing relations between the two nations.

8. Until 1974, immigration was handled through the Bureau de Main d'Oeuvre. From 1974 to 1981, an offer of employment and a housing certificate were required.

9. These figures are derived from village records kept in relation to the repatriation system.

10. Amkan was in a "free zone" (*zone libre*) during the war, and it served as a "host" village. Other villages, whose locations made them difficult to control, were declared "forbidden zones" (*zones interdites*), and their populations were forced to relocate to host villages, such as Amkan, or to resettlement camps. See Bourdieu and Sayad 1964.

11. On the FLN's control over the distribution of resources, see Mahé 2001: 481.

12. Many of these efforts were mandated by the World Bank and the International Monetary Fund as part of "structural adjustment" programs.

13. Bourdieu's description of the house draws on an earlier ethnography of the Kabyle house (Maunier 1926; see also Maunier 1925), but does so selectively. In particular, Maunier described a gender division of labor that is less rigid than in Bourdieu's discussion (see esp. Maunier 1926: 29, 67). Alternative ethnographic trajectories of the house, which Bourdieu does not consider, view it in terms of hygiene (Hanoteau and Letourneux 1872–73; Rémond 1933) or, more importantly, discuss changes in Kabyle housing styles due to European influence as early as the 1920s (Bernard 1921; A. Berque 1936; Maunier 1926: 36, 48; Rémond 1933).

14. For a photograph showing the center beam of the house in relation to the pillars, see Abouda 1985: 53.

15. Fadhma and her brother, both long-term residents of France, generally spoke in French together.

16. On the tajmaᶜat in relation to the precolonial Kabyle social system, see Mahé 2001: 78–144. On the tajmaᶜat and the French colonial administration, see Mahé 2001: 245–272. On the tajmaᶜat and the Berber Cultural Movement, see Mahé 2001: 488–495. On the tajmaᶜat's relations with cultural associations and with the political parties of the 1990s, see Mahé 2001: 546–556.

17. As early as 1946, ways of speaking at village assemblies were being turned into heritage. With encouragement by the missionaries (Pères Blancs), a Kabyle

man reconstructed a session of a village assembly, which was published by the missionary journal *Fichier de documentation berbère*. See Lanfry 1959 [1946].

18. *Lqanunat,* Village "Tamkant" ("Amkan"), village archives.

19. In Amkan, this tax was 5 or 10 dinars per person in 1993, depending on the project.

20. See Mahé 2001: 490–492 for a vivid example of the application of quarantine in another village, which ended only with the payment of a fine of two cattle by the ostracized individual.

21. The phenomenon of younger men taking control of the tajmaᶜat after 1989 was widespread, as was the practice of limiting ostentatious displays of wealth. See Mahé 2001: 547–553.

22. Traditionally, marabouts were exempt from attendance at the tajmaᶜat and from collective labor. With the changes in the tajmaᶜat after 1989, this began to shift; see Mahé 2001: 490. In Amkan, marabout families were among the most active in tajmaᶜat affairs during my stay.

23. In earlier decades, the village committee in Paris also provided services to newly arriving immigrants, including helping them find a job and housing and providing them with a stipend for living expenses. Because the nature of immigration has changed considerably, these services are rarely necessary today.

24. In 1994, repatriation costs ranged from 13,000–26,000 francs per corpse.

25. Reglement Générale, Paris, May 15, 1977, Village of "Amkan," village archives.

26. This might occur, for example, if a woman marries into a town or city without its own repatriation system (such as Algiers).

27. For a description of the three-day wedding see Goodman 1999 and Mahfoufi 1991; see also Laoust-Chantréaux 1990.

28. See Goodman 1999 for a description of a café wedding.

29. If the bride is from the village, her relatives will also be invited; if she is from a different village, only her closer family will attend, and on the second night only. In addition to invited guests, uninvited men from the village (and sometimes, from a neighboring village) may be present at the evening urar, but must watch from a distance and may not dance. Uninvited women may not attend.

30. On the dance economy, see Goodman 1999 and Mahfoufi 1991.

31. Michael Herzfeld (1987) uses the term *disemia* to describe the "expressive play of opposition that subsists in all the varied codes through which collective self-display and self-recognition can be balanced against each other" (Herzfeld 1987: 114).

4. Collecting Poems

1. I have treated Hanoteau's material in two earlier publications. Goodman 2002b emphasizes the ways in which poetry was used to construct Kabylia as an object of ethnographic knowledge and explores what the collection reveals

about the colonel's position in Kabyle society, including extended discussion of his primary informant, the marabout Si Moula n Ait Ameur. Goodman 2002c foregrounds the ways the poems participated in the French civilizing mission.

2. Adolphe Hanoteau began his military career in 1836 and was sent to Algeria in 1846, where he spent most of his career in the Offices for Indigenous Affairs, or Bureaux Arabes (Gouvernement Général de l'Algérie n.d.). In 1859, after serving eight years under General Daumas at the Bureau Politique des Affaires Arabes in Algiers, Hanoteau was posted to the Kabyle town Dra-el-Mizan, where he was named Commander-in-Chief (*Commandant Supérieur*) of the Bureau Arabe (Office for Indigenous Affairs). Shortly thereafter, he was tapped to head up the Bureau Arabe in the important military outpost of Fort Napoléon, where he served as bureau chief from 1860 to 1862. In 1863, Hanoteau relocated to Algiers, where his work on customary law became known to his colleagues; in 1864 he was released from his regular duties to write a volume on Kabyle law for publication (Hanoteau and Letourneux 1872–73; see Ageron 1960: 334; Mahé 2001: 204). I refer to him as "the colonel" in this chapter because that was his rank in the period that concerns me.

3. These dates are from Hanoteau's personnel dossier, Gouvernement Général de l'Algérie n.d.

4. Carette's "Etudes sur la Kabilie proprement dite" was, before Hanoteau's work, the most influential of these proto-ethnographies (Carette 1847–48); Carette was also a *Polytechnicien* (Lorcin 1995: 276 n.71). See also Aucapitaine 1857; Daumas and Fabar 1847.

5. The Ministry's refusal to associate itself with Hanoteau's project is surprising in light of the fact that the regime of Napoleon III had decreed in 1852, over ten years earlier, that school inspectors and other researchers should start collecting French folklore to be published in a volume entitled *Recueil des poésies populaires de la France* [Collection of Popular Poems of France] (Rearick 1974: 162–163; note the resemblance to Hanoteau's title, *Poésies populaires de la Kabylie du Jurjura*).

6. After the series of fourteen poems, Hanoteau placed two more in Part I. The first is about the death of a Turkish caïd (administrator) in the region. The second, interestingly, is a women's lament about a Kabyle man who was executed by the French. This is the only poem by women that Hanoteau placed in Part I; see my discussion of the "Lament for Dahman-ou-Meçal" below.

7. The choice of the Roman over the Arabic alphabet is, of course, deeply ideological and continues to be a subject of dispute not only between Berbers and Arabs but also among different Berber populations.

8. Twenty-three of Part III's twenty-five poems address these topics.

9. Poem 16 in Part I, 154–160. This is the only poem in Part I attributed to women.

10. For extended analysis of this poem, see Goodman 2002b. I have retained Hanoteau's orthography for the terms *imedjd'ab* and *Aissaoua*.

11. It is unclear to me which school Chaker is referring to. Colonna (1975) dates

the first state-run school in the region to 1881, when a school opened in the village of Taourirt-Mimoun (At Yenni), but Boulifa would have enrolled in school a decade or so before that date. It is likely, then, that Boulifa attended a Christian school run either by the Jesuits, who opened the first school in 1873, or by the Pères Blancs, who closely followed.

12. As one of the first Kabyle teachers of the Berber language, Boulifa developed Kabyle grammar books (Boulifa 1910, 1913) to support his classes. Boulifa also wrote a history of the region from what some have seen as a Kabyle-centric perspective (Boulifa 1925, reedited in 1999); see Chaker 2001a: 120–123.

13. Boulifa (1990) tells us that the poems were collected by students and other young people from the village of Adni; Boulifa then tried to "authenticate" them by reading them to the poet himself (in a few cases), or to those who knew the poet well. The poems that could not be "authenticated" were relegated to Part II, along with poems from other authors; see Boulifa 1990 [1904]: 67.

14. *Afrique Action,* December 5, 1960, reproduced in Institut du Monde Arabe 1994: 73.

15. As her extraordinary autobiography testifies (F. Amrouche 1988 [1968]), Jean's mother experienced profound alienation from and marginalization within her native Kabylia. A child born out of wedlock in a society where civil status and moral stature were conveyed through paternal lineage, Fadhma At Mansour (1882–1967) had no choice but to enter the mission schools at the age of four; at age seventeen, she would convert to Christianity. Her literacy—rare for a woman at the time—allowed her to serve in the highly unusual role of a female public scribe. After marrying a Christian man, she spent forty years outside of her country, in Tunisia. There she penned her life story as well as several original poems.

16. Interview with Taos Amrouche, "D'un jour à l'autre," recorded and broadcast April 4, 1968, produced by Hélène Turner and Jean-François Noel. INA387L454.

17. Taos Amrouche's recordings of Kabyle music include Amrouche 1966, 1968, 1971, 1974, 1975a, 1975b, 1977.

18. Interview with Taos Amrouche. INA387L454.

19. Personal interview with SACEM representative, July 11, 1994; I believe the songs would have been declared in the public domain but could not verify this. Transcriptions were by French ethnomusicologists Yvette Grimaud and Georges Auric. At the time Taos was working, there was no Algerian copyright agency.

20. Taos Amrouche, "Que fait-on pour la langue berbère?" In *Combat,* November 18, 1956. Reproduced in Institut du Monde Arabe 1994: 89–90.

21. Interview with Taos Amrouche on "Les couleurs de l'été," recorded and broadcast September 29, 1968, France Culture, produced by De Beer and Crémieux. INA186L91.

22. *Le grain magique: Contes, poèmes, proverbes berbères de Kabylie.* This collection provides stories, poems, and proverbs in French translation only, with

limited commentary (a two-page prologue situates them in relation to such collections as the Mother Goose rhymes). Reprinted in 1979.

23. Interview with Taos Amrouche. INA186L91. (Emphasis added.)

24. Interview with Taos Amrouche. INA186L91.

25. Cited in Abdoulaye Fall, "'Chants berbères' par Marguerite Taos Amrouche, ce soir au théâtre Sorano." In *Dakar matin,* April 20, 1966. Reproduced in Institut du Monde Arabe 1994: 106.

26. Mammeri and his colleagues were unable to locate Kabyle texts for all of Amrouche's poems.

27. Mammeri was referring to Victor Hugo's poem about the 1815 battle of Waterloo.

28. For more on Mammeri, as well as a partial list of his works, see Bellil and Chaker 2001 and Chaker 2001b; see also Colonna 2003.

29. By Mammeri's day, the Kabyle region had formed the object of countless ethnographic studies. Bibliographies of French studies of Kabylia include Brenier-Estrine 1994, 1995; Chaker 1991; Galand 1979; Lacoste 1962.

30. Ben Mohamed, personal communication by e-mail, September 18, 2001.

31. These notes are entirely in Berber, with a single exception. In Poem 28, Mammeri provided a note explaining the word *angal/tangalt* in Kabyle; he then added that "in French" (*s tfransist*), the word meant "symbol" or "allusion" (1980: 132 n. 94). This suggests that while Mammeri assumed that Berber readers understood French (a plausible assumption, since public education in Algeria at the time was carried out partly in French), the reverse assumption was not made.

32. For extended analysis of this poem, see Goodman 2002b.

33. Mammeri did occasionally situate the poems on the French pages within a dialogue, but he used the literary *passé simple* to frame the dialogue. See, for example, Poem 43 (Mammeri 1980: 167–171).

34. Salem Chaker, a former student and colleague of Mammeri, describes Mammeri's configuration of two publics in different terms, but he conveys a similar meaning. For Chaker, the Kabyle text "addressed itself first of all to [Mammeri's] own people"; in so doing, it "brings to life and fastens in memory . . . an exceptionally [rich] heritage." In contrast, the French translation "brings . . . the testimony and the song of a people" to "universal knowledge [*la connaissance universelle*]" (Chaker 2001b: 163).

35. This was almost as true of Arabic in the initial years of Algerian independence. See Pervillé 1996: 436.

5. Authoring Modernity

1. Interviews with Ben Mohamed in Paris took place on December 1, 1992; December 23, 1992; June 21, 1993; August 18, 1994; and October 30, 1996. These formal interviews were supplemented by a number of informal conversations and e-mail exchanges. Interviews with Idir in Paris took place on February 10, 1994 and November 4, 1996.

2. For an ethnomusicological study of Kabyle women's genres, see Mahfoufi 1991 and Mecheri-Saada 1979.

3. *Isefra* was released in 1976 on EMI/Pathe Marconi (C 066–14334) and in 1991 on Blue Silver (035.4 BSD 127).

4. Text copyrighted by Mohammed Benhammadouche (Ben Mohamed). Reproduced with permission.

5. Tanina: A mythical female bird who chose from among all the birds to mate with the eagle, who was the strongest. See Mammeri 1980: 226–257.

6. I found the line "I am walking in the plain" in what women presented to me as a "traditional" poem, and it also occurs in Yamina 1961 [1953]: 115–117. Ben no doubt had heard this line and substituted it here; he said that he often could no longer tell what was his and what was traditional.

7. The melody on the tape Ben used does not match Idir's melody. It is common in Kabylia to find similar words set to different melodies in different villages.

8. Personal communication, Boualem Rabia; cf. Messick 1987.

9. I can attest that these lines are sung by the woman on the Ait Hichem tape from which Ben worked.

10. Text copyrighted by Mohammed Benhammadouche (Ben Mohamed). Reproduced with permission. Recorded on EMI/Pathe Marconi (C 066–14334) and in 1991 on Blue Silver (035.4 BSD 127).

11. Recorded on the LP *Ay arrac-nneγ* (Editions Azwaw, Paris, 1979, AZW 021); the album credits Idir for the music, Ben Mohamed (Mohammed Benhammadouche) for the text.

12. The translation "Mr. Joe Saint" was developed in relation to three texts: (1) the Berber poem—"si winnat" could be literally glossed as "Saint Whatever"; (2) an existing French translation of the poem by Ben Mohamed, in which he used the term "Monsieur Un Tel" (Mr. So-and-So); and (3) my discussion of the poem with Ben Mohamed, in which we used the term "Sidi Machin" (Saint What's-His-Name). "Mr. Joe Saint" is my attempt to convey the sense of irreverence and parody that was communicated to me in this discussion. See Goodman 1998.

13. Text copyrighted by Mohammed Benhammadouche (Ben Mohamed). Reproduced with permission.

14. The French text, by Ramdane Sadi (producer of Kabyle concerts and recordings), reads as follows: "Au loin! Allez-vous en! Laissez-moi méditer en paix. . . . Détournez-vous loin de moi! Moi, je transcende vos peccadilles humaines. . . . Moi, je médite, moi! Moi, je ne fais pas de politique, moi!" (Translation on the jacket of the LP *Ay arrac-nneγ*, Editions Azwaw, Paris, 1979, AZW 021.)

15. On Ccix Muḥend U Lḥusin, see Mammeri n.d.

6. Copyright Matters

1. In considering this range of commentary, I am not interested in pointing an accusatory finger at anyone. Rather, I attempt to understand how the moral

and creative character of songwriters is being constructed and evaluated in relation to the ways they register their songs at the copyright agency.

2. Interview with Idir, Paris, February 10, 1994.

3. Interview with Ammar Arab, Kabyle video producer, Paris, July 19, 1994.

4. "Cheikha Cherifa à l'Olympia," VHS, released January 1994.

5. Like new Kabyle song, contemporary rai draws heavily on earlier rai songs, which were the province of women and sung in bars and at weddings. See Virolle 1995; see also Gross et al. 1994 and Schade-Poulsen 1999.

6. The French copyright agency SACEM resolves such cases by conducting a comparative expert analysis based on a system of fine gradations. Two works can be determined to be identical, in which case the second artist must pay full royalties to the first. Or they can be deemed similar with some differences; the degree of the similarity is fixed as a percentage by the analysts, and the second artist pays that percentage of royalty fees to the first.

7. In an important exception, Jessica Litman argues that the public domain is what enables the fiction of authorship as "ineffable creation from nothing" (1990: 1023).

8. See Feld 1996 for a fascinating account of the multiple appropriations of pygmy songs by differently positioned individual and corporate interests.

9. Much valuable scholarship has been devoted to how copyright law is fundamentally at odds with indigenous modes of organizing and regulating the circulation of cultural texts (see, for example, Bigenho 2002; Coombe 1998; McCann 1993; Seeger 1992; and the essays in Frith 1993 and Ziff and Rao 1997). My intention is not to challenge this important work but rather to propose that indigenous groups may also be appropriating some of the categories of copyright law to their own ends.

10. Certain forms of indigenous expression can be legally protected as "cultural property." Material artifacts are the primary targets of cultural property law; indigenous texts are generally unprotected. Like intellectual property law, cultural property law is also based on Western assumptions (such as, for instance, a distinction between "art" and "culture"); for an in-depth discussion, see Coombe 1998, chap. 5. Because my interlocutors talked about copyright law without separating intellectual from cultural property, I do not emphasize the distinction.

11. On the differences between French and Anglo-American copyright law, see Goldstein 2003, chap. 5. For detailed discussion of French copyright law as concerns music, see Gautreau 1970.

12. Moral rights are detailed in Gautreau 1970: 36–52.

13. The author may cede patrimonial rights to a third party. See Gautreau 1970: 69–86.

14. Gautreau concurs (1970: 65, n. 3), linking the extension of patrimonial rights to increases in life expectancy in developed countries.

15. Interview, M. Menant, Services Juridiques, SACEM, Paris, July 27, 1994.

16. The copyright declaration may also be split between text and melody, with

one attributed to the public domain and the other to the author (of new text) or the composer (of new music), as the case may be. See Feld 2000: 161 on the exploitive potential of the category of "arranger."

17. Interview, M. Menant, Services Juridiques, SACEM, Paris, July 27, 1994. Gautreau uses these terms somewhat differently; see Gautreau 1970: 32–33.

18. On the administration of French copyright law in Algeria, see Bendimered 1970, esp. 9, where he notes that Algerian artists were protected by French copyright law of 1957, which became Algerian law as of December 31, 1962.

19. Although ONDA was created in 1973, it dispersed no royalties to authors until 1976, when they were paid retroactively; see the unattributed article, "Première répartition des redevances," *Algérie actualité* 624 (September 29–October 5, 1977): 13. On the creation of ONDA, see Moussaoui 1980a: 18 (sidebar).

20. On reproduction and representation, see Gautreau 1970: 52–63.

21. The information on royalty payments in this paragraph is drawn from a personal interview with Mennane Benhamed at SACEM in August 1994.

22. According to reporter Kémal Bendimered, many producers in Algeria use the public domain attribution as a loophole to avoid paying full royalties to authors or composers (Bendimered 1970: 18).

23. Whether such authorizations are actually requested, and whether they are ever refused, would require further investigation.

24. The original singer's descendants may, however, come forward and, with appropriate proof, declare on their honor that the song belonged to one of their forebears. Such a case will be investigated, and if it is determined in the plaintiff's favor, appropriate financial amends must be made.

25. Mehenna Mahfoufi.

26. For a detailed account of women's village performances, including song texts and musical transcriptions, see Mahfoufi 1991.

27. When the bride leaves her home, women of the groom's family sing songs of joy, while women from the bride's family sing songs of loss and sadness.

7. Staging Gender

1. At a national level, political parties are the chief venues where these debates unfold, with ultrasecularist parties like the RCD (Rassemblement pour la Culture et la Démocratie) pitting themselves against various Islamist and centrist groups—initially, the FIS (Front Islamique de Salut, subsequently banned); later, Islamist parties like Hamas and En-nahda; and eventually, even the more centrist Kabyle-dominated party, the FFS (Front des Forces Socialistes).

2. For some of the first accounts of what took place in October 1988, see Afaq Ichtirakia n.d.; Aissou et al. 1988; and Charef 1990, among others.

3. Algerian Law 87–15 of July 21, 1987 granted the right to form locally based, nonpolitical associations without obtaining prior governmental authorization. Algerian Law 90–31 of December 4, 1990 extended this right to nationally based associations.

4. In Algeria, many other kinds of associations also formed at this time; on women's associations, see Benzerfa-Guerroudj 1993.

5. Mahé notes 400 village cultural associations at the time of his writing (presumably the late 1990s) (Mahé 2001: 470), yet he also says that nearly every village had its own association (2001: 546), which would suggest a figure considerably higher than 400.

6. The Amazigh Cultural Association of America (ACAA) was founded in 1992. In Canada, several cultural associations had formed earlier, such as Averroës and Tiddukla n Imazighen du Québec. During the 1990s and early 2000s, a number of others formed in Canada, including Tiruggza and Centre Amazigh de Montréal.

7. Alain Mahé contends that via the cultural associations, young women are "bursting into" (*faire irruption sur*) village public space (2001: 546). My own assessment is more cautious.

8. An *aggus* is also fastened around a new bride's hips as she makes her ritual trip to the village fountain, where she draws water for a young boy to drink—an obvious symbol of fertility.

9. In a personal interview, Amkan, September 1993.

10. My discussion in this section, as well as all quotations, are based on my line-by-line transcription of the meeting as it unfolded. I was not able to record all statements in their entirety.

11. Zahra was referring to French Law 81–909 of October 9, 1981, which modified the law of July 1, 1901, concerning the rights of associations organized by foreigners in France. See Benamrane 1983: 358.

12. My discussion in this section, as well as all quotations, are based on my line-by-line transcription of the meeting as it unfolded. I was not able to record all statements in their entirety.

13. My discussion in this section, as well as all quotations, are based on a transcript from my tape-recording of the full meeting.

14. This "kingdom" is known as the Royaume de Koukou.

8. Village to Video

1. On October 29, 1985, Aït Menguellet was arrested on a trumped-up charge of illegal arms possession (he had several hunting rifles in his home) and sentenced to three years in prison, ostensibly for dedicating one of the songs at his August 8 concert to the singer Ferhat Imazighen Imula, himself in jail since July 17, 1985 for his role in creating the Algerian League of Human Rights (LADH) in June 1985. See Collectif Contre la Répression en Algérie 1985: 148, 152.

2. In the spring of 1991, Islamist activists from the Front Islamique de Salut (FIS) attacked one of Aït Menguellet's concerts at the Atlas Theater in Algiers.

3. Among the most prominent Kabyle cultural figures to be assassinated were novelist and cultural critic Tahar Djaout (May 26, 1993) and new Kabyle singer Matoub Lounes (June 25, 1998).

4. Personal interview, Tizi Ouzou, Algeria, September 28, 1993.

5. Aït Menguellet tunes his guitar as follows: The second and fourth frets are further subdivided into two smaller frets, which enables quarter-tones; the six guitar strings are tuned E-A-D-G-C-F (instead of the western E-A-D-G-B-E).

6. Aït Menguellet was instrumental in forming and helping to finance several choruses in Algeria under the auspices of the Association M'Barek Aït Menguellet (Hamroun 1992). In 1991, he performed in Tizi Ouzou, Algeria with one of the choruses from that association (M.T. 1991). In 1992, he performed in Paris with the Tasga chorus from the Berber Cultural Association and the Shawi dance troupe Amendil (Mezouane 1992). See also Aït Menguellet 1990.

7. Aït Menguellet dedicated each of the concerts to a renowned Kabyle singer or cultural figure; these included Kamal Hamadi, Taleb Rabah, Cherif Kheddam, Idir, and Ben Mohamed.

8. Two men later claimed that they had asked the manager if they would be paid and were told they would be, but that "it wouldn't be much."

9. My host cited the same proverb when I attempted to negotiate payment for the lodging his family provided me. I knew that I was expected to reciprocate in some way, but attempting to collapse our relationship into a monetary transaction by discussing it up-front was almost insulting to him. Moreover, payment (which I did eventually make on the night before I left, framing it as a gift to be used to dig a well) was not enough. If I didn't also maintain the relationship, I would break the trust they placed in me by allowing me to share their home. See also Bourdieu's comments on the same proverb (Bourdieu 1977: 173).

10. I witnessed and experienced this mode of negotiation on a number of occasions in both Algeria and France. For example, my host told me about construction work that a contractor in the Algerian village had done on my host's house. After the work was finished, the contractor refused to tell my host how much he wanted for the work until more than two years had passed—despite repeated requests to do so from my host. Once the contractor provided a bill, my host then delayed paying him for two years. The difficulty of negotiating a fee for one's labor was also evident in a play that young men of the village's cultural association in Algeria wrote and staged in 1993. The play was about two men who perform some work and then try all kinds of ruses to get the money they think they are owed. I also found that I could not generally reimburse my consultants "directly" (i.e., with a prenegotiated wage for their assistance). They refused payment, so I had to find alternative ways to give them what I felt they deserved.

11. The men were unhappy with the conditions as well, but I spent far less time with them than I did with the women, so it is with the women that my focus lies.

12. Ammar Arab, video producer, explained to the women's chorus that they were considered "extras" (*figurantes intelligentes*) by French law and thus could not claim rights to their image.

13. A Kabyle dance troupe had initially been engaged, but withdrew at the last minute from the performances.

14. Jansen (1987: 183) reports that older Algerian women claim to be able to assess a girl's moral character from the way she pours coffee.

15. See Jansen 1987, chap. 8.

16. The song *Mi d-i-tenniḍ* (When You Told Me . . .) was previously performed as part of the larger work *Abrid t_temzi* (The Path of Youth) in Paris on June 28 and July 5, 1990, and recorded on Aït Menguellet 1990.

17. The song *Lγerba n 45* (Exile of 1945) was recorded on Aït Menguellet 1992 with the participation of the Tasga chorus.

18. The women may have had less to lose than the men did. That is, the women were able to use payment for the video as an "arm" (in the words of one) precisely because they had a culturally sanctioned way out: they could always claim that their fathers did not approve. Two women did claim to require their fathers' permission (which was granted), but they appeared to do so as a stalling device to gain time in which to consolidate their position. In other words, that the women felt less obligated to appear in the video than the men did allowed them more play with the situation. The men had more "face" to lose.

Epilogue

1. Berber could be taken as an oral elective on the baccalaureate exam in France as early as the 1950s, but not until 1995 was it offered as a standardized written exam.

Works Cited

A.B.A. 1984. Orchestre mécanique. *Algérie actualité* 957, February 16–22.

Abouda, Mohand. 1985. *Axxam: Maisons kabyles, espaces et fresques murales.* Goussainville, France: n.p.

Abu-Lughod, Lila. 1986. *Veiled Sentiments: Honor and Poetry in a Bedouin Society.* Berkeley and Los Angeles: University of California Press.

Achab, Ramdane. 1996. *La néologie lexical berbère (1945–1995).* Paris and Louvain: Editions Peeters.

A.D. [presumably Abdelkrim Djilali]. 1984. Sous le pavés, le plagiat. *Algérie actualité* 957 (February 16–22).

Ageron, Charles-Robert. 1960. La France a-t-elle eu une politique kabyle? *Revue historique* 1960 (April): 311–352.

———. 1976. Du mythe kabyle aux politiques berbères. In *Le mal de voir: Ethnologie et orientalisme: politique et épistémologie, critique et autocritique . . . Contributions aux colloques: Orientalisme, africanisme, américanisme (9–11 mai 1974); Ethnologie et politique au Maghreb (5 juin 1975),* 331–348. Paris: Cahiers Jussieu, Union Générale d'Editions.

———. 1991 [1964]. *Modern Algeria: A History from 1830 to the Present.* Trenton, N.J.: Africa World Press.

Aissou, Abdel et al. 1988. *Octobre à Alger.* Paris: Editions du Seuil.

Aït Amrane, M. Idir. n.d. *Mémoire: Au lycée de Ben-Aknoun 1945, Ekkr a mmis oumazigh.* Privately published.

Ait Ferroukh, Farida. 1994. Ethnopoétique berbère: Le cas de la poésie orale kabyle. Ph.D. diss., Université de la Sorbonne Nouvelle Paris III.

Ait Menguellet, Azzedinne. 1993. Aït Menguellet: Le poète et la terre. *L'Evènement* (Algiers), 110.

Aït Menguellet, Lounis. 1990. *Abrid t-temzi . . .* Paris: AdAC Amacahu and Akfadu Music.

———. 1992. *Awkni Xda'a Rabbi.* Akbou, Algeria: Editions Aqbu.

———. 1994. *Aït Menguellet à l'Olympia.* Paris: Triomphe Musique.

Alencastre, Amilcar. 1969. Le Brésil: Présence de l'Afrique en Amérique. In *Premier festival culturel panafricain: Communications,* vol. 2, 353–354. Algiers: Société Nationale d'Edition et de Distribution.

Algerian Constitutional Council. 1996. *The Constitution of the People's Democratic Republic of Algeria.* Algiers: Algerian Constitutional Council.

A.M. (presumably Achour, Mouloud). 1973. Séminaire national sur la musique: Rompre avec le conservatisme. *Algérie actualité* 384 (February 25–March 3).

Amrouche, Fadhma A. M. 1988 [1968]. *My Life Story: The Autobiography of a Berber Woman.* D. S. Blair, trans. London: The Women's Press.

Amrouche, Jean El-Mouhoub. 1988 [1939]. *Chants berbères de Kabylie (Edition bilingue).* Paris: L'Harmattan.

———. 1994. *Un Algérien s'adresse aux Français, ou l'histoire d'Algérie par les textes (1943–1961)*, ed. T. Yacine. Paris: L'Harmattan/Awal.

Amrouche, Marguérite Taos. 1966. *Chants berbères de Kabylie*. Boîte à Musique. BAM-LD 101.

———. 1968. *Chants de procession: Méditations et danses berbères*. SM-30, A280.

———. 1971. *Chants de l'Atlas: Traditions millénaires des berbères de l'Algérie*. Arion-30 U 103.

———. 1974. *Incantations, méditations et danses sacrées berbères*. Arion-34 233.

———. 1975. *Chants berbères de la meule et du berceau*. Arion-34 278.

———. 1977. *Taos Amrouche au Théâtre de la Ville*. Arion-34 407.

———. 1979 [1966]. *Le grain magique: Contes, poèmes, proverbes berbères de Kabylie*. Paris: Maspéro.

Amselle, Jean-Loup. 2001. *Branchements: Anthropologie de l'universalité des cultures*. Paris: Flammarion.

Anderson, Benedict. 1991 [1983]. *Imagined Communities: Reflections on the Origin and Spread of Nationalism*. London: Verso.

Appadurai, Arjun. 1990. Disjuncture and Difference in the Global Cultural Economy. *Public Culture* 2 (2): 1–24.

Arnaud, Jacqueline. 1992. Entretien avec Ben Mohamed. In *Littérature et oralité au Maghreb: Hommage à Mouloud Mammeri*, 163–183. Itinéraires et Contacts de Cultures. Paris: L'Harmattan.

Askew, Kelly M. 2002. *Performing the Nation: Swahili Music and Cultural Politics in Tanzania*. Chicago and London: University of Chicago Press.

Aucapitaine, Baron Henri. 1857. *Le pays et la société kabyle (expédition de 1857)*. Paris: A. Bertrand.

Azar. 1990 [1980]. *Amawal n Tmazight Tatrert (Lexique de berbère moderne)*. Bgayet (Bejaia), Algeria: Azar, Editions de l'Association Culturelle Tamazight.

Azem, Slimane. 1984. *Izlan: Receuil de chants kabyles*. Paris: Numidie-Music.

Bakhtin, Mikhail M. 1981. *The Dialogic Imagination*, trans. Caryl Emerson and Michael Holquist. Austin: University of Texas Press.

———. 1984. *Problems of Dostoevsky's Poetics*. Minneapolis: University of Minnesota Press.

———. 1986. *Speech Genres and Other Late Essays*, trans. V. W. McGee. Austin: University of Texas Press.

Basagana, Ramon, and Ali Sayad. 1974. *Habitat traditionnel et structures familiales en Kabylie*. Algiers: Société Nationale d'Edition et de Distribution.

Bauman, Richard. 1977. *Verbal Art as Performance*. Prospect Heights, Ill.: Waveland Press.

———. 1993. The Nationalization and Internationalization of Folklore: The Case of Schoolcraft's "Gitshee Gauzinee." *Western Folklore* 52 (April): 247–269.

———. 1995. Representing Native American Oral Narrative: The Textual Practices of Henry Rowe Schoolcraft. *Pragmatics* 5 (2): 167–183.

Bauman, Richard, and Charles Briggs. 1990. Poetics and Performance as Critical Perspectives on Language and Social Life. In *Annual Review of Anthropology*, vol. 19, 59–88.

———. 1999. Language Philosophy as Language Ideology: John Locke and Johann Gottfried Herder. In *Regimes of Language: Ideologies, Polities, and Identities*, ed. P. V. Kroskrity, 139–204. Santa Fe, N.M., and Oxford: School of American Research Press.

———. 2003. *Voices of Modernity: Language Ideologies and the Politics of Inequality.* Cambridge: Cambridge University Press.

B.D. 1992. Idir au New Morning. *Libération* (February 8–9).

Bellil, Rachid, and Salem Chaker. 2001. Mouloud Mammeri, directeur du CRAPE (Alger). In *Hommes et femmes de Kabylie*, vol. 1, ed. S. Chaker, 167–169. Aix-en-Provence, France: Edisud.

Benamrane, Djilali. 1983. *L'émigration algérienne en France (passé, présent, devenir).* Algiers: Société Nationale d'Edition et de Distribution.

Benaziez, S. 1979. Disque: A la portée de tous. *Algérie actualité* 696 (February 15–21).

Bendimered, Kémal. 1969. Premier festival national de la musique et des chants populaires. *Algérie actualité* 203 (September 7–13).

———. 1970. Maisons de disques et . . . "sociétés pirates." *Algérie actualité* 270 (December 20–26).

———. 1975. L'Algérie sur un miroir décennal. *Algérie actualité* 505 (June 22–28).

Bendix, Regina. 1997. *In Search of Authenticity: The Formation of Folklore Studies.* Madison: University of Wisconsin Press.

Benzaghou, Djamel. 1977. Réalisme et authenticité. *Algérie actualité* 604 (May 13–19).

Benzerfa-Guerroudj, Zineb. 1993. Les associations féminines en Algérie. *Journal of Maghrebi Studies* 1–2 (1): 17–26.

Berger, Harris M., and Giovanna P. Del Negro. 2002. Bauman's "Verbal Art" and the Social Organization of Attention: The Role of Reflexivity in the Aesthetics of Performance. *Journal of American Folklore* 115 (455): 62–91.

Berkani, Derri. 1972. *Taos Amrouche: Chants berbères de Kabylie,* dir. D. Berkani. Paris: Institut National Audiovisuel.

Bernard, Augustin. 1921. *Enquête sur l'habitation rurale des indigènes de l'Algérie.* Algiers: Fontana.

Berque, Augustin. 1936. L'habitation de l'indigène algérien. *Revue africaine* 78: 43–100.

Berque, Jacques. 1955. *Structures sociales du Haut-Atlas.* Paris: Presses Universitaires de France.

Bertucelli, Jean-Louis. 1970. *Remparts d'argile (Ramparts of Clay),* dir. J.-L. Bertucelli. Tunis, Tunisia: Office Nationale de Commercialisation et d'Industrie Cinématographique (ONCIC). 85 mins.

Bessaoud, Mohand Arab. 1963. *Heureux les martyrs qui n'ont rien vu.* Colombes: Imprimerie Cary.

Bhabha, Homi. 1994. Of Mimicry and Man: The Ambivalence of Colonial Discourse. In *The Location of Culture.* London and New York: Routledge.

Bhabha, Homi K., ed. 1990. *Nation and Narration.* London and New York: Routledge.

Bigenho, Michelle. 2002. *Sounding Indigenous: Authenticity in Bolivian Music Performance.* New York: Palgrave.

Blidi, Maâchou. 1978. Et pour quelques pas de plus. . . . *Algérie actualité* 664 (July 6–12).

———. 1980. Tizi-Ouzou: La sérénité. *Algérie actualité* 756 (May 1–7).

Boulifa, Si Ammar Ben Saïd. 1910 [1897]. *Une première année de langue kabyle (dialecte zouaoua) à l'usage des candidats à la prime et au brevet de kabyle.* Algiers: A. Jourdan.

———. 1913. *Méthode de langue kabyle: Cours de deuxième année (Etude linguistique et sociologique sur la Kabylie du Djurdjura).* Algiers: A. Jourdan.

———. 1925. *Le Djurdjura à travers l'histoire (depuis l'antiquité jusqu'à 1830): Organisation et indépendance des Zouaoua (Grande Kabylie).* Algiers: Bringau.

———. 1990 [1904]. *Recueil de poésies kabyles.* Paris: Awal.

Bourdieu, Pierre. 1958. *Sociologie de l'Algérie.* Paris: Presses Universitaires de France.

------. 1962 [1958]. *The Algerians,* trans. A. C. M. Ross. Boston: Beacon Press.

------. 1977. *Outline of a Theory of Practice,* trans. R. Nice. Cambridge: Cambridge University Press.

------. 1979 [1970]. The Kabyle House or the World Reversed. In *Algeria 1960,* 133–153. Cambridge: Cambridge University Press.

------. 1990. *The Logic of Practice,* trans. R. Nice. Stanford: Stanford University Press.

Bourdieu, Pierre, and Abdelmalek Sayad. 1964. *Le déracinement: La crise de l'agriculture traditionnelle en Algérie.* Paris: Les Editions de Minuit.

Brah, Avtar. 1996. *Cartographies of Diaspora: Contesting Identities.* London and New York: Routledge.

Brenier-Estrine, Claude. 1994. *Bibliographie berbère annotée, 1992–1993.* Aix-en-Provence, France: Institut.de Recherches et d'Etudes sur le Monde Arabe et Musulman (IREMAM), Universités d'Aix-Marseille.

------. 1995. *Bibliographie berbère annotée, 1993–1994.* Aix-en-Provence, France: Institut de Recherches et d'Etudes sur le Monde Arabe et Musulman (IREMAM), Universités d'Aix-Marseille.

Brett, Michael, and Elizabeth Fentress. 1996. *The Berbers.* Oxford: Blackwell.

Briggs, Charles. 1993. Metadiscursive Practices and Scholarly Authority in Folkloristics. *Journal of American Folklore* 106 (422): 387–434.

Briggs, Charles, and Richard Bauman. 1992. Genre, Intertextuality, and Social Power. *Journal of Linguistic Anthropology* 2 (2): 131–172.

Bulletin d'études berbères. 1972–73. Une expérience pédagogique à Vincennes: Le Groupe d'Etudes Berbères. *Bulletin d'études berbères* 1: 4–14.

Burke Lefevre, Karen. 1992. The Tell-Tale "Heart": Determining "Fair" Use of Unpublished Texts. *Law and Contemporary Problems* 55 (2): 153–183.

Butler, Judith. 1999 [1990]. *Gender Trouble: Feminism and the Subversion of Identity.* New York and London: Routledge.

Cabral, Amilcar. 1973. *Return to the Source: Selected Speeches by Amilcar Cabral.* New York and London: Monthly Review Press with Africa Information Service.

Camps, Gabriel. 1987. *Les Berbères: Mémoire et identité.* Paris: Editions Errance.

Carette, Ernest. 1847–48. *Etudes sur la Kabilie proprement dite.* Vols. 1–2. Paris: Imprimerie Nationale.

Carlier, Omar. 1984. La production sociale de l'image de soi: Note sur la "crise berbériste" de 1949. *Annuaire de l'Afrique du Nord* 23: 347–371.

------. 1995. *Entre nation et jihad: Histoire sociale des radicalismes algériennes.* Paris: Presses de Sciences Po.

Carmichael, Stokely. 1965. *Stokely Speaks: Black Power Back to Pan-Africanism.* New York: Random House.

Chachoua, Kamel. 1996. Les enfants de chuhada: Fils de veuves ou fils de martyrs? *Monde arabe Maghreb-Machrek* 154: 31–39.

------. 2001. *L'islam kabyle: Religion, état et société en Algérie.* Paris: Maisonneuve et Larose.

Chaker, Rachid. 1982. Journal des événements de Kabylie (mars–mai 1980). *Les temps modernes* 39 (432–433): 383–436.

Chaker, Salem. 1987a. L'affirmation identitaire berbère à partir de 1900: Constantes et mutations (Kabylie). *Revue de l'occident musulman et de la méditerranée* 44 (2): 13–33.

------. 1987b. Amaziɣ (Amazigh), "(le/un) Berbère." In *Encyclopédie berbère,* vol. 4, 562–568. Aix-en-Provence, France: Edisud.

———. 1989. *Berbères aujourd'hui*. Paris: L'Harmattan.

———. 1991. *Une décennie d'études berbères (1980–1990): Bibliographie critique: langue, littérature, identité*. Algiers: Bouchène.

———. 1995. Berber Language and Political Identity in Algeria and Morocco. Talk delivered at Massachusetts Institute of Technology, Cambridge, Mass., April 25.

———. 1996. *Manuel de linguistique berbère*. Vol. 2, *Syntaxe et diachronie*. Algiers: ENAG Editions.

———. 2001a. Boulifa Si Amar-ou-Saïd (1865–1931): Le grand précurseur berbérisant. In *Hommes et femmes de Kabylie*, vol. 1, ed. S. Chaker, 119–123. Aix-en-Provence, France: Edisud.

———. 2001b. Mouloud Mammeri (1917–1989): Le berbérisant. In *Hommes et femmes de Kabylie*, vol. 1, ed. S. Chaker, 162–166. Aix-en-Provence, France: Edisud.

Chaker, Salem, ed. 2004. Kabylie. In *Encyclopédie berbère*, vol. 26, 3986–4093. Aix-en-Provence, France: Edisud.

Charef, Abed. 1990. *Algérie '88: Un chahut de gamins . . . ? Octobre*. Algiers: Laphomic.

Chatterjee, Partha. 1993. *The Nation and Its Fragments: Colonial and Postcolonial Histories*. Princeton, N.J.: Princeton University Press.

Cherbi, Moh, and Arezki Khouas. 1999. Chanson kabyle et identité berbère: L'œuvre de Lounis Aït Menguellet. Paris: Editions Paris-Mediterranée.

Cherifa. 1994. *Cheikha Cherifa à l'Olympia*. Paris: n.p.

Clancy-Smith, Julia. 1996. The Colonial Gaze: Sex and Gender in the Discourses of French North Africa. In *Franco-Arab Encounters: Studies in Memory of David C. Gordon*, ed. L. C. Brown and M. Gordon, 201–228. Beirut, Lebanon: American University of Beirut.

Clifford, James. 1983. On Ethnographic Authority. *Representations* 1: 118–146.

Clifford, James, and George E. Marcus, eds. 1986. *Writing Culture: The Poetics and Politics of Ethnography*. Berkeley: University of California Press.

Collectif Contre la Répression en Algérie. 1985. *Algérie: Les droits de l'homme (Revue de presse)*. Paris: Collectif Contre la Répression en Algérie.

Collins, John. 1993. The Problem of Oral Copyright: The Case of Ghana. In *Music and Copyright*, ed. S. Frith, 146–158. Edinburgh, Scotland: Edinburgh University Press.

Colonna, Fanny. 1975. *Instituteurs algériens 1883–1939*. Paris: Presses de la Fondation Nationale des Sciences Politiques.

———. 1996. Sur le passage de l'émeute à l'attentat collectif. *Monde arabe Maghreb-Machrek* 154: 40–47.

———. 2003. The Nation's "Unknowing Other": Three Intellectuals and the Culture(s) of Being Algerian, or the Impossibility of Subaltern Studies in Algeria. *Journal of North African Studies* 8 (1): 155–170.

Contribution au débat socio-culturel en Algérie: Un texte d'Alger. 1976. *Bulletin d'études berbères* 9–10: 7–51.

Coombe, Rosemary C. 1998. *The Cultural Life of Intellectual Properties: Authorship, Appropriation, and the Law*. Durham, N.C., and London: Duke University Press.

Cornell, Vincent J. 1998. Realm of the Saint: Power and Authority in Moroccan Sufism. Austin: University of Texas Press.

Crapanzano, Vincent. 1992. *Hermes' Dilemma and Hamlet's Desire: On the Epistemology of Interpretation*. Cambridge, Mass., and London: Harvard University Press.

Dallet, Jean-Marie. 1982. *Dictionnaire Kabyle-Français*. Paris: SELAF (Société d'Etudes Linguistiques et Anthropologiques de France).

Daumas, Général Eugène. 1912. La femme arabe. *Revue africaine* 56: 1–154.

Daumas, Général Eugène, and M. Fabar. 1847. *La Grande-Kabylie: Etudes historiques.* Paris and Algiers: Hachette.

Déjeux, Jean. 1975. Principales manifestations culturelles en Algérie depuis 1962. In *Culture et société au Maghreb,* 77–96. Paris: CNRS (Editions du Centre National de la Recherche Scientifique).

———. 1982. Le débat culturel en Algérie, 1979–1982. *L'Afrique et l'Asie modernes* 133 (2e trimestre): 3–22.

De la culture. 1968. *Révolution africaine* 276: 39.

Depestre, René. 1969. Les fondements socio-culturels de notre identité. In *Le premier festival culturel panafricain: Communications,* vol. 2, 250–254. Algiers: Société Nationale d'Edition et de Distribution.

Djaad, Abdelkrim. 1979. Idir, entre l'aède et le show. *Algérie actualité* 720 (August 2–8).

Djaout, Tahar. 1993. La famille qui avance et la famille qui recule. *Ruptures* 20 (May 25–31).

Duranti, Alessandro, and Charles Goodwin, eds. 1992. *Rethinking Context: Language as an Interactive Phenomenon.* Cambridge: Cambridge University Press.

Duvignaud, Jean. 1970 [1968]. *Change at Shebika: Report from a North African Village,* trans. F. Frenaye. Austin: University of Texas Press.

Eickelman, Dale. 1976. *Moroccan Islam: Tradition and Society in a Pilgrimage Center.* Austin: University of Texas Press.

———. 2002. *The Middle East and Central Asia: An Anthropological Approach.* 4th ed. Upper Saddle River, N.J.: Prentice Hall.

Etienne, Bruno, and Jean Leca. 1975. La politique culturelle de l'Algérie. In *Culture et société au Maghreb,* 45–76. Paris: CNRS (Editions du Centre National de la Recherche Scientifique).

Faigre, Marc. 1985. *Jean Amrouche: L'éternel Jugurtha (collected writings).* Marseille: Archives de la ville de Marseille.

Fairley, Jan, and David Horn, eds. 1987. Latin America. *Popular Music* 6 (special issue).

Fanon, Frantz. 1963. On National Culture. In *The Wretched of the Earth,* 206–248. New York: Grove Press.

Feld, Steven. 1988. Notes on World Beat. *Public Culture* 1 (1): 31–37.

———. 1996. pygmy POP: A Genealogy of Schizophonic Mimesis. *Yearbook for Traditional Music* 28: 1–35.

———. 2000. A Sweet Lullaby for World Music. *Public Culture* 12 (1): 145–171.

Feraoun, Mouloud. 1954. *Le fils du pauvre.* Paris: Editions du Seuil.

———. 1960. *Les poèmes de Si Mohand.* Paris: Editions de Minuit.

Ferguson, James. 1997. The Country and the City on the Copperbelt. In *Culture, Power, Place: Explorations in Critical Anthropology,* ed. A. Gupta and J. Ferguson, 137–154. Durham, N.C., and London: Duke University Press.

Ferhat Imazighen Imoula. 1979. *Tizi bb wassa.* Paris: Imedyazen.

Fonds Ministériels. n.d. Documents des services métropolitaines successifs en charge de l'Algérie. FM/f80/1732. Aix-en-Provence, France: Centre des Archives d'Outre-Mer.

Foucault, Michel. 1977 [1969]. What Is an Author? In *Language, Counter-memory, Practice,* ed. D. F. Bouchard, 113–138. Ithaca, N.Y.: Cornell University Press.

Frith, Simon, ed. 1993. *Music and Copyright.* Edinburgh: Edinburgh University Press.

Front de Libération Nationale (FLN). 1964a. *La Charte d'Alger: Ensemble des textes adoptés par le 1er Congrès du Parti du Front de Libération Nationale.* Algiers: FLN, Commission Centrale d'Orientation.

——. 1964b. *Colloque national sur la musique algérienne.* Algiers: FLN, Section des Affaires Culturelles.

——. 1964c. *La Constitution.* Algiers: FLN.

——. 1971. *Aspects essentiels de la Révolution Culturelle.* Algiers: FLN.

——. 1976. *Charte nationale.* Algiers: République Algérienne Démocratique et Populaire.

Galand, Lionel. 1979. *Langue et littérature berbères: Vingt-cinq ans d'études.* Paris: Editions du Centre National de la Recherche Scientifique (CNRS).

Gautreau, Michel. 1970. *La musique et les musiciens en droit privé français contemporain.* Paris: Presses Universitaires de France.

Gellner, Ernest. 1969. *Saints of the Atlas.* Chicago: University of Chicago Press.

Genevois, Henri (Père). 1962. *L'Habitation kabyle,* no. 75. Fort National, Algeria: Fichier de Documentation Berbère.

Gilsenan, Michael. 1982. *Recognising Islam: Religion and Society in the Modern Arab World.* New York: Pantheon Books.

Goffman, Erving. 1981. *Forms of Talk.* Philadelphia: University of Pennsylvania Press.

Goldstein, Paul. 2003. *Copyright's Highway: From Gutenberg to the Celestial Jukebox.* Stanford: Stanford University Press.

Goodman, Jane E. 1998. Singers, Saints, and the Construction of Postcolonial Subjectivities in Algeria. *Ethos* 26 (2): 204–228.

——. 1999. Refracting Berber Identities: Genre, Intertextuality, and Performance in Kabylia and the Kabyle Diaspora. Ph.D. diss., Brandeis University.

——. 2002a. Berber Popular Music. In *Garland Encyclopedia of World Music,* vol. 6: *The Middle East,* ed. Virginia Danielson, Scott Marcus, and Dwight Reynolds, 272–277. New York and London: Routledge.

——. 2002b. The Half-Lives of Texts: Poetry, Politics, and Ethnography in Kabylia (Algeria). *Journal of Linguistic Anthropology* 12 (2): 157–188.

——. 2002c. Writing Empire, Underwriting Nation: Discursive Histories of Kabyle Berber Oral Texts. *American Ethnologist* 29 (1): 86–122.

——. 2003. The Proverbial Bourdieu: Habitus and the Politics of Representation in the Ethnography of Kabylia. *American Anthropologist* 105 (4): 782–793.

Gordon, Wendy. 1989. An Inquiry into the Merits of Copyright: The Challenges of Consistency, Consent, and Encouragement Theory. *Stanford Law Review* 41: 1343–1469.

Gouvernement Général de l'Algérie. n.d. Affaires indigènes. Officiers et personnels. Haa-Har. Vol. Alg/gga 18h/73. Aix-en-Provence, France: Centre des Archives d'Outre-Mer.

Grandguillaume, Gilbert. 1983. *Arabisation et politique linguistique au Maghreb.* Paris: Maisonneuve et Larose.

Gross, Joan, David McMurray, and Ted Swedenburg. 1994. Arab Noise and Ramadan Nights: Rai, Rap, and Franco-Maghrebi Identity. *Diaspora* 3 (1): 3–39.

Guilbault, Jocelyne. 1993. On Redefining the "Local" through World Music. *The World of Music* 35 (2): 33–47.

Hamroun, Smaïl. 1992. Une interview de Lounis Aït Menguellet. *Le pays* 49 (April 11–17).

Hanks, William F. 1996. *Language and Communicative Practices.* Boulder, Colo.: Westview Press.

Hannerz, Ulf. 1989. Notes on the Global Ecumene. *Public Culture* 1 (2): 66–75.

——. 1992. *Cultural Complexity: Studies in the Social Organization of Meaning.* New York: Columbia University Press.

Hanoteau, Adolphe. 1858. *Essai de grammaire kabyle: renfermant les principes du langage parlé par les populations du versant nord du Jurjura et spécialement par les Igaouaouen ou Zouazoua*. Algiers: Bastide.

———. 1860. *Essai de grammaire de la langue tamachek': renfermant les principes de ce langage berbère parlé par les Imouchar' ou Touareg*. Paris: Imprimerie Impériale.

———. 1867. *Poésies populaires de la Kabylie du Jurjura*. Paris: Imprimerie Impériale.

Hanoteau, Adolphe, and Aristide Letourneux. 1872–73. *La Kabylie et les coutumes kabyles*. 3 vols. Paris: Imprimerie Nationale.

Harbi, Mohammed. 1980. Nationalisme algérien et identité berbère. *Peuples méditerranéens* 11: 31–37.

Héron, Pierre-Marie. 2000. *Les écrivains à la radio: Les entretiens de Jean Amrouche*. Montpellier, France: Centre d'Etude du XXᵉ siècle/Université Paul-Valéry.

Herzfeld, Michael. 1987. *Anthropology through the Looking-Glass: Critical Ethnography in the Margins of Europe*. Cambridge: Cambridge University Press.

———. 1996. National Spirit or the Breath of Nature? The Expropriation of Folk Positivism in the Discourse of Greek Nationalism. In *Natural Histories of Discourse*, ed. M. Silverstein and G. Urban, 277–298. Chicago and London: University of Chicago Press.

———. 1997. *Cultural Intimacy: Social Poetics in the Nation-State*. New York and London: Routledge.

Hoffman, Katherine E. 2003. Moving and Dwelling: Building the Moroccan Aselhi Homeland. *American Ethnologist* 29 (4): 928–964.

Humblot, Catherine. 1978. Idir, Algérien et Berbère . . . *Le Monde*, April 20.

Idir. 1976a. *A vava inouva*. 33 rpm. Paris: EMI/Pathe-Marconi. C 066-14334.

———. 1976b. Muqleɣ. In *A vava inouva*. Idir. Paris: EMI/Pathe-Marconi. C 066-14334.

———. 1979. *Ay arrac-nneɣ*. 33 rpm. Editions Azwaw. AZW 021.

———. 1991. *A vava inouva*. Compact disc recording. Paris: Blue Silver Distribution. 035.4.BSD 127.

Idir and Ben Mohamed. 1973. *A vava inouva*. 45 rpm. Algiers: Les Disques Oasis. 11.001.

Imedyazen. 1981a. *Préparation du dossier culturel: Séminaire de Yakouren (du 1er au 31 août 1980)*. Paris: Imedyazen.

———. 1981b. *Tafsut Imazighen (Printemps berbère)*. Paris: Imedyazen.

Institut du Monde Arabe (IMA). 1994. *Fadhma et Taos Amrouche: Beautés de roche et de source*. Paris: Institut du Monde Arabe.

Irvine, Judith T., and Susan Gal. 2000. Language Ideology and Linguistic Differentiation. In *Regimes of Language: Ideologies, Polities, and Identities*, ed. P. Kroskrity, 35–84. Santa Fe, N.M.: School of American Research Press.

Ivy, Marilyn. 1995. *Discourses of the Vanishing: Modernity, Phantasm, Japan*. Chicago and London: University of Chicago Press.

Jabbour, Alan. 1982. Folklore Protection and National Patrimony: Developments and Dilemmas in the Legal Protection of Folklore. *Copyright Bulletin* 17: 10–14.

Jansen, Willy. 1987. *Women without Men: Gender and Marginality in an Algerian Town*. Leiden: E. J. Brill.

Jaszi, Peter. 1991. Toward a Theory of Copyright: The Metamorphoses of "Authorship." *Duke Law Journal* 1991: 445–502.

Julien, Charles-André. 1994 [1951]. *Histoire de l'Afrique du Nord: Des origines à 1830*. Paris: Editions Payot et Rivages.

Kapchan, Deborah. 1996. *Gender on the Market: Moroccan Women and the Revoicing of Tradition*. Philadelphia: University of Pennsylvania Press.

Khaldun, Ibn. 1925. *Histoire des Berbères et des dynasties musulmanes de l'Afrique septentrionale,* trans. De Slane, 4 vols. Paris: Paul Geuthner.

Khellil, Mohand. 1979. *L'exil kabyle: Essai d'analyse du vécu des migrants.* Paris: L'Harmattan.

Kirshenblatt-Gimblett, Barbara. 1998. *Destination Culture: Tourism, Museums, and Heritage.* Berkeley: University of California Press.

Ki-Zerbo, Joseph. 1969. Positions et propositions pour une néo-culture africaine. In *La culture africaine: Le symposium d'Alger, 21 juillet–1er aout 1969, Algiers, Algeria, 1969,* 341–345. Algiers: Société Nationale d'Edition et de Distribution.

Lacoste, Camille. 1962. *Bibliographie ethnologique de la Grande Kabylie.* Paris: Mouton.

Lacoste-DuJardin, Camille. 1976. *Un village algérien: Structures et évolution récente.* Algiers: Société Nationale d'Edition et de Distribution.

Lakoff, Robin Tolmach. 2000. *The Language War.* Berkeley: University of California Press.

Lanfry, Jacques. 1959 [1946]. *L'assemblée du village,* no. 62, trans. J. Degezelle. Fort National, Algeria: Fichier de Documentation Berbère.

Lange, David. 1982. Recognizing the Public Domain. *Law and Contemporary Problems* 44 (4): 147–178.

———. 1992. At Play in the Fields of the Word: Copyright and the Construction of Authorship in the Post-literate Millennium. *Law and Contemporary Problems* 55 (2): 139–151.

Laoust, Emile. 1993. *Noces berbères: Les cérémonies du mariage au Maroc. Textes bilingues et documents inédits,* ed. C. Lefebure. Aix-en-Provence, France: Edisud.

Laoust-Chantréaux, Germaine. 1990. *Kabylie côté femmes: La vie féminine à Aït Hichem, 1937–1939.* Aix-en-Provence, France: Edisud.

Latour, Bruno. 1993. *We Have Never Been Modern,* trans. C. Porter. Cambridge, Mass.: Harvard University Press.

Lazreg, Marnia. 1994. *The Eloquence of Silence: Algerian Women in Question.* New York: Routledge.

Lee, Benjamin. 1997. *Talking Heads: Language, Metalanguage, and the Semiotics of Subjectivity.* Durham, N.C., and London: Duke University Press.

Lindstrom, Lamont. 1992. Context Contests: Debatable Truth Statements on Tanna (Vanuatu). In *Rethinking Context: Language as an Interactive Phenomenon,* ed. A. Duranti and C. Goodwin. Cambridge: Cambridge University Press.

Litman, Jessica. 1990. The Public Domain. *Emory Law Journal* 39: 965–1023.

Litzinger, Ralph A. 2000. *Other Chinas: The Yao and the Politics of National Belonging.* Durham, N.C., and London: Duke University Press.

Lorcin, Patricia M. E. 1995. *Imperial Identities: Stereotyping, Prejudice, and Race in Colonial Algeria.* London and New York: I. B. Tauris.

———. 1996. The Soldier Scholars of Colonial Algeria: Arabs, Kabyles and Islam: Military Images of France in Algeria. In *Franco-Arab Encounters: Studies in Memory of David C. Gordon,* ed. L. C. Brown and M. S. Gordon, 128–150. Beirut, Lebanon: American University of Beirut.

Maggi, Wynne. 2001. *Our Women Are Free! Gender and Ethnicity in the Hindukush.* Ann Arbor: University of Michigan Press.

Mahé, Alain. 2001. *Histoire de la Grande Kabylie, XIXᵉ–XXᵉ siècles: Anthropologie historique du lien social dans les communautés villageoises.* Paris: Bouchène.

Mahfoufi, Mehenna. 1991. Le répertoire musical d'un village berbère d'Algérie. Université de Paris X, Laboratoire "Etudes d'ethnomusicologie" (CNRS/UPR 165).

———. 2002. *Chants kabyles de la guerre d'indépendance.* Paris: Editions Séguier.

Mammeri, Mouloud. 1969. *Les isefra de Si Mohand-ou-Mhand.* Paris: La Découverte.

———. 1976. *Tajerrumt n tmazight: tantala taqbaylit.* Paris: Maspéro.

———. 1980. *Poèmes kabyles anciens.* Paris: Maspéro.

———. 1985. *L'ahellil du Gourara.* Paris: Maison des Sciences de l'Homme.

———. 1989. Une expérience de recherche anthropologique en Algérie. *Awal* 5: 15–23.

———. 1991a. Dialogue sur la poésie orale en Kabylie (conversation with Pierre Bourdieu). In *Culture savante, culture vécue: Etudes 1938–1989,* 93–123. Algiers: Tala.

———. 1991b. Problèmes de prosodie berbère. In *Culture savante, culture vécue: Etudes 1938–1989,* 84–92. Algiers: Tala.

———. n.d. *Inna-yas Ccix Muhend (Cheikh Mohand a dit).* Privately published.

Manuel, Peter. 1987. Marxism, Nationalism and Popular Music in Revolutionary Cuba. *Popular Music* 6 (2): 161–178.

———. 1993. *Cassette Culture: Popular Music and Technology in North India.* Chicago: University of Chicago Press.

Marcus, George E., and Michael M. J. Fischer. 1986. *Anthropology as Cultural Critique: An Experimental Moment in the Human Sciences.* Chicago and London: University of Chicago Press.

Masqueray, Emile. 1983 [1886]. *Formation des cités chez les populations sédentaires de l'Algérie,* ed. Fanny Colonna. Paris: Edisud.

Massignon, Louis, and Adolphe Gérolami. 1930. Les kabyles dans la région parisienne. *Revue des études islamiques* 4: 160–169.

Maunier, René. 1925. Les rites de construction en Kabylie. *Revue de l'histoire des religions* 91–92: 12–29.

———. 1926. *La construction collective de la maison en Kabylie.* Paris: Université de Paris, Institut d'Ethnologie.

McCann, Anthony. 2001. All That Is Not Given Is Lost: Irish Traditional Music, Copyright, and Common Property. *Ethnomusicology* 45 (1): 89–106.

Mecheri-Saada, Nadia. 1979. Chants traditionnels de femmes de Grande Kabylie: Etude ethnomusicologique. Master's thesis, Sorbonne.

Mehta, Uday S. 1997. Liberal Strategies of Exclusion. In *Tensions of Empire: Colonial Cultures in a Bourgeois World,* ed. F. Cooper and A. L. Stoler, 59–86. Berkeley: University of California Press.

Meintjes, Louise. 1990. Paul Simon's "Graceland," South Africa, and the Mediation of Musical Meaning. *Ethnomusicology* 43 (1): 37–73.

Mekhlef, Abderrahmane. 1969. La voie est tracée. *Algérie actualité* 217 (December 14–20).

Memmi, Albert. 1969. Culture et tradition. In *La culture africaine: Le symposium d'Alger, 21 juillet–1er aout 1969, Algiers, Algeria, 1969,* 259–262. Algiers: Société Nationale d'Edition et de Distribution.

Merdaci, Noureddine. 1978. Les voies de l'authenticité. *Algérie actualité* 672 (August 31–September 6).

Messadia, Mohamed-Chérif. 1967. Notre culture est révolutionnaire. *Révolution Africaine* 177 (June 10–16).

Messaoudi, Khalida, and Elisabeth Schemla. 1995. *Unbowed: An Algerian Woman Confronts Islamic Fundamentalism,* trans. A. C. Vila. Philadelphia: University of Pennsylvania Press.

Messick, Brinkley. 1987. Subordinate Discourse: Women, Weaving, and Gender Relations in North Africa. *American Ethnologist* 14: 210–225.

Mézouane, Rabah. 1992. Le triomphe d'Aït Menguellet. *Le soir d'Algérie* (May 10).

Mills, Sherylle. 1996. Indigenous Music and the Law: An Analysis of National and International Legislation. *Yearbook for Traditional Music* 28: 57–86.

Mitchell, Timothy. 1988. *Colonising Egypt.* Berkeley, Los Angeles, and Oxford: University of California Press.

Miyaji, Mieko. 1976. *L'émigration et le changement socioculturel d'un village kabyle (Algérie).* Tokyo: Institute for the Study of Languages and Cultures of Asia and Africa.

Montagne, Robert. 1954. *Etude sociologique de la migration des travailleurs musulmans d'Algérie en métropole.* Paris: Direction des Affaires d'Algérie du Ministère de l'Intérieur (Bureau des Affaires Sociales Musulmanes).

Moussaoui, Djouher. 1980a. Le droit d'auteur. *Algérie actualité* 747 (February 7–13).

———. 1980b. Qu'est-ce que l'ONDA? *Algérie actualité* 747 (February 7–13).

M.T. 1991. Retour fracassant de Aït Menguellet. *Horizons* (March 24).

Nacib, Youssef. 1993. *Anthologie de la poésie kabyle.* Algiers: Editions Andalouses.

———. 2002. *Slimane Azem le poète.* Algiers: Editions Zyriab.

Ndoye, Babacar. 1989. Protection of Expressions of Folklore in Senegal. *Copyright* (December): 374–378.

N.S. [presumably Nadjib Stambouli]. 1984. L'O.N.D.A. civique. *Algérie actualité* 957 (February 16–22).

Office National des Statistiques. 2002. *Quelques indicateurs économiques: Statistiques sociales–Population et démographie.* Electronic document: www.ons.dz/them_sta. htm, accessed June 3, 2003.

Organisation de l'Unité Africaine (OUA). 1969a. Ariadne's Thread: From the Drums of the Niger River to the Art of Archie Shepp. *First Pan African Cultural Festival New Bulletin* 6: 36–38 (English ed.).

———. 1969b. La culture face à la science. *Le premier festival culturel panafricain: Bulletin d'information* 2: 8–9.

———. 1969c. Le programme algérien au premier festival culturel panafricain. *Le premier festival culturel panafricain: Bulletin d'information* 5: 43–46.

Ouary, Malek. 1974. *Poèmes et chants de Kabylie.* Paris: Librairie Saint-Germain-des-Prés.

Ouazani, Chérif. 1988. La tourmente paisible: Rencontre avec Lounis Aït Menguellet. *Algérie actualité* 1168 (March 3–9).

Ouazani, Chérif, and Mohamed Hamdi. 1992. A vava inouva: Idir vrai. *Algérie actualité* 9371 (January 23–29).

Ouerdane, Amar. 1990. *La question berbère dans le mouvement national algérien, 1926– 1980.* Quebec: Septentrion.

Ourad, Meziane. 1984. Aït Menguellet: "L'homme poème." *Algérie actualité* 978 (July 12–18).

Parker, Andrew, Mary Russo, Doris Sommer, and Patricia Yeager, eds. 1992. *Nationalisms and Sexualities.* New York and London: Routledge.

Pels, Peter, and Oscar Salemink. 2000. *Colonial Subjects: Essays on the Practical History of Anthropology.* Ann Arbor: University of Michigan Press.

Pemberton, John. 1987. Musical Politics in Central Java (or How Not to Listen to a Javanese Gamelan). *Indonesia* 44: 17–29.

———. 1994. *On the Subject of "Java."* Ithaca, N.Y., and London: Cornell University Press.

Pervillé, Guy. 1996. The "Francisation" of Algerian Intellectuals: History of a Failure? In *Franco-Arab Encounters: Studies in Memory of David C. Gordon,* ed. L. C. Brown and M. Gordon, 415–445. Beirut, Lebanon: American University of Beirut.

Première répartition des redevances. 1977. *Algérie actualité* 624 (September 29–October 5).

Rabia, Boualem. 1993. *Le viatique du barde: Recueil de poésies kabyles des Aït Ziki*. Paris: L'Harmattan/Awal.

Raheja, Gloria Goodwin. 1996. Caste, Colonialism, and the Speech of the Colonized: Entextualization and Disciplinary Control in India. *American Ethnologist* 23 (3): 494–513.

Rearick, Charles. 1974. *Beyond the Enlightenment: Historians and Folklore in Nineteenth-Century France*. Bloomington: Indiana University Press.

Redjala, Ramdane. 1988. *L'opposition en Algérie depuis 1962*. Paris: L'Harmattan.

Rémond, Martial. 1933. *Au coeur du pays kabyle*. Algiers: Baconnier-Hélio.

Révolution Démocratique Africaine (RDA). 1970. Intervention de la délégation guinéenne au festival d'Alger. *Révolution Démocratique Africaine* 35: 23–57.

Roberts, Hugh. 1983. The Economics of Berberism: The Material Basis of the Kabyle Question in Contemporary Algeria. *Government and Opposition* 18 (2): 218–235.

Rose, Mark. 1993. *Authors and Owners: The Invention of Copyright*. Cambridge, Mass., and London: Harvard University Press.

Sadi, Said. 1983. Entretien avec le Dr. Said Sadi. *Tafsut* 7: 37–54.

Sayad, Abdelmalek. 1977. Les trois "âges" de l'émigration algérienne en France. *Actes de la recherche en sciences sociales* 15 (June): 59–79.

Schade-Poulsen, Marc. 1999. *Men and Popular Music in Algeria: The Social Significance of Rai*. Austin: University of Texas Press.

Schein, Louisa. 1999. Performing Modernity. *Cultural Anthropology* 14 (3): 361–395.

Scott, David. 1999. *Refashioning Futures: Criticism after Postcoloniality*. Princeton, N.J.: Princeton University Press.

Seeger, Anthony. 1992. Ethnomusicology and Music Law. *Ethnomusicology* 36 (3): 345–359.

———. 1996. Ethnomusicologists, Archives, Professional Organizations, and the Shifting Ethics of Intellectual Property. *Yearbook for Traditional Music* 28: 87–105.

Seizer, Susan. 2000. Roadwork: Offstage with Special Drama Actresses in Tamilnadu, South India. *Cultural Anthropology* 15 (2): 217–259.

La semaine culturelle en question. 1981. *Algérie actualité* 803 (March 5–11).

Shannon, Jonathan H. 2003. Sultans of Spin: Syrian Sacred Music on the World Stage. *American Anthropologist* 105 (2): 266–277.

Silverstein, Michael. 1993. Metapragmatic Discourse and Metapragmatic Function. In *Reflexive Language: Reported Speech and Metapragmatics*, ed. J. A. Lucy, 33–58. Cambridge: Cambridge University Press.

Silverstein, Michael, and Greg Urban, eds. 1996. *Natural Histories of Discourse*. Chicago and London: University of Chicago Press.

Silverstein, Paul. 2002. The Kabyle Myth: Colonization and the Production of Ethnicity. In *From the Margins: Historical Anthropology and Its Futures*, ed. B. K. Axel, 122–155. Durham, N.C., and London: Duke University Press.

———. 2003. Martyrs and Patriots: Ethnic, National and Transnational Dimensions of Kabyle Politics. *Journal of North African Studies* 8 (1): 87–111.

———. 2004a. Of Rooting and Uprooting: Kabyle Habitus, Domesticity, and Structural Nostalgia. *Ethnography* 5 (4).

———. 2004b. *Algeria in France: Transpolitics, Race, and Nation*. Bloomington: Indiana University Press.

Slim. 1981. Note de service. *Algérie actualité* 803 (March 5–11).

Slimani-Direche, Karima. 1997. *Histoire de l'émigration kabyle*. Paris: L'Harmattan.

Slyomovics, Susan. 1995. "Hassiba Ben Bouali, If You Could See Our Algeria": Women and Public Space in Algeria. *Middle East Report* 192: 8–13.

———. 1998. *The Object of Memory: Arab and Jew Narrate the Palestinian Village.* Philadelphia: University of Pennsylvania Press.

Société Nationale d'Edition et de Distribution (SNED). 1969. *La culture africaine: Le symposium d'Alger, 21 juillet–1er aout 1969. Premier festival culturel panafricain d'Alger.* Algiers: Société Nationale d'Edition et de Distribution.

Spender, Dale. 1982. *Women of Ideas and What Men Have Done to Them: From Aphra Behn to Adrienne Rich.* London: Routledge and Kegan Paul.

Stewart, Susan. 1994. *Crimes of Writing: Problems in the Containment of Representation.* Durham, N.C., and London: Duke University Press.

Stoler, Ann Laura, and Frederick Cooper. 1997. Between Metropole and Colony: Rethinking a Research Agenda. In *Tensions of Empire: Colonial Cultures in a Bourgeois World,* ed. F. Cooper and A. L. Stoler, 1–58. Berkeley, Los Angeles, and London: University of California Press.

Tafsut. 1981a. Faire le point. *Tafsut* 3: 42.

———. 1981b. Pétition de la communauté universitaire de Tizi-Ouzou en faveur des détenus de Bejaia. *Tafsut* 3: 10.

———. 1981c. Qu'est-ce que le Mouvement Culturel Berbère? *Tafsut* 2: 13.

Taleb-Ibrahimi, Ahmed. 1973. Déclaration du ministre de l'information et de la culture à l'ouverture du séminaire. *Algérie actualité* 384 (February 25–March 3).

———. 1981 [1972]. Une révolution globale. In *De la décolonisation à la révolution culturelle: 1962–1972,* 213–216. Algiers: Société Nationale d'Edition et de Distribution.

Taleb-Ibrahimi, Khaoula. 1995. *Les Algériens et leurs langues.* Algiers: El Hikma.

Talha, Larbi. 1989. *Le salariat immigré dans la crise: La main-d'œuvre maghrébine en France (1921–1987).* Paris: Editions du CNRS (Centre National de la Recherche Scientifique).

Taylor, Charles. 1999. Two Theories of Modernity. *Public Culture* 11 (1): 153–174.

Tsing, Anna. 1993. *In the Realm of the Diamond Queen: Marginality in an Out-of-the-Way Place.* Princeton, N.J.: Princeton University Press.

———. 2000. The Global Situation. *Cultural Anthropology* 15 (4): 327–360.

Tumas-Serna, Jane. 1992. The "Nueva Canción" Movement and Its Mass-Mediated Performance Context. *Latin American Music Review* 13 (2): 139–157.

Turner, Victor. 1986. *The Anthropology of Performance.* New York: PAJ Publications.

Urban, Greg. 1996. Entextualization, Replication, and Power. In *Natural Histories of Discourse,* ed. M. Silverstein and G. Urban, 21–44. Chicago: University of Chicago Press.

———. 2001. *Metaculture: How Culture Moves through the World.* Minneapolis: University of Minnesota Press.

Van der Veer, Peter. 1995. *Nation and Migration: The Politics of Space in the South Asian Diaspora.* Philadelphia: University of Pennsylvania Press.

Van Nieuwkerk, Karin. 1995. *"A Trade like Any Other": Female Singers and Dancers in Egypt.* Austin: University of Texas Press.

Venuti, Lawrence. 1992. *Rethinking Translation: Discourse, Subjectivity, Ideology.* London and New York: Routledge.

Virolle, Marie. 1995. *La chanson raï: De l'Algérie profonde à la scène internationale.* Paris: Karthala.

Wallis, Roger, and Krister Malm. 1984. *Big Sounds from Small Peoples: The Music Industry in Small Countries.* Constable and London: Constable and Co.

Warner, Michael. 2002. Publics and Counterpublics. *Public Culture* 14 (1): 49–90.

Westermarck, Edward. 1914. *Marriage Ceremonies in Morocco.* London: Macmillan.

White, Hayden. 2002. The Illusion of Historical Perspective. Talk delivered at Indiana University, Bloomington, Indiana, April 11, 2002.

Williams, Raymond. 1973. *The Country and the City.* London: Chatto & Windus.

Woodmansee, Martha. 1984. The Genius and the Copyright: Economic and Legal Conditions of the Emergence of the "Author." *Eighteenth-Century Studies* 17 (4): 425–448.

Yacine, Tassadit. 1989. *Aït Menguellet chante . . .* Paris: La Découverte/Awal.

———. 1990. Aux origines de la quête: Mouloud Mammeri parle. . . . *Awal* (édition spéciale): 67–77.

Yamina. 1960 [1953]. *Le mariage en Kabylie,* première partie, no. 68, trans. S. L. de Vincennes. Fort National, Algeria: Fichier de Documentation Berbère.

———. 1961 [1953]. *Le mariage en Kabylie,* deuxième partie, no. 70, trans. S. L. de Vincennes. Fort National, Algeria: Fichier de Documentation Berbère.

Zemp, Hugo. 1996. The/An Ethnomusicologist and the Record Business. *Yearbook for Traditional Music* 28: 36–56.

Ziff, Bruce, and Pratima V. Rao. 1997. *Borrowed Power: Essays on Cultural Appropriation.* New Brunswick, N.J.: Rutgers University Press.

Index

Bauman, Richard, 18, 22, 61, 104, 121, 167. *See also* Briggs, Charles
Ben Badis, Shaykh, 55
Ben Djedid, Chadli, 14, 44
Ben Mohamed: *A vava inouva* (song) (with Idir), 39, 49–52, 61–68; *Cfiɣ* (song) (with Idir), 122, 132–136; "Constitutive Cultural Elements of the New Algerian Man," 205*n*16; *L'émission du matin* (radio program), 64; *Isefra* (song) (with Idir), 122, 123–132; *Isiditen* (poem), 136; *Journey into the World of Poets and Poetry* (radio program), 64–65; *Muhend-nneɣ* (song) (with Idir), 122, 136–143, 212*n*12; and Pan-African Festival, 53; source texts and reworkings, 120–126, 129, 131, 133–135, 139
Benzaghou, Djamel, 60
Berber Academy, 37, 38–40, 202*n*15
Berber Academy of Cultural Research and Exchange (ABERC), 37–38
Berber Cultural Association (ACB), 176, 179, 216*n*6
Berber cultural associations: in Algeria, 40–41; increase in, 1; Paris developments, 37–40, 203*n*18; recent global implications, 197–199; youth activism of, 166–167
Berber Cultural Movement (MCB), 12, 37, 46, 48
Berber history, 5–7
Berber House, 77–80
Berber identity: and Algerian nationalism, 10–12; in Amrouche's song collections, 106–111; axes of differentiation, 196, 199; Berber House, 77–80; in Boulifa's *Recueil de poésies kabyles,* 103–106; branching interconnections metaphor of, 15–18, 197–198; cultural identity, 3–5, *98;* cultural organizations in the 1960s and 1970s, 37–41; and ethnographic projects, 50–52; folklore, 57–59; global attention and gains, 197–199; in Hanoteau's *Poésies populaires de la Kabylie du Jurjura,* 99–103; Idir and revalorization of Berber heritage, 19–20; Imazighen, 11; and Islamism, 4, 14; Kabyle village as locus of, 68; in Mammeri's *Poèmes kabyles anciens,* 29, 112–119; and new Kabyle song, 1, 3, 5, 11–12, 20, 22–23, 172; public performances of, 195–196; and religion, 4–5; and social morality, 80–83; women and songs, 154–155
Berber language: Berber language family, 6, 201*n*2; in colonial period, 34; postcolonial marginalization, 11–12, 56–57; in schools, 197; Tamazight, 1, 11–12, 197; triangulation, with Arabic and French, 55–57; varieties or "dialects," 6–7, 34
Berber populations, 4–6
Berber Spring (Tafsut Imazighen): about, 2, 22, 30–34, 202*n*7; Algerian embassy protest (1980), 30, 201*n*2; Anti-Repression Committee, 44, 46; and Arabization of public schools, 33–37; and Berber cultural associations, 40–41; and Black Spring, 32; framing of, by Kabyle writers, 48; press coverage and human rights focus, 45–48; strikes organized, 43–44; and student governance associations, 41–45
Berber Studies Group (GEB), 40
Berber village: patrilineages, marabouts vs. Kabyles, 10, 80; performance politics, 155–161; relations of respect, 166–167, 173–174, 181–182, 185; social morality, 80–83
Bererhi, Adelhak, 44
Bessaoud, Mohand Arab, 38, 202*n*14
Bhabha, Homi, 16, 21, 143
"Black Spring," 32
Boudiaf, Mohammed, 14
Boulifa, Si Ammar Ben Saïd, 103–106, 209*n*11, 210*nn*12–13
Bourdieu, Pierre, 40, 51, 71, 72, 77–78, 190
Bouteflika, Abdelaziz, 197
Brah, Avtar, 196, 199
branching interconnections (branchements) (Amselle), 15–18, 197–199
Briggs, Charles, 18, 22, 61, 64, 104, 121. *See also* Bauman, Richard
Bulletin d'études berbères (Bulletin of Berber Studies) (journal), 40
Bureau Arabe, 99, 209*n*2
Butler, Judith, 171

Cabral, Amilcar, 22, 118
Canada, 215*n*6
Carette, Ernest, 209*n*4
Carmichael, Stokely, 53
Centre de Recherches Archéologiques, Préhistoriques, et Ethnologiques (CRAPE), 112–113
Cfiɣ (song) (Ben Mohamed and Idir), 122, 132–136
Chadli, Ben Djedid, 14
Chahine, Youcef, 205*n*14
Chaker, Rachid, 203*nn*23,26,30
Chaker, Salem, 32, 42, 57, 202*nn*8,13, 203*n*27, 211*n*34
Chants berbères de Kabylie (J. Amrouche), 107–109, 112

234 *Index*

(poem), 102, 115; "Lament for Dahman-
ou-Meçal" (poem), 102; poem collection,
99–103, 208*n*1, 209*n*2; *Poésies populaires de
la Kabylie du Jurjura,* 99
henna ceremony, 156–158
Herder, Johann Gottfried, 18
Herzfeld, Michael, 72, 97; "disemia," 92,
208*n*31; "structural nostalgia," 72, 206*n*4
High Council of State (HCE), 14
Hoffman, Katherine, 72
Houses of Culture, 60, 206*n*26

Ibadites, 6
Ibn Khaldun, 1
Idir: *A vava inouva* (song) (with Ben
Mohamed), 49–50, 61–68, 204*n*1; *Cfiγ*
(song) (with Ben Mohamed), 122, 132–
136; cultural pilgrimages, 61; *Ers-ed ay Iḍes,*
65; *Isefra* (song) (with Ben Mohamed), 122,
126–131; *Muhend-nneγ* (song) (with Ben
Mohamed), 122, 136–143; *Muqleγ,* 30; origins and creativity issues, 146; and Pan-
African Festival, 54; and revalorization
of Berber heritage, 19–20; *Tamacahuṭ n
tsekkurt,* 154
idyllic chronotope (Bakhtin), 63
"If We Stay Like This We Will Not Thrive"
(poem), 115
Imazighen, 11
Imazighen Imoula (group), 40, 44
Imazighene (journal), 38–39, 202*n*15
Imedyazen (The Poets), 40
Imoula, Ferhat Imazighen, 12
indigenous texts. *See* oral texts
"Insurrection of 1856" (poem), 102, 115
intellectual property. *See* copyright issues
internally persuasive discourse (Bakhtin), 68
International League of Human Rights, 46
interpretation, 108, 142–144
Intertextuality: and authorship, 161; and
emergence of modern social orders, 198;
entextualization, 101–103, 106, 115–119,
199; hierarchies of difference, 19; intertextual gaps, 120–126, 129, 131, 133–135, 139;
narrated event vs. event of narration, 63;
oral texts and modernity, 149–155, 213*n*7
Isefra (song) (Ben Mohamed and Idir), 122,
123–132
Isiditen (poem) (Ben Mohamed), 136, 143
Islam: and Algerian nationalism, 10–12; Arab-
Berber commonalities, 4–5; Berbers and
Kabyle Myth, 9–10
Islamic Salvation Army (AIS), 14

Islamic Salvation Front (FIS), 13–14, 214*n*1
Islamism, 4, 10–15, 165–166, 214*n*1
Iṭij (Sun) (journal), 38–39, 202*n*15
Ivy, Marilyn, 55

Jara, Victor, 206*n*31
Jews, North African, 201*n*4
Journey into the World of Poets and Poetry
(radio program) (Ben Mohamed), 64–65
Junqua, Daniel, 46

Kabyle Myth, 7–10, 71, 104–105
Kabyle texts. *See* oral texts
Kabyle village, *79. See also* Amkan village
study—Algeria; Berber House in, 77–83;
ethnographic literature on, 70–72, 206*n*1;
as locus of Berber culture, 68, 93; social
morality, 80–83; song performance settings,
155–160; and state development policies
and practices, 76–77
Kabylia: and Arabization efforts, 36–37;
bardic tradition, 187; Berber Spring in,
31–34; civilizing mission to, 99–103; and
ethnographic projects, 50–52; French colonization, 7; Kabyle radio, 64–65; law, 9, 104;
music and folklore, 57–59; and nationalist
movement, 10–12; performance economy
in, 155–161; public domain in discourse,
153–155; religious practices in colonial
period, 102
Kahina, 31
Khaldun, Ibn, 1
Ki-Zerbo, Joseph, 53–54

Lakehal, Ammar, 36, 39, 46–47
"Lament for Dahman-ou-Meçal" (poem), 102
language politics: Agraw calls for Berber national language, 38; Algerian national language clash, 32, 55–57; Arabization of
schools, 34–37; Berber language family,
201*n*2; Mammeri's work on Berber grammar, 112–113; and nationalism, 10–12;
Tifinagh alphabet dissemination, 12, 39,
202*n*16
Larba n At Iraten cherry festival, 33, 202*n*6
Latour, Bruno, 15
law: in Kabylia, 9, 104
Lee, Benjamin, 63
"Let Us Remember Our Country" (radio program), 107
Letourneux, Aristide, 83
Lγerba n 45 (song) (Aït Menguellet), 217*n*16
Libana (group), 18, 19

project of society, 12, 14, 165
public domain. *See* copyright issues

Rabia, Boualem, 39, 146, 187, 212*n*8
radio, 40, 64, 66–67; *L'émission du matin* (Ben Mohamed), 64; *Journey into the World of Poets and Poetry* (Ben Mohamed), 64–65; "Let Us Remember Our Country" (T. Amrouche), 107
rai songs, 147, 213*n*5
Ramparts of Clay (documentary), 50, 204*n*3
Recueil de poésies kabyles (Boulifa), 103–106
Redjala, Ramdane, 40
Reform Islam, 10–11
relations of respect, 80–83, 166–167, 173–174, 181–182, 185
religion. *See* Islam; saint veneration (marabouts)
religious formulas, in songs, 125–126
Remitti, Cheikha, 147, 153
reproduction and representation, 152–153
Rose, Mark, 160
Royal Institute of Amazigh Culture, 197

Sabatier, Camille, 104
SACEM (Société des Auteurs, Compositeurs et Editeurs de Musique), 147, 152–153, 213*n*6
Sadi, Ramdane, 212*n*14
Sadi, Said, 13
saint veneration (marabouts), 9–10, 139–143
Saint-Simonianism, 99–100, 103
Sayad, Abdelmalek, 86
Scott, David, 55, 205*n*19
Secularism, 12–14, 214*n*1
Seminar of Yakouren, 46
Senghor, Léopold Sédar, 111
Shawiya, 6
Shebika, 50–52
Shenwa, 6
Shepp, Archie, 53
Si Mohand, 104
"si winnat" (poem), 212*n*12
Sidi Muḥend u Salaḥ, 136, *137*
Sidi Yaḥya Lɛidali, 136
Silverstein, Michael, 63
Silverstein, Paul, 7, 72
Simon and Garfunkel, 65
Simone, Nina, 53
Slim, 60
Slimani-Direche, Karima, 202*nn*11–12,15
Slyomovics, Susan, 72
social morality, in village, 80–83. *See also* relations of respect

Socialist Forces Front (FFS), 13, 43, 214*n*1
SONELEC factories, 43, 44
songs. *See also* oral texts: *A vava inouva* (Ben Mohamed and Idir), 39, 49–52, 55–59, 61–68, 204*n*1; *Cfiɣ* (Ben Mohamed and Idir), 122, 132–136; intertextual gaps in reworkings, 120–123, 129, 131, 133–135, 139; *Isefra* (Ben Mohamed and Idir), 122, 123–132; *Muhend-nneɣ* (Ben Mohamed and Idir), · 122, 136–143; origins and copyright issues, 145–161; village performance settings, 155–160
Soviet Union, 204*n*11
Stewart, Susan, 78
"structural nostalgia" (Herzfeld), 72, 206*n*4
stylization (Bakhtin), 61

Tafsut ("Spring") (journal), 31, 46
Tafsut Imazighen. *See* Berber Spring (Tafsut Imazighen)
tagmaṭ, 135
tajmaɛat (men's assembly), 8, 83–89, *84*, 134–135, 178
Taksebt village model, 69
Taleb-Ibrahimi, Ahmed, 56, 205*n*23
Tamacahuṭ n tsekkurt (song) (Idir), 154
Tamazight, 1, 11–12, *35*, 197; Tifinagh alphabet dissemination, 12, 39, 202*n*16
tameɣra (wedding festival), 89–93, *91*, 155–158, *157, 171*
tanina, 126, 212*n*5
Tasga chorus, 216*n*6
ṭṭɛeyen, 156
texts. *See* oral texts
tibuɣarin, 123
ticeṭṭaḥin, 193
Tifinagh alphabet dissemination, 12, 39, 202*n*16
Tilelli chorus, 1–2, 5, 14, 170–175
Tisuraf (Small Steps) (journal), 40
Tizi bb wass-a (song) (Ferhat), 172
Tizi Ouzou: 1978 Folklore Festival, 61; events around Berber Spring, 41–45; University of Tizi Ouzou Hasnaoua, 33, 202*n*8
Touré, Ahmed Sékou, 204*n*8
transduction (Urban), 108
Tsing, Anna, 16, 167
Tuareg populations, 6, 12

U.N. Committee for Economic, Social and Cultural Rights, 197
"An Unequal Struggle" (poem), 115
UNESCO, 46

Union Nationale de Jeunesse Algérien
(UNJA), 41–42, 203n24
University of Algiers, 40
University of Tizi Ouzou Hasnaoua, 33, 41–
48, 202n8
university system, in Algeria: modes of student governance, 41–45
Urban, Greg, 17, 21, 108

weddings. *See tameɣra* (wedding festival)
women, Kabyle. *See also* oral texts: agricultural work, 76–77; authorship and copyright issues of songs, 153–155, 159–160; in Boulifa's poetry collection, 105–106; in Hanoteau's poetry collection, 101; intertextual gaps in new Kabyle song, 120–123, 126–129, 133–135; and musical tradition, 58;

performance politics, 155–161, 184–196; relations of respect, 80–83, 166–167, 173–174, 181–182, 185; saint veneration and modernity, 139–140; *tameɣra* (wedding festival), 89–93, *91*, 155–158, *157*; village performance settings, 155–160
World Amazigh Congress, 197
World Conference Against Racism, 197
world music, 5, 18–20, 65, 148, 206nn30–31

Yamina, 136, 137, *137*, 147, 156, 159
Yugurten (group), 39, 146
Yugurtha, *31*, 201n4
Yusef U Qaci, 114

zawiyas, 10

JANE E. GOODMAN is Associate Professor of Communication and Culture at Indiana University. While training to become a cultural anthropologist, she also performed with the women's world music group Libana.